Aging and Milieu

Environmental Perspectives on Growing Old

In Memoriam:
Florine Livson
June 9, 1925–June 3, 1981

Florine Livson made the last of her many distinguished contributions to the field of gerontology at the 1981 West Virginia University Gerontology Conference on Aging and Milieu. She was murdered in Berkeley on June 3, 1981—just days after the conference ended. This book is dedicated to the memory of our colleague and friend, whose death by violence cheated her of the opportunity to grow old in the healthy milieu described in these pages. We who knew and loved her have lost a very dear friend; the field of adult development and aging has lost a scholar. As social gerontologists we are reminded that optimism about the possibilities for a healthy old age is not enough; it is our responsibility as scholars not only to mourn our colleague's death but also to cry out in protest against a society where murder is not rare. The poet's obligation, as Berthold Brecht described it in 1936, is ours as well:

They won't say: The times were dark.
Rather: Why were their poets silent?

NANCY DATAN

Aging and Milieu

Environmental Perspectives on Growing Old

EDITED BY

GRAHAM D. ROWLES

Department of Geology and Geography
West Virginia University
Morgantown, West Virginia

RUSSELL J. OHTA

Department of Psychology
West Virginia University
Morgantown, West Virginia

ACADEMIC PRESS

A Subsidiary of Harcourt Brace Jovanovich, Publishers

New York　　London

Paris　San Diego　San Francisco　São Paulo　Sydney　Tokyo　Toronto

ACADEMIC PRESS, INC.
111 Fifth Avenue, New York, New York 10003

United Kingdom Edition published by
ACADEMIC PRESS, INC. (LONDON) LTD.
24/28 Oval Road, London NW1 7DX

Library of Congress Cataloging in Publication Data
Main entry under title:

Aging and milieu.

   Includes index.
   1. Aging--Environmental aspects--Congresses.
2. Environmental psychology--Congresses. 3. Aged--
Social conditions--Congresses. 4. Relocation (Housing)
—Congresses. I. Rowles, Graham D. II. Ohta,
Russell J. III. Title: Aging and milieu. [DNLM:
1. Geriatrics--Congresses. 2. Environment--Congresses.
3. Social environment--Congresses. WT 30 A2667 1981]
HQ1061.A446 1982   305.2'6   82-16347
ISBN 0-12-599950-X

PRINTED IN THE UNITED STATES OF AMERICA

83 84 85 86   9 8 7 6 5 4 3 2 1

Contents

I

AGING AND MILIEU: CONCEPTIONS

12176

II
THE OLD-PERSON–ENVIRONMENT TRANSACTION

III

SOCIAL PERSPECTIVES ON MILIEU

IV

CHANGING MILIEU: PERSPECTIVES ON RELOCATION

V

PERSPECTIVE

Contributors

Numbers in parentheses indicate the pages on which the authors' contributions begin.

NANCY DATAN (29), Department of Psychology, West Virginia University, Morgantown, West Virginia 26506

SANDRA C. HOWELL (97), Department of Architecture, Massachusetts Institute of Technology, Cambridge, Massachusetts 02139

BOAZ KAHANA (205), Department of Psychology, Oakland University, Rochester, Michigan 48063

EVA KAHANA (205), Elderly Care Research Center, Department of Sociology, Wayne State University, Detroit, Michigan 48202

ROBERT KASTENBAUM (3), Adult Development and Aging Program, Arizona State University, Tempe, Arizona 85287

KATHLEEN C. KIRASIC (83), Department of Psychology, Old Dominion University, Norfolk, Virginia 23508

M. POWELL LAWTON (41), Philadelphia Geriatric Center, Philadelphia, Pennsylvania 19141

FLORINE B. LIVSON[1] (131), Institute of Human Development, University of California, Berkeley, Berkeley, California 94720

NANCY LOHMANN (17), School of Social Work, West Virginia University, Morgantown, West Virginia 26506

ROGER LOHMANN (17), School of Social Work, West Virginia University, Morgantown, West Virginia 26506

[1]Deceased.

LUCILLE NAHEMOW (171), Gerontology Center, West Virginia University, Morgantown, West Virginia 26506

RUSSELL J. OHTA (83, 231), Department of Psychology, West Virginia University, Morgantown, West Virginia 26506

ANDREW C. OSTROW (153), School of Physical Education, West Virginia University, Morgantown, West Virginia 26506

LEON A. PASTALAN (189), College of Architecture and Urban Planning, and Institute of Gerontology, University of Michigan, Ann Arbor, Michigan 48109

VICTOR REGNIER (63), Housing Research and Development Program, and School of Architecture, University of Illinois at Urbana–Champaign, Urbana, Illinois 61801

GRAHAM D. ROWLES (111, 231), Department of Geology and Geography, West Virginia University, Morgantown, West Virginia 26506

Preface

This volume represents an effort to forge new directions in the rapidly expanding domain of aging–environment research. The contributors are drawn from a variety of disciplines ranging from clinical psychology to architecture, from physical education to social work. Each presents evidence and insight regarding the critical role of context in determining the experience of old age. Although the contexts explored vary—from the medical clinic to the rural community to the national political arena—each essay contained in this book focuses on one facet of the subtle interplay between person and environment.

There is a voluminous literature in environmental psychology and gerontology on the aging–environment theme. Much of this literature focuses on the transaction between the old person and the built, or architectural, environment. The intent of the West Virginia Gerontology Conference, which provided the impetus for this volume, was to assemble leading contributors to this literature and scholars from related research disciplines and to ask them to think beyond the perspectives for which they have become renowned—to share the new directions in which their own thinking and research has been progressing. Our request was that they "focus on the environmental context of aging, not merely considered from a physical or architectural perspective but rather in terms of the old person's total milieu—physical, social, cultural, clinical, phenomenological, and so on." The response to this request exceeded our expectations, as is evidenced in the following pages.

The essays are presented in a sequence providing a thematic progression. Part I explores alternative conceptions of aging and milieu. Through Robert Kastenbaum's indictment of therapeutic pretensions of many clinical milieu, Roger and Nancy Lohmann's broad overview of the social policy environment, and Nancy Datan's phenomenological interpretation of the intergenerational context of the aging experience, we are provided with a clear indication of both the substantive breadth and the pertinence of the volume's primary focus.

Part II builds on familiar themes within the environmental psychology orientation that has characterized much research on the old-person–environment transaction. The growing sophistication of research in this domain is revealed as Powell Lawton grapples with issues of personal activity patterns in time and space as these relate to well-being. Victor Regnier introduces significant new themes in exploring functional and symbolic components of old people's neighborhood cognitive maps. Russell Ohta and Kathleen Kirasic, probing the issue of environmental learning, conclude that the elderly may have far greater environmental negotiation abilities than we have assumed. Finally, Sandra Howell's provocative essay confronts the thorny issue of environmental meaning as she illustrates the difficulty of pinning down often acknowledged, but generally elusive, components of attachment to place.

Part III comprises a series of attempts to move beyond the confines of the environmental psychology rubric. Contributors focus on social dimensions of milieu. Each chapter reinforces the notion that the social context is a critical filter mediating and conditioning the symbiotic relationships between the old person and the built environment. Graham Rowles explores spatial dimensions of social support and social meanings of place in a rural community. He illustrates how such supports and meanings become translated into a variety of specific support systems attuned to individual needs and environmental circumstances. Florine Livson's chapter probes the implications of changing sex roles as these influence the older woman's adaptation within a societal social milieu that historically has demeaned the status of older women. Andrew Ostrow examines the role of societal expectations and preconceptions and traces the implications of "appropriate behavior" stereotypes as these influence old people's participation in sport activities. Lucille Nahemow concludes this section by poignantly illustrating the way in which mutual expectations implicit within the social ambience of a clinical interaction constrain the patient–physician relationship. The tragedy of alienation between people from different worlds is made embarassingly apparent.

Although the dynamism of old-person–milieu transactions is stressed throughout this volume, it is the particular concern of Part IV. Leon

Pastalan, synthesizing the contributions of a central paradigm, reviews the way in which the literature on relocation of the elderly has embraced a series of perspectives ranging from the view that relocation is de facto a negative experience for old people to more positive perspectives, which have incorporated fuller consideration of the diverse circumstances under which the relocation decision is made. In the context of the ongoing relocation debate, it is appropriate to follow this contribution with an unashamedly optimistic account of the extremely successful adaptation of old people who relocate following retirement and find new direction and richness in their lives. Eva and Boaz Kahana's study not only adds a new dimension to the relocation debate but also brings into question some basic but untested assumptions permeating research into the old-person–environment transaction.

It would be pretentious to claim to synthesize such a diversity of perspectives within a single coherent concluding statement. Rather, in Part V we seek to provide a summary of several themes that emerged from the conference and to indicate some directions worthy of attention in future research.

Although this volume provides a wide array of perspectives on milieu, it is certainly far from comprehensive in treating the topic and its implications for the quality of life in old age. One omission is particularly ironic in view of a tragedy that cast a pall over the aftermath of an otherwise highly successful conference. The brutal and senseless murder of Florine Livson just a few days after the conclusion of the conference provided a tragic reminder that the milieu of aging in America is one pervaded by fear. We may create built environments attuned to the needs and capabilities of elderly people. Our efforts may improve the therapeutic ambience of clinical settings. We may even succeed in changing societal attitudes that limit the environmental participation of old people. However, in the numb exchange of shocked and angry phone calls among conference participants that ensued following news of Florine's death, the relative importance of such contributions was brought into clear focus. A societal milieu in which old people, and many young ones, live in a state of perpetual fear for their lives is no milieu at all.

As a group, the conference participants dedicate this book to the fond memory of our friend and respected colleague Florine B. Livson.

GRAHAM D. ROWLES
RUSSELL J. OHTA

Acknowledgments

The success of the second West Virginia University Gerontology Conference can be attributed to many individuals who, in various ways, provided us with their valuable time and effort. First and foremost, we are indebted to a talented and cooperative group of speakers who took time from their busy schedules to be a part of the conference and did much to make it a convivial experience for all the participants. Our gratitude for financial support is extended to the Administration on Aging (grant no. 03AT111) and to Ray Koppelman, vice president for energy studies, Graduate Programs and Research, West Virginia University, who provided supplementary funding. We would like to express special appreciation to the graduate student hosts—Linda Holt and Dean Rodeheaver, Department of Psychology, and Pat Ice, Department of Geology and Geography—without whom the conference could not have been conducted so smoothly. Finally, our thanks go to Betty Maxwell for handling many of the administrative headaches associated with organizing a conference, to Ruth Rowles for cartographic contributions, and to Rita Rendina for assisting with preparation of the manuscript.

I

AGING AND MILIEU: CONCEPTIONS

1

Can the Clinical Milieu Be Therapeutic?

ROBERT KASTENBAUM

The world is designed for my constant comfort, security, and delight.

Those who agree strongly with this statement are the most elite graduates of the Candide Academy for Studies of Never-never land. The rest of humanity has learned a different lesson, starting in the cradle. Life at times is dangerous, unpredictable, confusing, and disappointing. This acknowledgment of the disparity between ideal and actual finds expression in the Garden of Eden from whence we came and in the Heaven that is our destination (although both are enveloped for some within the shadow of doubt). The desire for comfort, security, and delight has also sponsored many attempts to alter reality, whether through the steam engine and the computer or through alcohol and other drugs. This chapter considers one of the other approaches toward preserving ourselves in a world that bruises and destroys when we would have it protect. The therapeutic tradition historically has mingled elements of medicine, suggestion, and healing (Kastenbaum, Barber, Wilson, Ryder, & Hathaway, 1981). Often the focus has been on a particular form of treatment. Almost as often, the effect of the treatment could be attributed, in part, to the shared climate of expectations. We are talking of *milieu*, the "medium" or surroundings within which specific events occur. A therapeutic milieu can be understood as a microcosm created to provide comfort, security, and regeneration when the larger world has proven inhospitable. This chapter examines selected aspects of the therapeutic and clinical milieu (which are not identical) for old people with special needs.

AGING AND MILIEU:
ENVIRONMENTAL PERSPECTIVES
ON GROWING OLD

TYPES OF CLINICAL AND THERAPEUTIC MILIEU
FOR THE AGED

Here is not a catalog, but a brief sampling of clinical or therapeutic environments that aged men and women have inhabited. The variety of the examples selected will help bring out some dimensions and processes.

Thursday State Hospital[1]

The geriatric unit in this state mental hospital is housed in a building that had seen many years of previous use as a prison and which has since received little modification or renovation for its current purpose. Physically and programmatically, the geriatric service is wildly out of compliance with national standards. It is a filthy and foul-smelling place which successfully resists such cleaning as is attempted. The sloping, uneven floors and poor lighting add to the environmental hazards, but the most frequent cause of injury is assault. Patients who are strong, mobile, and psychotic mix with those who are frail or suffering senile dementia. Clinical services are rudimentary. Individual treatment plans do not exist nor do such services as occupational, physical, or recreational therapy. The master's degree psychologist and the social worker do what they can to intervene in emergencies and keep the situation from completely exploding, but both are clearly at the end of their own frustration tolerance and would probably not be replaced if they left. Nursing is critically understaffed. Although some staff members are dedicated and competent, many of the attendants are unstable people with undependable attendance and work patterns. Unmistakably, there is a constant atmosphere of tension, oppression, and menace. Visitors—including family members—are treated rudely by the unit physician and discouraged from "butting in."

One senior staff member admits that "incidence reports" are filed only sporadically because nothing is done about them and because "they are not really *incidents*. It's all a pattern, a jungle, a zoo. You could walk around and record incidents all day long." Even so, a visitor could find 16 documented reports of physical injuries suffered by patients within the most recent 3-week period. *Not* included in these reports were incidents such as the following:

> The physician is completing his rounds. The dank corridor is lined with geriatric and other disabled patients who sit facing a blank tile wall. Some patients are tied to their wooden chairs. He approaches the last patient in the row. For a moment the physician stands silently in front of the old man.

[1]Thursday State Hospital and Sunset View Nursing Home refer to real places; the names are fictitious.

Suddenly he seizes one of the patient's arms and twists it behind his back. "Oscar, you little old bastard, you bastard! You better be a good boy today. You damn well better!" Having delivered this message, the physican squeezes the old man's shoulders, knocking him back and forth in the chair. "Sure you will, won't you, Oscar? You're going to be a real good boy today!"

This is an example of a clinical milieu that is not therapeutic in effect. Instead of providing an alternative to harsh reality, this geriatric unit is itself a killer world.

The Temples of Healing

Old and young alike find their way to one of the temples dedicated to and manifesting the healing powers of Aesculapius. Sick, pained, and frightened by their illnesses, they are encouraged to undertake the journey by those who have already received help and by respected authorities who praise the healing potencies. Although the journey itself may be arduous, they feel increasingly hopeful as they proceed, telling each other stories of miraculous cures. The temple itself is a beautiful and impressive place. The travelers are welcomed by priest–physicians who interview them and listen sympathetically to their medical histories. The temple walls themselves seem to be part of the treatment, covered as they are with hundreds of testimonials from previous patients.

The program designed to return to the patients to health reaches into almost every aspect of their lives, waking and sleeping. Patients and physicians pray together. Under supervision, the patients perform bathing rituals in water celebrated for its healing properties. They receive soothing rhythmic massages and are anointed with special oils, fed a special diet, and given exercises to perform (Caton, 1900). Treatment is both specific and general. Sacred snakes, for example, might coil their cool and curing bodies around the body of an arthritis sufferer. Specific instructions might be given to help the patient dream of the healing that will take place during sleep. The general or milieu treatment for all patients includes soft music and soothing breezes flowing between the temple columns, and the overall atmosphere of restfulness and serenity. It is altogether too beautiful, too healthy, too restful, too holy, and too confident an environment for a person to remain tense and frightened. Old as well as young had no choice but to feel better.

Here, then, is an example of a therapeutic milieu that history claims was very effective. Although it had components that can be recognized as clinical, the overall atmosphere did not resemble the typical clinical milieu we know today.

Sunset View Nursing Home

This contemporary residential facility for the frail and impaired elderly operates at close to 100% capacity. It has a clean and organized look. One does not sense menace or detect violence, neglect, and disorder. Yet there is also little sense of vitality, spontaneity, or community spirit. Above all, there is a lack of purpose, direction, and reason for getting up in the morning. Individual staff and residents at times break through this pattern of nonpurpose and nonrelatedness, but the milieu in general retains its peculiar suspension-of-life ambience.

Remaining in compliance with a many-tiered structure of rules, regulations, and procedures occupies much of the administrative and direct-care staff's time. The staff often feel as limited in flexibility and decision-making oppportunity as do the residents. Seligman (1975) and others have called attention to the enforced passivity and "learned helplessness" often experienced by residents of nursing homes. Similar analyses might usefully be performed on the situation of the staff as well.

As in many hospitals and extended care facilities, the staff who spend the most time in direct contact with the residents are at the lowest steps in the professional hierarchy and are paid accordingly. They often ex-perience their work as difficult and frustrating and feel that their efforts are not well appreciated—that they are "flunkies" looking after the discarded of society. At times their frustration, coupled with a lack of good models for interaction with the elderly, leads them to speak in the presence of their patients in such ways as the following (quotes):

> "Look at the mess you made! You'd think I didn't have anything else to do but clean up after you!"
> "This one, she can't talk. She doesn't know what you are saying."
> "She doesn't know any better. You can't tell her anything."
> "Can you do anything with this one? Boy, what a troublemaker she is!"
> "You should have seen her when she first came here, but look at her now!"
> "The poor thing would be better off going in her sleep."

All of these comments, by the way, were completely understood by the patients even though the staff member often assumed otherwise.

Sunset View does have its clinical and even its therapeutic components. In a fundamental sense, however, it is no milieu at all. The residents are suspended in a floating world that bears little relationship to their previous lives and in which most of their deepest thoughts, feelings, and values are irrelevant. They are spared the squalor and physical abuse of Thursday

State Hospital but are just as far removed from the psychological, social, and spiritual resources of the ancient Greek temple.

Highland Heights

Some 200 disabled adults, most of them elderly and strong candidates for a Sunset View placement, live independently in Fall River's Highland Heights Apartments. The building was constructed specifically to meet the needs of people with substantial physical impairments. Additionally, it includes an outpatient clinic with physical therapy, occupational therapy, and other services available to the tenants. There are also meeting halls, a congregate dining room for those who choose to eat together, and a variety of other spaces for ancillary services. A general hospital is right next door.

The project started with the hope "that the basic features of this type of housing—the specialized architecture, outpatient clinic, and other ancillary services—would not only enhance functioning in activities of daily living, but also would foster a more normal social life, promote physiological and psychological well-being, and provide a viable alternative to institutionalization for persons who required a specialized environment but did not need the 24-hour care of a chronic hospital or nursing home [Sherwood, Greer, Morris, & Mor, 1981, p. 7]."

This proved to be the case. Old men and women are living independently, pursuing their individual life-styles, and cultivating friendships with each other. Follow-up study (Sherwood *et al.*, 1981) has shown high morale and less mortality than would have been expected for a population with this level of impairment. Furthermore, this social experiment has even proven to be cost-effective: The elderly and other disabled adults were selective and sparing in their use of services instead of absorbing everything available, as some doubters had predicted. It actually cost less, considering all sources of expenditure, for these people to live independently in a service- and security-enriched environment than it would have cost for them to join the dispirited ranks of the institutionalized.

Highland Heights, then, is essentially a normal milieu, a sample of the larger social world, but one which *functions* as "normal" by virtue of some special planning and enrichments. It is not a clinical milieu as such, although optional clinical components are available. It is not a therapeutic milieu in the sense of an environment created specifically to cure and regenerate, although some therapeutic effects can be seen, especially in prevention of further impairment. The professional presence is peripheral and low-profile, yet the outcomes in physical and psychosocial well-being surpass what is achieved at health care facilities such as Thursday State Hospital and Sunset View.

Where the Heart Is

Under ordinary circumstances, the home is neither a clinical nor therapeutic milieu. It is, well, just home! It is the preferred environment for most old people, including those with serious infirmities and limitations. The sense of comfort and well-being is a milieu effect generated by the home environment, when a person can function to at least some degree in his normal capacity. Too often, however, this capacity is severely diminished because the old person has difficulty in managing the tasks of daily life and because fears of crime, harassments, and humiliation have created a pattern of social isolation. At the extreme, the old person is living alone in a fortress–home in which the defenses are crumbling.

A deft professional touch can make the difference between continued life satisfaction and survival on the one hand and stress and deterioration on the other. The systematic friendly visiting program described by Mary Anne Mulligan (1980), for example, illustrates how this can be done. She and her colleagues demonstrated the value of this program with isolated old people living in high crime section of New York City. This area is considered so dangerous that visitors always traveled in pairs and did not always feel secure even then. The old men and women visited in this program showed "a steady improvement in personal appearance and the condition of the home [p. 93]."

Mrs. K., for example, at the first meeting, worse a soiled and tattered dress, her hair was unkempt, and she seemed depressed. Her room was cluttered, dirty, and much in need of repairs. Subsequently, her appearance improved markedly; she began dressing up and having her hair cut and set, because "I knew you were coming." She also cleaned the room and had the walls repainted. Furthermore, Mrs. K. became more outgoing and pleasant toward others and started to attend meetings at a community center.

Unfortunately, this kind of program has yet to be become a permanent, well-supported component of our system for extending care to the elderly. In conjunction with adult day-care centers (e.g., Weiler & Rathbone-McCuan, 1978) and other relatively new developments, it is possible to bring just enough professional assistance to the home and neighborhood setting to sustain the old person without the stress and loss occasioned by relocation. An effective out-reach program, then, can prevent or delay the need for an old person to be in a clinical milieu.

SOME CONCEPTUAL AND PRAGMATIC ISSUES

Holistic Care in a Fragmented System?

The holistic care movement has breathed new life into the cliché of "treating the whole person." The holistic approach makes use of a sometimes bewildering variety of specific techniques, but it essentially emphasizes self-in-environment and is an alternative to a simplistic cause–effect view of action and to its parallel in symptom-specific medical treatment. The holistic approach bears a closer resemblance to field models of action and process. It is simultaneously quite contemporary in its concept of cause and process and quite old-fashioned in its assumptions about harmonious living. The holistic method does not neglect specific interventions to alleviate specific problems, but the overall intent is to help the person live in both inner and outer harmony.

For the distressed, frightened, or impaired old person, the holistic approach would seem to be especially appropriate:

1. The problems are often interconnected and require attention to the entire pattern rather than independent details.
2. The old person has a wealth of experience and personal resources that can be called upon to restore harmony.
3. "Successful outcome" is not necessarily defined in terms of longevity or the remission of a particular symptom, but rather in the ability to withstand crisis, deprivation, and tragedy, and to maintain a sense of personal value.

These remain realistic goals in many circumstances where "cure" and "recovery" are not likely.

Unfortunately, the fragmentation, contradictions, and dislocations within our society in general interfere with the development of holistic care for the elderly. We have the ability to create an effective clinical milieu as well as a variety of nonclinical therapeutic environments and to maintain and enrich existing normal support systems. In practice, we often fail for such reasons as the following:

1. Service delivery systems available to older Americans are divided and compartmentalized. We have "acute" and "long-term" care agencies and regulations, with each further subdivided into "physical" and "mental" components, and both of these are subdivided into institutional or community-based services. These distinctions often are frustratingly inappropriate to an actual situation. Whatever is gained by rigid distinctions between acute and long-term care or between physical and mental

problems is destroyed by the stupidities and miseries induced by this approach. Entitlements to services are often difficult to ascertain, and the services themselves often unavailable in a timely and appropriate fashion. The individual is caught in a complex and rather arbitrary grid of entitlements and regulations. His or her life is disrupted and undermined by the many bureaucracies. The "system," such as it is, simply does not acknowledge the old person as a distinctive and complete person. This inherent defect in the system generates endless practical difficulties for the old person, the family, and potential caregivers.

2. The caregivers themselves are further differentiated and fragmented by their respective guilds and by their own pressures to specialize. Who can provide what service to whom and how often sometimes becomes a more critical consideration than the overall well-being of the client. There are services, for example, that a visiting nurse might be willing to perform for an elderly client but which are forbidden by regulatory policy or reimbursement formula. The continuing trend toward specialization in the human service fields is a particular hardship for the aged. Fancy specialists seldom want to devote themselves to their specific part of the total problem. There are few fancy generalists available to help the old person understand and cope with the entirety of his or her problems.

3. The campaign for "cost-containment" in health care is wreaking additional damage on many older people. An example is the nationwide crusade to "deinstitutionalize." This complex topic cannot be dealt with thoroughly here. One implication is especially relevant, however. As the patient census drops in a mental hospital, staff members usually are transferred to community services or are discharged. The facility tends to decline rapidly with respect to both physical plant and clinical programming. Emphasis is on releasing patients permanently and unless some unusually strong and effective staff members remain on the scene, the hospital becomes a shell of its former self, providing a less adequate level of care (Kastenbaum, in press). Only recently have investigators started to analyze carefully which patients are left behind. Many older patients will be found in this residual group, since they are seldom welcome back in the community. Furthermore, the empty beds in the state mental hospital become a convenient final destination for old people who are still in the community but who are becoming "troublesome." Paradoxically, substandard care in a state mental hospital does not necessarily yield a "bottom line" savings. These facilities, themselves aging, frequently are very inefficient to operate and may become even more costly as the patient census declines.

4. The clinical milieu too frequently remains poisoned by ageism on the

societal level. The geriatric unit at Thursday State Hospital, for example, receives only those job applicants who have been turned down by every other department. The physician who abused Oscar is one such example. He is an alcoholic with limited frustration tolerance who blows up at patients, staff, and relatives alike. Yet this once-able physician actually does care about his patients and rules his province with fierce pride, although erratically. If he were dismissed and the situation otherwise remained unimproved, the next physician forced into the geriatric unit would probably invent his or her own form of escapism. What meets the eye, ear, and nose on this unit is appalling. The destructive milieu, however, does not begin here: This is merely where the sludge and poison collects. The hospital has systematically neglected and downgraded the geriatric unit, and behind the hospital stands a state mental health administration equally disinterested in quality care of the aged, and on and on, through echelons of governmental negativism and indifference, resting at last on the shoulders of the citizens themselves.

5. Specialized environments for the frail and impaired aged tend to confirm and intensify their isolation. Many, though not all, such environments are physically set apart from the community. The control function is almost entirely in the hands of people younger than the patients. This is so obvious as to almost escape notice. It is the obverse of the school situation where authority is invested in elders. In both the juvenile and the geriatric settings there is marked age-associated inequality, although in different directions. This situation does not have to be perpetuated. Geriatric patients could share in the power, which has the double advantage of relieving some of the workload of the staff and helping to maintain a sense of competence and efficacy for the elderly. Too often, specialized environments punish individualistic and assertive behavior. Mishara and Kastenbaum (1980), for example, found that the most intact and "normal" patients in a geriatric ward were those who engaged in self-destructive behavior as their only apparent alternative to passivity and surrender. To cite just one further aspect of the typical geriatric setting, we often see the clinical ambience minus the clinical benefits. The person who is a patient only temporarily can adjust to the unfamiliar and unlovely hospital routines knowing that this is only an interlude. Some comfort and individuality is sacrificed; however, in fair return the person receives state-of-the-art medical and nursing care. By contrast, the geriatric milieu is a long-term or permanent arrangement for many people, and the clinical ambience is not counterbalanced by superb care. Perhaps the most infuriating note from the standpoint of the patient is the attitude that "this is all for your own good." It is not—and everybody knows it.

Making the World Right Again

Much of what has been said up to this point is discouraging, but none of it is beyond redemption. Creation of a humane and effective clinical milieu requires facing up to such harsh realities, and worse. What do we want to accomplish with a clinical milieu? "Making the world right again" is the basic task, or so I suggest.

The frail and impaired old person has any number of sorrows, losses, frustrations, and fears, as well as an array of physical ailments. The therapeutic environment will need to provide treatments, replacements, and compensations. Good dental and podiatric care, for example, can prevent much discomfort and help the individual maintain an independent life-style. There is still a place for specific treatments to prevent or alleviate specific problems. Nevertheless, the best treatments will eventually be overmatched by weakness and deterioration. Specificity is essential, but it is not enough. There must also be a general comfort to soothe the general distress. In its finest moments, the modern hospice provides such a milieu (Cohen, 1979; Hamilton & Reid, 1980). A prevailing attitude of trust and serenity—often illuminated by some form of faith—helps the dying person to bear whatever suffering cannot be relieved by attentive medical and nursing care. Geriatric care can take heart from the hospice example and also acquire some useful techniques, even though the two types of situations cannot be equated.

We are indebted to the pioneering work of Hans Selye (1956) who demonstrated the importance of "nonspecific" factors in illness. His approach, bolstered by extensive research, introduced many new elements but also refurbished earlier traditions of healing. The "syndrome of just being sick," as Selye (1956, p. 79) once put it, can be observed in every geriatric setting. On top of specific ailments and disabilities there is often a pervasive sense of "not rightness." It seems to me that this represents more than a sense of personal not rightness. It is a falling out of love with the universe as well. One common expression of this sense is "The whole damn world has gone wrong ... It maybe never was much good anyway, and I am just lost, lost, lost." Another form is "The world has nothing to do with me any more. I mean nothing to the world and it means nothing to me." In both instances, the individual has suffered a disruption in his or her basic sense of being in the world. This person may never have heard of "existential despair," but he or she is suffering from it every day.

The usual environmental response to this profound sense of not rightness involves some mixture of the following ingredients: neglect, social withdrawal, medication, and more neglect. This response seldom works. It does not always stand up to a rigorous "cost-effectiveness" analysis either, because this kind of pattern often intensifies dependency and therefore also increases the burden on staff which in turn leads to a high and costly turnover rate.

The "just being sick" syndrome can be countered effectively by a milieu that accentuates the positive. This approach makes use of time-proven elements from the healing and suggestive therapy disciplines, including what has become known as "the placebo effect" (Frank, 1961; Shapiro, 1971). The goal is to develop a systematic and encompassing network of positive expectations on the part of everyone in the environment. Earlier, for example, I offered some verbatim statements spoken to or in the presence of geriatric patients. These were more than negative statements: They were, in effect hexes. Important people—the authorized staff who control and patrol the environment—were attesting to the patients' inadequacies. "You cannot do that any more! You are not worth talking to! You would be better-off dead!" These messages confirm the patients' own doubts and fears. They are *instructions*, instructions to be passive and ineffectual. The effect of these hexes often is intensified by the reduced dimensions of the geriatric patients' world. The old person lives within an impoverished sensory and interpersonal field. His "experiential tone" may have become dulled through monotony, absence of achievable goals, desire to reduce the perception of distress, and by the side effect of drugs. Within this altered state of consciousness, the few words spoken in his presence by "important people" may have an inordinate effect. It might be compared in some respects to so-called hypnotic suggestions in which a person perceived as powerful makes confident judgments and demands on a person who perceives himself to be in the other's power.

Positive suggestion can have an equal response in the opposite direction. Ideally, every person in the milieu carries the message of confidence and positive expectation in every interaction with the geriatric patient. This attitude must be conveyed in action, gesture, and tone of voice as well as words. A series of studies of this idea introduced alcoholic beverages in a social setting into geriatric facilities (Mishara & Kastenbaum, 1980). The situation itself spoke directly to the patients, telling them that they were acknowledged to be mature people capable of giving as well as receiving enjoyment on an adult level. Many other ways can be found to create a set of environmental expectations that foster self-confidence and hopefulness.

Some geriatric patients appear too deteriorated to respond favorably—or even to acknowledge—a positive milieu. In such instances, skillful caregivers can establish what might be called a "primary milieu" or "two-person world." I have had the opportunity to observe some of our Cushing Hospital therapists do just this. They have found ways to reach and gain the trust of many old men and women who had seemed to be unable or unwilling to enter into new relationships. These therapists are people with unusual sensitivity and empathy. Often they seem to intuit emotional pain and to establish quickly a therapeutic alliance. After discussing a series of such cases and studying the transcripts, it became clear that their specific techniques include:

1. Speaking aloud the patient's own thoughts and feelings, until the patient is able to express them for himself or herself
2. Emphasizing that they are there just for the patient and for what the patient wants to do with his or her life
3. Explaining to the patient what has been happening to his or her mind and body
4. Touching, holding, hugging—whatever form of physical contact is most acceptable to and appreciated by a man or woman who may not have received affectionate physical contact in years
5. Encouraging the patient to use abilities, both physical and mental, that he or she had given up on
6. Providing a safe context in which the patient can make little experiments in rehabilitation. Often this is as simple—yet as powerful—as getting up the courage to speak again, or taking a pencil in hand and writing his or her own name.
7. Teaching relaxation techniques, preferably to the point where the patient can induce a relaxed state by himself or herself
8. Developing guided imagery exercises to help the patient to transcend the bleakness of the immediate situation, to recover valuable memories, or to facilitate rehabilitation. In one instance, guided imagery seemed to make the difference in enabling an old man to avoid the need for double amputation of his legs (Kastenbaum *et al.*, 1981). This man was able to comprehend and apply guided imagery even though he was (correctly) diagnosed as afflicted with an organic brain syndrome.
9. Making it clear to the patient, again and again, that the therapist considers the patient to be a person of real value, somebody the therapist respects and truly wants to be with. It should be emphasized that the therapists are sincere—they do respect and value their patients, seeing much more in them than casual observation reveals.
10. Pointing out to the patient that what has been achieved in rehabilitation or increased life satisfaction has come through the patient's own strengths—his underestimated powers of physical healing, his determination, or his faith. Every relevant opportunity is taken to help the patient realize that goodness and strength can still be found within himself.

A truly therapeutic milieu for geriatric patients does not try to replace what cannot be replaced or hold back what cannot be resisted. What it does accomplish is to help the old person *reconnect*. Given respect, affection, and encouragement, starting from a primary 2-person milieu and building into a larger network, the old person realizes again what has been good and strong about his life. At the same time he regains something of his faith in the world's goodness. This has been made possible through the mediation of the primary therapist. Patient and therapist both know very well that the world has its dangerous and unyielding side, but together they have created a microcosm that truly is designed for their mutual comfort, security, and delight.

REFERENCES

Caton, R. *The temples and ritual of Asklepios.* London: C. J. Clay & Sons, 1900.

Cohen, K. P. *Hospice: Prescription for terminal care.* Germantown, Md.: Aspens Systems Corporation, 1979.

Frank, J. D. *Persuasions and healing.* Baltimore: Johns Hopkins University Press, 1961.

Hamilton, M., & Reid, H. (Eds.), *A hospice handbook.* Grand Rapids, Mich.: William B. Eerdmans, 1980.

Kastenbaum, R. Healthy, wealthy and wise: Health care provision for the elderly from a psychological perspective. In G. Sanders & J. Suls (Eds.), *Social psychology of health and illness.* New York: Lawrence Erlbaum Associates, in press.

Kastenbaum, R., Barber, T. X., Wilson, C., Ryder, B. L., & Hathaway, L. B. *Old, sick, and helpless: Where therapy begins.* Cambridge, Mass.: Ballinger Publications, 1981.

Mishara, B. L., & Kastenbaum, R. *Alcohol and old age.* New York: Grune & Stratton, 1980.

Mulligan, M. A. Reduction and prevention of isolation in the community aged: Friendly visiting. In R. Bennett (Ed.), *Aging, isolation and resocialization.* New York: Van Nostrand Reinhold, 1980.

Seligman, M. E. P. *Helplessness.* San Francisco: W. H. Freeman, 1975.

Selye, H. *The stress of life.* New York: McGraw–Hill, 1956.

Shapiro, A. K. Placebo effects of medicine, psychotherapy, and psychoanalysis. In A. E. Bergin & L. Garfield (Eds.), *Handbook of psychotherapy and behavior change: An empirical analysis.* New York: Wiley, 1971.

Sherwood, S. Greer, D. S., Morris, J. N., & Mor, V. *An alternative to institutionalization: The Highland Heights experiment.* Cambridge, Mass.: Ballinger Publications, 1981.

Weiler, P. G., & Rathbone-McCuan, E. *Adult day care.* New York: Springer, 1978.

2

Aging and the Social Policy Milieu

ROGER LOHMANN   NANCY LOHMANN

WHITHER 1984?

Concern for the policy implications of the expanding body of gerontological knowledge has been one of the characteristic features of aging
studies. The first series of handbooks on the subject, published in 1959
and 1960, contained articles on income, housing, and government programs along with reports of basic research data (Binstock & Shanas, 1976;
Birren, 1959; Burgess, 1960; Tibbitts, 1960). The Gerontological Society
has always been structured into four main sections: the biological sciences;
clinical medicine, social and behavioral sciences; and social research,
policy, and practice. It is quite fitting, therefore, that attention be devoted
to the subject of social policy in a conference concerned with the
emerging environmental perspective on aging.

Social policy means different things to different authors. Although it is
apparently unfashionable in the new world of political conservatism, our
concern in this chapter is primarily the public social policy as an
environment of human aging. Within the public sector, social policy is a
matter not only of legislation, but also increasingly of administrative and
judicial decision making as well. To a very considerable degree, it is also an
economic issue of the levels and uses of tax revenues.

In relation to the theme of this book, one might take either of two
perspectives toward social policy:

1. *Milieu policy:* Concern for those legislative, administrative, and

17

AGING AND MILIEU:
ENVIRONMENTAL PERSPECTIVES
ON GROWING OLD

judicial actions designed to improve the well-being of the old by modifications in their physical, social, or phenomenological environments.

2. *Policy as milieu:* Public decisions and actions that form part of the context or backdrop for the world of the everyday life of older persons.

Although there are some intriguing threads of suggestion in the present environmental literature, which suggest possible future lines of development, and also a number of organizational and community level innovations with "environmental interventions," it is premature to speak of "environmental policy" affecting the aged population. Therefore, we shall restrict ourselves in this context to discussing policy as part of the milieu of human aging.

THE POLICY MILIEU

In contrast to some other dimensions of milieu, the social policy milieu for the aged is one characterized by a large and presently increasing risk. For example, any older person currently facing a retirement decision in the United States must recognize that there is a great public furor over the alleged insolvency of the Social Security trust fund. This has led to proposals for modifications in current benefit groups, cost of living adjustments, and levels of payments. In this context, any older worker lacking a detailed working knowledge of the system is hard pressed to make any accurate assumptions about expected retirement income levels.

By their very nature, public social policies always involve a certain element of risk. They are typically enacted by partisan supporters in a climate characterized by controversy and opposition rather than consensus. The hope is that, after enactment and implementation, consensus for the policy will grow and opposition will weaken and fade. Indeed, this is often the case.

Two additional possibilities are always present in public policy situations, however: One is that the policy simply will not work as intended, and the other is that after some time opposition may reemerge and grow, eventually overwhelming the working consensus in support of existing policy.

The social policy of aging, and perhaps most existing social policy seems at the moment to be faced with both of these possibilities simultaneously. The political rise of the "New Right" and the apparent exhaustion of New Deal liberal democratic idealism have been much documented in the news media. Equally important, however, is the growing record of evaluation studies and critisms which support the case that, however well intended, current social policies for the aged have not been successful in achieving the ends to which they were directed.

Because of this twofold shift, which amounts to a political collapse of key constituency support together with a growing loss of confidence by some of the very groups that have traditionally "certified" the respectability of liberal social policy, it seems reasonable to predict a period of great ferment in social policy for the aged. In the American social policy context, change ordinarily occurs in one of three ways. By far the most common form of change is incremental change, such as year-to-year modifications in guidelines, legislative amendments, and budget increments. Rapid change ordinarily occurs in brief spurts, with the enactment of major new pieces of legislation or landmark court rulings. A few incremental and rapid changes also bring about deeper changes, which involve modifications in the very understandings and assumptions underlying the working consensus in a given policy arena. We may be facing the possibility of such an era of deep change in social policy at present, as the entire spectrum of existing social policies and the underlying values they represent appear to be under attack by the "new conservatives."

It was fairly certain that the 1982 federal budget—which incorporates the "block grant" approach to consolidating numerous social programs—will bring major incremental changes in program guidelines and funding patterns, if only because of the budget reductions that are included. In addition, some rapid changes can be expected to result from Congressional actions such as the elimination of CETA, Legal Services, and other programs which have been of marginal benefit to older recipients. However, the depth of change in the policy milieu of the aged has yet to be gauged.

In addition to the likelihood of change in aging policy, it seems quite likely at the moment that any deeper changes in policy which do occur will almost certainly move aging policy in a more conservative direction, if only because of the paucity of credible liberal reform ideas and political support cited earlier. Among other things, this is likely to mean: (a) less reliance on government in general, and the federal government in particular, in policy strategies; (b) elimination or reduction of political, economic, and social redistributive tendencies, such as they are, in existing policy; (c) a reemphasis on "traditional" welfare notions of worthiness, custody, and familial and community responsibility as elements in serving the old; and (d) generally more restrictive and limited conceptions of eligibility and benefit.

We will not attempt to assess or predict the full range of possible implications of the new political strength of the Right, or of the professional and scholarly criticism of aging policy. Such a task is well beyond the limitations of this chapter, and elements of any present predictions would likely be rendered obsolete day by day. We wish instead to highlight certain central elements of existing aging policy and raise certain questions which require consideration in the context of policy change.

Income Policy

By far the most important area of social policy concern for the aged is income maintenance policy, if only because an estimated 30 million retired persons receive all or a major portion of their income through the Social Security system (Brotman, 1980). Policy in this area has been evolving incrementally since the 1930s but always in the direction of gradually increased benefits, expanded eligibility, broadened coverage, and cost of living adjustments. Despite 45 years of continuous tinkering, however, the system is still incomplete as an antipoverty policy for the old because there are still sizable numbers of older poor persons in our society. Current estimates are that roughly 15% of the older population has an income below the accepted "poverty line," whereas an additional 15% are classified as "near poor" (Brotman, 1980).

Critical to an understanding of the continuing nature of old-age poverty in the United States is the realization that the phenomenon is not evenly distributed among the old. Instead, those who are black, Spanish-surnamed, female, or living in rural areas are disproportionately poorer than the older population as a whole (Brotman, 1980; Schultz, 1980). Furthermore, the economic aspect of life for these older groups is clear: Working life begins at an early age, often at minimal or lowest possible compensation with inadequate or nonexistent fringe benefits, continues unabated until health-related retirement with minimum Social Security payments, supplemented by Supplemental Security Income (SSI), Medicaid, food stamps, and other public subsidies, and terminates in an extended illness (probably related to the same factors that forced retirement) bringing death at an age significantly lower than the life expectancy of the general population. It is pure political fantasy to suggest that massive cutbacks in public social welfare expenditures will not adversely affect these and other "worthy poor." The real questions are how many of the older poor will be hurt and how extensively?

The present outlook for improving the condition of the older poor is decidedly pessimistic. There is little realistic chance of further improvements for the older poor in income maintenance policy in the foreseeable future. Instead, the rise of the New Right appears to have already succeeded in minimizing or eliminating the problem of poverty as a legitimate concern for public social policy reform. Also, systematic under-payment of women, minorities, and rural residents for work comparable to that done by men, whites, and urban residents is a problem that shows no sign of abatement. Thus, it is very likely that the problem of old-age poverty for these subgroups has been integrated into the very fabric of contemporary society and can only be dealt with through one form or another of income redistribution, for which there is precious little political support at the moment.

Housing Policy

The housing data for older people in general are not as stark as those for income. About 10% of all housing occupied by the old is inadequate (Brotman, 1980). To an even greater extent than the income problem noted earlier, the housing problem of the aged falls disproportionately more heavily on the minority old. Among the black and Hispanic old, only about one in five has a chance to enjoy adequate housing (Brotman, 1980). Also, housing problems for the old are much worse in rural areas.

To a considerable extent, the housing problem of the old in the United States has been treated as a subset of the income problem, primarily because of the significance of housing as a commodity for most individuals and families. From this vantage point, one would expect that the housing problems of the old would be a function of economic status, and primarily important in the context of economic policy. Inadequacies in housing are seen as a by-product of personal income, and primary attention is directed toward policies that address the production and consumption aspects of housing as a commodity. Various policy strategies have been tried: government provision of housing; public subsidies for market and non-profit developers; tax incentives such as the controversial middle-class mortgage deduction on federal income taxes; and a "trickle down" laissez-faire approach which assumes that used housing will eventually work its way down to lower income consumption levels through the workings of an the marketplace.

There has even been the semblance of an "environmental policy" approach which has appeared in the case of federal housing policy for the old. Since the 1960s, those concerned with the policy implications of housing for the elderly have not only been concerned with the economic issue of production and consumption, but also with the "qualitative" issue of the living environments of older persons. Although this approach has made some impact through the process of designing public and private nonprofit housing units and nursing homes, it is also apparent that much remains to be done in this area and that a significant proportion of the housing created explicitly for the old using public funds has been poorly designed, inadequately constructed, and offers an indifferent legacy to the future.

Services Policy

Carol Estes, in *The Aging Enterprise* (1979), has declared that services policy for the old is a failure, and we are inclined to agree with her. Public policy support for services to the old in the United States is predominantly offered through three principle legislative avenues: Medicare and Medicaid, Titles XVIII and XIX of the Social Security Act, Title XX of that same act, which provides funding for social services, and Title III of the Older Americans Act, which provides support for nutritional and social services through the "Aging Network." Medicare provides approximately $19 billion annually for health care for those over 65. Medicaid expenditures total approximately $6.7 billion annually—of which approximately 21% is explicitly for the old. Title XX funds approximately $2.9 billion annually for the purchase of services by state departments of welfare—a major part of which is for older constituents. In this category, the Aging Network spends a rather paltry $400 million, but the program is symbolically important as legislation intended specifically for the benefit of the aged.

"Deinstitutionalization" or keeping the old out of institutions and living independently has allegedly been a major objective of national aging policy since the 1960s. This is explicitly recognized in the legislative language of both Title XX and the Older Americans Act. Despite such legislative intent, however, it is abundantly clear to anyone who chooses to examine the issue closely that national public policy also incorporates enormous and powerful incentives favoring institutionalization of the old, and that, unless and until these are overcome, the "deinstitutionalization movement" is destined to remain largely rhetoric. In particular, Medicare and Medicaid create enormous financial incentives against home-delivered and community-based care, as various critics have been pointing out since the 1960s (Anderson & Stone, 1969; Morris, 1979). Furthermore, Medicare and Medicaid also support a bizarre labeling process in which the chronic health conditions of the old are often "acute-ized" into reimbursible short-term illnesses and redefined into purely medical conditions in order to be eligible for public reimbursement. As evidence of the general lack of impact of deinstitutionalization policy, the number of nursing home beds in the United States actually increased from 815,000 in 1969 to 1.3 million in 1977 (U.S. Government Commerce Department, 1979).

In both Title XX and the Aging Network, political and organizational considerations have typically transcended individual client needs and expectations in determining the allocation of funds. Title XX ostensibly provides support for state welfare departments to purchase services which they deem to be needed in their states; however, in most instances such determinations are a mere by-product of a bargaining process where by the best mobilized, most skillful and politically influencial deliverers can ordinarily expect to gain the largest share of available funds. Meanwhile, the Administration on Aging (AOA) has been preoccupied for some time with the organizational and political dimensions of creating an "Aging Network" and dramatically less concerned with the types of services delivered—and the agencies have been extremely prolific at this. With $400 million a year, the AOA has spawned a five-layered national system: Before any services are ever provided, the discretionary funds appropriated by Congress must be acted upon by (*a*) the national AOA; (*b*) 10 regional AOA offices; (*c*) 55 state aging agencies; (*d*) approximately 600 area aging agencies (AAA); and (*e*) thousands of "local projects" at varying levels of autonomy from the AAA's. It is appropriate to ask, in this context, if there really are that many matters to be decided for $400 million.

Title XX, like Medicaid, is not explicitly aging legislation. However, it is particularly relevant to the old because of its goal of preventing premature institutionalization. It is likely also to be a portent of things to come under the proposed Reagan community block grant approach. Thus, it is of no small interest that in some states there has been marked tendency toward children's services in Title XX decision making, whereas in others Title XX has been the arena for extended conflict between interests and agencies favoring the young versus those favoring the old.

The fundamental paradox of national service policies remains: Because of the traditions of American federalism, the federal government has been legislatively limited to a largely fiscal role in subsidizing services; yet the very bureaucratic processes that support "grantsmanship," "contracts-manship," and "third-party reimbursement" have given a strong policy role to administrative officials and an equally strong role to agency and program recipients. What results is often a kind of quasi-market approach to social policy—an approach which has largely failed to produce nationally coherent service policy.

Symbolic Policy

A significantly less studied, but equally interesting, dimension of aging policy is what can be termed *symbolic policy*. We use this term in two related senses: First, there are the relatively benign propoganda efforts of the AOA and others to shape a "more favorable public attitude toward the aged." The Ruth Gordon poster circulated nationally in May 1981 for Senior Citizens Month is an example of this approach. The public television series *Over Easy* with Hugh Downs is another example. These approaches combine elements of romanticism, sympathy, and nostalgia in efforts to try to recapture the high esteem in which the old were allegedly once held in our society. On the whole, such efforts constitute little more than well-intended efforts to recapture some past "golden age" and introduce more caring and concern for the plight of others into public society.

Symbolic policy also encompasses another related, but far more pernicious, dimension—what Butler (1975) calls "the pacification politics" of aging. The apparent objective here is for a variety of elites—most notably federal- and state-elected officials, bureaucrats, and national interest group officials—to create the illusion of widespread involvement and participation by older people in policy decision-making processes. The presumed motivation behind these efforts is twofold: To ensure individual and organizational positions and to prevent or mitigate the effects of genuine political activism by, or involving, the old. Anyone who has ever become involved with the various White House Conferences on Aging, for example, knows it is a sham to suggest that the nation's old are identifying their problems and calling for action. Likewise, legislative goals for Medicare, Medicaid, Title XX, the Older Americans Act, and National Housing Acts, to mention just a few, serve no apparent purpose other than assuring the naive and the gullible that public officials are "looking out for the folks back home."

Although it can be objected that these are "goals" to be aspired to or striven for, and not operational objectives, it can also be conjectured that the principal reasons for such formulations are to foster the "politics of quiescence"—in this case to politically pacify the old. The spectre of another Townsend movement, with hundreds of thousands of older persons mobilized, marching, and voting their convictions looms large over Washington and state capitals everywhere. Apparently, old people with various serious and even life-threatening problems should be content with their fate simply because Washington has identified their plight as a high priority.

Taken together, then, the present social policy picture is not one to inspire great confidence in our collective problem-solving capability as a society—the Stockman budget cutters notwithstanding. Despite, or perhaps because of, public income support policies, we have created an apparently permanent underclass of older poor who are predominantly female, minority, and rural as a permanent fixture of American life. The "living environments" approach has made relatively little permanent impact on a national housing policy that is predominantly economics- and construction-oriented. Services policy is poorly conceived and misfocused, and the considerable propaganda resources of the federal government are being divided between the laudable end of creating better public support for the old and the less laudable end of "fostering contentment" and political pacification among the old.

CONCLUSIONS

So what does all this mean? It is well within the realm of reason, for example, that the passionate frenzy of the new conservatives could achieve their avowed goals and virtually eliminate all vestiges of the present social policy system for the old in the next 3–5 years, perhaps replacing it with increased reliance on family, community, and state systems. Similarly, it is very conceivable that bureaucratic and interest group alliances can survive politically, emerging in 1982 or 1984 unscathed, and that the present configurations of Social Security, SSI, Medicare, Medicaid, Title XX, National Housing Act, Older Americans Act, and the other less prominent components of national aging policy will define the bounds of social provisions for the old for the remainder of the century. Although it might resolve the question of emergent opposition to present aging policy, it would leave unresolved the equally vexing problem of the collapse of confidence in present policy. Before we as a society can expect to have a set of coherent, meaningful policies for the aged, a number of the major issues raised by critics must be resolved. In particular, three basic sets of issues need to be resolved: Who benefits? How are Benefits Delivered? Who Pays?

Who Benefits?

One of the most basic questions to be applied to the present system is who are the real beneficiaries of Medicare, Medicaid, Title XX, the Older Americans Act, and other, minor pieces of social legislation affecting older persons? Is it older persons or middle-class and middle-aged service providers who really benefit from these programs? This question has been raised by Estes and others, and needs to be addressed. Is it really that the middle-aged get incomes and the old get symbols under present policy?

Furthermore, which of the old really benefit under such social legislation—the young-old or the old-old; the healthy or the frail; those with acute or those with chronic illnesses; those with low, middle, or high incomes; urban, rural, or suburban groups; whites, blacks, or other ethnic minorities? Part of the present problem with social policy is the tendency to answer "all of the above" to such questions—and then to fail to follow through.

How are Benefits Delivered?

Another set of issues concerns the questions of who does what under public policy auspices and who pays the bill. In this area, the Reagan–Stockman approach has once again made the role of government, and the role of the federal government in particular, a basic issue in social policy—to a degree that it has not been for several decades. However, even if one opts for a massive "reprivatization" of human services, in which voluntary and for-profit entities assume all major present public policy roles, a host of public policy questions remain. The nursing home industry in the United States, for example, is probably the single most privately held sector of the total array of human services. It is also an area suspected of widespread abuse and neglect of patients, and the clamor for inspection, regulation, and control of these private institutions is ongoing.

One of the current lines of though is that many of the problems of professional and bureaucratic service delivery systems would be eliminated or minimized by encouraging "natural helping systems." In part, of course, this approach is a disingenuous attempt to cope with the consequences of funding cutbacks—to get for free what once was paid for. A variety of fascinating experiments and demonstrations has been conducted in this area; it is, however, premature to suggest that the "natural supports" model can be the basis for public policy response to the problems of the aged. Not that many years have passed since the natural supports notion of family responsibility was eliminated from public welfare legislation in most states.

Who Pays and How?

The "bottom line" on public policy options is, of course, the fundamental question of who pays for services and benefits and how payment is made. From the vantage point of sources, there are three principal options: private (market) purchases; public subsidies from tax revenues; and voluntary contributions.

Basic to the new political economy of the Reagan era are the arguments that (a) the federal government should not support social programs for constitutional and philosophical reasons; (b) current expenditures in this area are bad for the economy; and (c) social expenditures merit lower priority than a major defense build-up.

It is important to note, however, that this leaves two options and not just one: Private social welfare efforts are typically assumed to be voluntary and nonprofit in nature; but "privatization" could also mean encouraging the growth of entrepreneurial, profitable enterprise to meet the needs of the elderly. This would constitute a major shift in orientation away from the current advertising and marketing thrusts upon such "created needs" as denture deodorants and skin dyes toward more pressing needs. Given the current income of the aged population, real opportunities for such an approach appear to exist in recreation and leisure time, housing, food and nutrition, health and personal care, and other areas. This approach has little applicability, however, for the roughly one-third of the old who are poor, or near poor, and for whom the expenditure for solving problems through private consumption is simply an unrealistic option. For this population, the Reagan-Stockman approach holds little promise other than through a new voluntarism which seeks to create programs and services funded by private donations and contributions. In the past, such ventures have been limited by the well-know difficulties of voluntary fund raising. Whether such difficulties could be overcome in a new era of private action remains to be seen.

The social policy milieu in which Americans grow old today is a very volatile environment indeed. In many respects, it may be the least predictable, most risky aspect of the current milieu of aging. The burden of this unpredictability will continue to weigh most heavily upon those who are currently old and uncertain of their fate and upon those approaching old age. However, ultimately the burden of this public policy uncertainty of the moment falls upon each of us as we seek to plan for or anticipate the events of old age, which are still several decades in the future. It would be an act of uncommon statesmanship to clarify and stabilize this environment as rapidly as possible.

REFERENCES

Anderson, N. N., & Stone, L. B. Nursing homes and public policy. *The Gerontologist,* 1969, 9, 214–218.

Binstock, R., & Shanas, E. (Eds.). *The handbook of aging and the social sciences.* New York: Van Nostrand Reinhold, 1976.

Birren, J. E. (Ed.). *Handbook of aging and the individual.* Chicago: University of Chicago Press, 1959.

Brotman, H. B. Every ninth American. *Developments in aging.* Washington, D. C.: U. S. Senate, 1980.

Burgess, E. W. (Ed.). *Aging in western societies.* Chicago: University of Chicago Press, 1960.

Butler, R. *Why survive? Being old in America.* New York: Harper and Row, 1975.

Estes, C. *The aging enterprise.* San Francisco: Jossey–Bass, 1979.

Morris, R. *Social policy of the welfare state: An introduction to policy analysis.* New York: Harper & Row, 1979.

Schultz, J. H. *The economics of aging* (2nd ed.). Belmont, Calif.: Wadsworth, 1980.

Tibbitts, C. (Ed.). *Handbook of social gerontology.* Chicago: University of Chicago Press, 1960.

U. S. Government Commerce Department. *Statistical abstract of the United States, 1979.* Washington, D. C.: U. S. Government Printing Office, 1979, 116.

3

Star-Crossed Love:
The Developmental Phenomenologies
of the Life Cycle

NANCY DATAN

My role in this chapter seems at first glance to be an appealing one: to stimulate the appetites by providing a glimpse into the personal milieu of aging —a sort of scientific voyeurism. At second glance, and more particularly upon critical reflection, however, this topic seems to me to represent a monstrous act of impertinence, the sort of scientific hubris to which gerontologists are particularly—and in my judgment, dangerously— prone. I am 40: In all honesty I have no idea at all what the personal milieu of aging must be like, although, like most gerontologists my age, I am seldom inhibited by my ignorance.

As our country's population ages, we will see the "graying" of society and, with it, significant social, political, and economic changes. I believe we will no longer be able to indulge in the luxury of ignorance masked with scientific measures. I am sometimes called the most pessimistic gerontologist in the country: This chapter will show the reader where I learned my pessimism.

I have undertaken this task with the help of two friends: my son Gidon, who is 13 years old, and his friend Leland, who is 88 years old. Six years ago, Robert Kastenbaum wrote to me that the *International Journal of Aging and Human Development* had accepted my article "Leland: A Love Story" for publication and in so doing would become the first gerontology journal to lose its mailing privileges and gain an X-rating. That article was a portrait, not of a man, but of a relationship. The man still lives, but a portion of the relationship has died, and in this chapter I shall chronicle the small deaths, of individuals and processes, which have occurred over

29

AGING AND MILIEU:
ENVIRONMENTAL PERSPECTIVES
ON GROWING OLD

the intervening years which have brought my son to the threshold of adolescence, me to middle age, and Leland to old age. My theoretical point of departure is a consideration of the life-cycle transformations in the three relational modes of the human personality—the narcissistic, the erotic, and the active—seen in the context of a social psychological model of proximity and contact across age groups (Nahemow & Lawton, 1975). My immediate point of departure will be the dialogue spoken in 1974 and published in 1975 which brings "Leland: A Love Story" to its conclusion. Step back with me in time, over about a mile in space—a mile that will soon prove longer than Leland and I had guessed.

> "I'm going to write my own companion piece to your essay," Leland tells me as this narrative takes shape, "but I shall begin at the end, as you pack your children and dog into the car and head for a new destination, leaving me behind."
> "Love stories always end in tragic separation. That's a comparatively benign conclusion, since each of us survives to find new companions. But what will you do if I don't depart according to your schedule?"
> "I'll have to find a new end for my beginning," says Leland [Datan, 1975, p. 290].

In 1974 Leland called our relationship a "facultative symbiosis"—a zoological term for a romance between two independent organisms who allowed themselves to enjoy a measure of interdependence. Some relationships, like good marriages and good gardens, thrive on constant contact. Ours did. When the house I was renting went up for sale and Leland advised against my purchasing it, neither of us guessed how vulnerable our symbiosis would prove.

Less than a year after our love story reached publication, I was indeed packing the children and the dog into the car and heading for a new destination, though it was not as distant as Leland had feared: It was only a mile up the hill to a newly purchased home. Leland was 83; my daughters were 13 and 11; my son was 8; our dog was 15; I was 35. Human development took my daughters into adolescence and away from their daily visits to Leland; old age took our dog away from all of us; the university routine brought me home in the evenings too weary for visits to a friend who was no longer next door. There seemed no way to recreate the casual intimacy we had taken for granted, so much deeper than the friendship of neighbors, but, it turned out, so completely dependent upon our proximity.

I learned this year that the distance between Leland and myself has been investigated by two of my colleagues who are contributors to this volume, Lucille Nahemow and Powell Lawton. They showed in 1975 that proximity increased the likelihood of friendship between persons of different ages. Conversely, they found that physical distance may combine with social psychological distance so that dissimilarity in age, sex, or race reduces the attraction between individuals—and thus the effort required to traverse the physical distance in order to establish or maintain a friendship may simply never be made.

Applying these findings to our own dilemma, then, it seems that the social psychology of proximity brought Leland and me together; developmental phenomenology, as I shall suggest, keeps us apart. For I am talking about a tie that is stronger than friendship: I am talking about love. Love has withstood the mile between myself and Leland, but, with the loss of a "shared living space," to borrow a phrase from Nahemow and Lawton (1975), the daily contact on which our friendship thrived has not.

In order to show how a mile can mean so much, I shall go beyond the social psychological model of Nahemow and Lawton and consider the developmental phenomenology of the life cycle, in order to suggest that the lack of synchrony in the developmental phenomenologies of middle- and old-age distances each from the other—at the expense of both. For this purpose, I shall integrate concepts from theorists of personality dynamics, developmental theorists of infancy, adolescence, and adulthood. Indeed, perhaps *integrate* is too grandiose a term for the modest synthesis I shall attempt; I shall take threads from assorted personality theories and weave them together in order to explore relationships among personality processes across the life span.

In this brief theoretical excursion, I shall bring together life-cycle perspectives on the dynamic transformations in personality which occur in the three great relational modes: the erotic, the active, and the narcissistic, as Freud (1961) terms them; or, as Bakan (1966), Gutmann (1980), and others describe them, the communal, the agentic or aggressive, and the narcissistic. Put more simply, I shall describe life-cycle transformations in three dimensions of individual experience: attachments to others, activity, and the sense of self. As is obvious, I use these concepts more loosely than many do, for the purpose of contrast among processes rather than for precision of definition of a single process. I hope to discover the interior experiences that accompany the social processes of different ages, and thus to come closer to understanding why a mile has proven such an obstacle to so close a friendship.

Let me preview and summarize the transformations in the three relational modes that occur as we look across the life cycle. Narcissism is first seen in infancy as primary infantile narcissism, reborn at adolescence as the adolescent's sense of omnipotentiality, reinvested in adulthood as one's child becomes the narcissistic extension of the self, finally reappearing in old age in subdued form as the preoccupations of the life review. Active engagement with the world begins modestly with the dependent infant who can cry, suckle, and smile. In time, if well fed, the infant grows into the autonomous adult, who in turn assumes responsibility for others, and, finally, with advancing old age and physical decline, once more becomes dependent. Erotic ties begin with the infantile, pregenital passions of the Oedipus complex, mature into the mutual genital love of adulthood and the ties of the parent to the child, and with old age undergo a regression to diffuse pregenital sensuality, together with the near-universal sexual deprivation consequent upon death of a spouse. In this preview, I have considered each of the three relational modes as it is transformed over the life cycle. I shall now consider these processes as they interact in each of the phases of the life cycle.

In infancy, we find the self at the center of all things. Primary narcissism is characteristic of infants, whose pre-Copernican view of the world is that it revolves about and for them. Early in development, however, primary narcissism is subdued by the many inevitable failures of even the most nurturant world: The food is never there before the hunger comes, and slowly the rhythm of frustration and gratification teaches the infant to value the nurturing parents. This, the beginning of the oedipal triangle, is also the beginning of object relations—or, more simply, love. At the same time that the developing infant is beginning to trust and depend upon the caretaking parents, paradoxically, the first steps toward autonomy are also being taken. Thus, early in life, primary narcissism is the natural state; slowly this yeilds to awareness of others and of dependence on them, together with the almost imperceptible beginnings of autonomous activity.

Moving on to the interface between adolescence and young adulthood, we find that dramatic transformations have occurred in the three relational modes. The narcissism of infancy has become the omnipotentiality of adolescence, soon to be focused in young adulthood on the developmental task of finding a place in the world—the very world that once seemed to revolve about the infant. The primitive object relations of the oedipal period have matured into a capacity for intimacy with a partner. Perhaps most significantly, the rudimentary steps toward autonomy begun in early childhood have culminated in an adult capable not only of caring for himself or herself, but also of looking after someone new, helpless, and, of course, narcissistic. Thus in adulthood, narcissism seems to have given way to nurturance and thus transformed into a narcissistic reinvestment in one's infant; dependency has been transformed into autonomy and then into responsibility for others; and the primal passions of the Oedipus complex have become the capacity for intimacy and the mutuality of adult genital love.

Proceeding once more, into the never-never land of the personality dynamics of later life, we find in middle age that sex-related differences reflect the narcissistic insults that physical aging brings. For women, physical aging threatens the capacity to love and be loved; for men, physical aging is a threat to the capacity to work. These statements represent my observations, not my endorsement; with Freud, I believe that love *and* work are the tasks of the healthy adult. As an observer of contemporary society, however, I consider that somehow the tasks of love and work have been bureaucratized, or so it seems: Women love; men work; and the vast marketplace of American advertising exploits the sex-specific anxieties of each as the narcissistic insults of aging begin (cf. Notman, 1980). Women learn from their mirrors that they will not be 21 forever but that their husbands might be induced to love them as much as before if they choose the right moisturizer; the Angel of Death snatches men in the middle of the coffee break, while divine voices assure them that their prudent selection of insurance will maintain their productivity without interruption.

The narcissistic insults of physical aging highlight the middle-age changes in activity and object relations. These interact for the parents of adolescent children: In middle age, the dependency of infancy and the autonomy of young adulthood, which have long since matured into responsibility for others, the oedipal passions, which have matured into genital love and the nurture of the next generation, and the infantile narcissism, which has been reinvested in the children, all undergo a swift obsolescence in middle age. For family development involves more than the parents: The developmental tasks faced by the adolescent children ensure that whatever stability the middle-aged parent has achieved will be very short-lived. I remember well when my own secondborn daughter, a newly blossomed adolescent, put her arm around me, and we smiled together into a mirror reflecting our faces as well as our relationship—or so I thought. Instead, my daughter smiled and said, "I'm so young and you're so old!"

The family life cycle brings the children to the omnipotentiality of adolescence just as their parents are confronting the finitude of middle and old age. Thus the narcissism once invested in the young child is threatened by the adolescent; the activity once expressed as responsibility for the children becomes superfluous as the children become responsible for themselves (although increasingly, and we shall see even more of this in the future, middle-aged parents become responsible for their own aging parents); and finally, the erotic ties of adult genital love may be vulnerable to the asynchrony between the sexes. The mid-life crisis in men's lives first received attention in a study of careers (Datan, 1981a, 1981b; Gould,

1978; Levinson, 1978; Sarason, 1977), whereas the salient mid-life changes in women's lives occur in family relations (Datan, 1981a; Datan, Antonovsky, & Maoz, 1981; Neugarten, 1968). Indeed, among the normative developmental life events for middle-aged women is the "rehearsal for widowhood" (Neugarten, 1968), a grim reminder that gender-related differences in biology, life-style, and expected age at marriage culminate in the expectation that most women whose marriages survive the middle years will outline their husbands by a decade or more (Lopata, 1980).

Now let us move into old age. I suggest that the normal process of the life review described by Robert Butler (1968) represents a reappearance of narcissism. The autonomy of young adulthood and the responsibilities of middle age slowly become the dependency of old age—altogether unlike the dependency of infancy, because the dependency of old age represents a fall from power, a reluctant acceptance of unwelcome physical, social, and economic limitations imposed on a body once fit for anything and a mind still likely to be fit for anything.

The genital eroticism of adulthood ebbs in later life, David Gutmann (1980) has claimed, and becomes a diffuse pregenital sensuality, the capacity to take an "incidental bonus of pleasure" from beauty, "the hunger of old men [p. 42]." As Robert Kastenbaum (1973) has remarked, the sexual fate of the aging individual is likely to be one of deprivation, due to the loss of a spouse and the consequent loss not only of an erotic partner but also of someone to cuddle with. When King David grew old, the Bible tells us, young Abishag[1] was brought to warm his bed; the double standard of aging has not changed very much over the several thousand intervening years, and most of the old today are women who are unlikely to look forward to the luxury of young boys to warm their chilled and aging flesh.

To recapitulate: In old age we see a resurgence of narcissism in the preoccupation with the life review, a return to dependency, and the prospect of erotic deprivation. This grim portrait should explain my reputation as one of the most pessimistic scholars in the field of gerontology. Having drawn the broad outlines, I would now like to add some color.

The outline of developmental dynamics that I have sketched here suggests a possible harmony between childhood and old age. I am not arguing Shakespeare's notion of a "second childhood"; indeed, I want to underscore the fact that the losses of later life do not parallel the expectations of childhood. Childhood ends with the achievement of

---

[1] I am indebted to Leland Taylor, whose poetry ranges to embrace this historical romance, for helping to preserve for the Bible its rightful place in contemporary psychology.

autonomous adulthood; old age begins with the dependencies of physical decline and terminates in death. Although the lack of equivalence is obvious, it is also true that the developmental phenomenologies of early and late life are compatible in a way that the phenomenologies of middle and late life are not.

The statements I have made are not merely pessimistic but frightening, and few gerontologists are eager to explore the final confrontation with biological decline and death. I was led to confront these issues through my son's friendship with Leland, for when Gidon grew old enough to realize that his best friend was 75 years older than himself, he also realized he would lose his friend to death. A part of any friendship is mutual respect for a friend's needs and weaknesses: On Leland's part, this has required tolerance for Gidon's enormous adolescent appetites, and he is sometimes caught publicly sneaking large supplies of candy bars into his shopping cart. On Gidon's part, he has made frank inquiries as to what to do if he comes for a visit and finds Leland unconscious and has even rehearsed phone calls to the Emergency Medical Squad. The candor of their reciprocal concerns is rare, as I shall show by comparison with other friendships.

Gidon and Leland celebrate their birthdays in April. This year Gidon celebrated his bar mitzvah. Leland is an atheist whose views on the topic of organized religion are firm and unfriendly, and he remarked that this bar mitzvah would be his final martyrdom to the social obligations incurred by his friendships with Jews. Nevertheless, his friendship with Gidon stood the test of 2 long hours of recitation in Hebrew; Gidon rarely paused for breath, and Leland never stopped smiling. No lasting conversion to ritual was worked by the ceremony itself, however; Leland declared at the reception afterward that he planned to pass on before the Cohens' sons reached bar mitzvah age.

At his own birthday party just a few days later, Leland stood by this declaration. A crowd of friends, whose mean age was less than half his 88 years, sang "Happy Birthday." As he thanked us, Leland declared that he did not intend to celebrate another birthday. This was greeted by hearty shouts of denial, and a friend remarked to me, "If you want to see him really angry, just tell him that's not for him to decide, but for God." But when I went over to join Leland, that was not what I told him. He took my hand and said that he hoped indeed that he would not survive into physical frailty and dependency, and, when, like everyone else, I tried to deny his dying, he said, "I think I have earned the right to look my own death in the face." Yes, he has, and, if I am ever to learn this for myself, it will be easier for me to learn from Leland, as Gidon has, than to struggle with death alone, imprisoned by the age-graded structure of contemporary Western society.

I think I have earned by now the title of most pessimistic gerontologist, and I would like to give credit where it is due. Leland was a pessimistic gerontologist before I ever met him—or, if you prefer, a poet of the final season of the life cycle. He and I have had a few similar experiences, and the distance between our responses—mine cautious and demographic; his poetic—will serve as my final illustration of the distance between the phenomenologies of middle and later life.

The object of these two encounters was identical; each of us ran across a chartered tour bus carrying old people. My own encounter occurred this year, on the road after taking my daughter to college and myself part way back again. A chartered bus load of "senior citizens" on tour pulled off the turnpike just when we did, and my husband and I found ourselves surrounded in the cafeteria line by old women—there were very few surviving husbands. It was a grim *memento mori* for me; I know that most of this country's old people are women, that statistical probability makes widowhood normative; that indeed, there, but for a few decades, go I. We were lightheaded after 10 hours on the road in a Volkswagon, or so I told myself at first, until I allowed myself to admit that giggling like a teenage in a high school cafeteria was a poor defense for an educated gerontologist against the fear of old age and widowhood.

Leland encountered a chartered busload of old people on tour also, but he did not giggle. He wrote a poem, in March 1973—3 months before we met—which he has allowed me to contribute to the gerontological literature.

> *Golden Agers' Trip*
>
> *Boldly painted banners across the chartered bus*
> *blast out the message*
> *Golden Age Autumn Foliage Tour.*
> *Sexagenarians septuagenarians octogenarians*
> *stumble like dusk-chilled bees*
> *crowding the entrance*
> *struggle to harvest the dwindling sweets of autumn*
> *seek tenuous warmth, nature's touted beauty*
> *an ante-climax to distract the eye of mind*
> *from winter's certain kiss of death*
> *embrace of dying.*
> *What evil calculating punster*
> *invented the foul pun Golden Age*
> *dubbing drab decades with an era's gloried name*
> *tempted the multigenarian to gulp pernicious pill*
> *destined to end*
> *in a bad trip?*
>
> —LELAND HART TAYLOR
> *(by permission)*

Why do Leland's many friends, who love his obscene limericks, refuse to listen to this poem, and sing "Happy Birthday" to him as though he will live forever? The easy answer is that if we allow ourselves to hear what we are being told so clearly, we must recognize that we are being asked to accept, even to share, the proximity of death. But it is hard to see how we could deny it, or why we would try. I shall attempt to answer this issue indirectly.

In 1973 Robert Butler described to me some new techniques in group therapy which were remarkably successful (see Butler & Lewis, 1977). He had found that age-heterogeneous groups potentiated the therapeutic interactions that occured more slowly in age-homogeneous groups. For years I thought this was a brilliant piece of research for the wrong reasons; I thought Butler had found a way to overcome the age segregation of American society. More recently I have concluded that what he accomplished was even more remarkable, though less original: He rediscovered the natural strengths of the extended family. Having been led to his concern for the old through his love for the grandfather who raised him (Butler, 1975), Robert Butler would appreciate the fact that my son made a very similar discovery. That the rest of us acknowledge our ties to the old so seldom is not only their loss, but also ours.

This chapter concludes with a confession. Of the two tasks I have set myself, I have so far admitted only to one, and that was the lesser task of painting, however incompletely, a portrait of one man's old age, through his poetry and through the eyes of those who love him. The larger task I attempted was to overcome the mile dividing Leland and me, to bridge the natural chasm between a productive, middle-aged professor of psychology and a retired professor of zoology. To put it another way, I tried to make work out of love, so as to legitimate the daily round of visits, and to make us, for a little while at least, neighbors again. At this second task I failed. We know one another too well, Leland and I; distance is no deterrent to our love, merely to our routines. So I captured his world for a little while, at least, but failed at the larger task when I tried to reenter it. The lesson I learned from having tried is that it is easier to be a creative gerontologist than to be a faithful friend.

REFERENCES

Bakan, D. *The duality of human existence.* Boston: Beacon Press, 1966.

Butler, R. N. The life review: An interpretation of reminiscence in the aged. In B. L. Neugarten (Ed.), *Middle age and aging.* Chicago: University of Chicago Press, 1968.

Butler, R. N. Personal communication, 1973. Subsequently published in R. N. Butler & M. I. Lewis. *Aging and mental health: Positive psycho-social approaches* (2nd ed.). St. Louis: C. V. Mosby, 1977.

Butler, R. N. *Why survive? Being old in America.* New York: Harper & Row, 1975.

Datan, N.   Leland: A love story. *International Journal of Aging and Human Development,* 1975, *6,* 283–291.

Datan, N. Coming undone. *Contemporary Psychology,* 1981, *26,* 460–461. (a)

Datan, N. Normative or not? Confession of a fallen epistemologist. In K. A. McCluskey & E. C. Callahan (Eds.), *Life-span developmental psychology: Non-normative life events.* New York: Academic Press, 1981. (b)

Datan, N., Antonovsky, A., & Maoz, B. *A time to reap: The middle age of women in five Israeli subcultures.* Baltimore: Johns Hopkins University Press, 1981.

Freud, S. *Civilization and its discontents.* New York: W. W. Norton, 1961.

Gould, R. L. *Transformations: Growth and change in adult life.* New York: Simon & Schuster, 1978.

Gutmann, D. L. The post-parental years: Clinical problems and developmental possibilities. In W. H. Norman & T. J. Scaramella (Eds.), *Mid-life: Developmental and clinical issues.* New York: Bruner–Mazel, 1980.

Kastenbaum, R. Epilogue: Loving, dying, and other gerontologic addenda. In C. Eisdorfer & M. P. Lawton (Eds.), *The psychology of adult development and aging.* Washington, D. C.: American Psychological Association, 1973.

Levinson, D. *The seasons of a man's life.* New York: Knopf, 1978.

Lopata, H. Z. The widowed family member. In N. Datan & N. Lohmann (Eds.), *Transitions of aging.* New York: Academic Press, 1980.

Nahemow, L., & Lawton, M. P. Similarity and propinquity in friendship formation. *Journal of Personality and Social Psychology,* 1975, *32,* 205–213.

Neugarten, B. L. The awareness of middle age. In B. L. Neugarten (Ed.), *Middle age and aging.* Chicago: University of Chicago Press, 1968.

Notman, M. T. Changing roles for women at mid-life. In W. H. Norman & T. J. Scaramella (Eds.), *Mid-life: Developmental and clinical issues.* New York: Bruner–Mazel, 1980.

Sarason, S. B. *Work, aging, and social change: Professionals and the one-life one-career imperative.* New York: Free Press, 1977.

II

THE OLD-PERSON–ENVIRONMENT TRANSACTION

4

Time, Space, and Activity

M. POWELL LAWTON

This chapter will discuss the activity patterns of older people as they are related to the broadest concept of well-being. *Activity* as discussed here may be defined as the time allocations of overt behaviors within specifiable environmental contexts. Thus the basic ingredients of the discussion to follow are time, space, activity, and well-being. For a variety of reasons these elements will not be given equal time. The focus will be on activity and well-being.

TIME AND ACTIVITY

The reason I choose to de-emphasize time is that, in contrast to Kastenbaum (1966) and many others, I suspect time of being primarily a yardstick by which activity can be measured rather than being a central construct around which people subjectively organize their own developmental stages or entire life spans.

To support this assertion one must first acknowledge the dialectic of objective versus subjective states, in this case, of time. Objective time is easy to define, since it is based on naturally occurring movement whose measurement constitutes no problem. Subjective time is a popular topic, of inherent interest and of presumed relevance for studying human development. The understanding of the processes of development themselves have been advanced greatly by the empirical and conceptual

41

AGING AND MILIEU:
ENVIRONMENTAL PERSPECTIVES
ON GROWING OLD

exploration of such constructs as time perspective and the personal and cognitive future (Kastenbaum, 1966).

However, my question is whether these subjective aspects of time are not better conceptualized in terms of events or activities whose meanings are transformed into personal terms by a variety of processes, only one of which is a subjective time metric. For example, the personal future, as operationalized by Kastenbaum requires the person to anticipate in fantasy an event with the self and/or others as actors (or, conceivably, some nonpersonal event) at some clock-time distance from the present. In addition to the event and the clock time, the response may be compounded with many elements of personal meaning, often with the self as an object, and it is this complex of elements that has been called subjective time. It seems to me to be stretching the point to refer to such complex and highly abstracted cognitive processes as "time." Rather, it would seem more important to understand and measure separately each component— the subjective time estimate, the event, and the subjective meanings attached to the event—and how they are related to another, than to try to subsume the totality under a single megaconstruct. The possible reward in increased knowledge will be greater if we learn more about how the events and the estimated time fit into the subjective meanings of the events than if we concentrate on the more global, and perhaps gerontologist-created, construct "time."

Clock time, according to Hendricks and Hendricks (1976), as "measured by arbitrary devices, comes to overshadow the role of the actor, man. . . . The conception of time as unilinear, externalized, and beyond the control of the actor curtails his creative role in the temporal experience [p. 30]." While these authors are arguing for the importance of the subjective experience of time, they have stated very well what clock time does: It "curtails," it sets limits, it bedevils, it acts as an environmental press on the behavior and the mental life of all. Part of the trick of living is to engage in fulfilling behaviors despite such external pacing. The tensions between clock time and subjective temporal perception is in the best dialectic tradition. It is of great importance to know how objective and subjective time duration are congruent and to which factors an observed incongruence is attributable.

As Hendricks and Hendricks (1976) suggest, to cast the person as the subjective "experiencer" of a time duration imposed by some arbitrary clock is to ascribe to him the role of a passive actor. However, if we redirect our thoughts to putting the person in the more active role, we leave the realm of time as such. If we direct our attention to the person as one who synchronizes his or her behavior with that of others, who does the scheduling, who makes plans, or who mentally schematizes his or her entire life span, the medium is *activity* (actual or fantasized) as allocated over clock time, not time in any abstract sense. Thus I am prepared, after noting clock time and perceived duration as temporal aspects existing to some extent in dynamic conflict, to move on to the relationship between space and activity.

SPACE AND ACTIVITY

The entire discipline of human geography is devoted to the study of the spatial aspects of behavior. Important advances in knowledge have been made toward understanding the spatial behavior of the aged (Golant, 1979; Regnier, 1976). Knowledge in this area is presently concentrated primarily on two levels: neighborhood resource use and migration (Golant, 1979). Beginnings have been made in relating these objective spatial behaviors to subjective spatial processes such as knowledge of the neighborhood and cognitive representations of these environments (Walsh, Krauss, & Regnier, 1981). There is a major lack in the knowledge of older people's activity within the space of their homes. We know to some extent the types of behaviors that occur in particular locations of planned housing for the elderly (Lawton, 1970) or institutions (Lawton, 1981; McClannahan & Risley, 1972) but have little information about the uses of spaces within the dwelling unit as studied by Altman (Altman & Gauvain, 1981; Altman, Nelson, & Lett, 1972) with respect to younger people. Similarly, despite the theoretical relevance of such proxemic concepts as privacy, personal space, crowding, and territorial behavior to older people (DeLong, 1970), few empirical studies (an outstanding exception is Rowles, 1978) have contributed to our understanding of this most microspatial level of either objective or subjective activity. So little information is available regarding place-specific behavior that the spatial aspect will be included only in very gross form.

This chapter will examine both the objective and subjective aspects of activity in search of new knowledge afforded by the congruity or incongruity between them. One feature that broadens the concern of this chapter as compared to much of the literature on activities and aging is its definition of activity to include all forms of behavior (see Lawton, 1978, for further discussion of the importance of time use of all types for the aged). "Leisure" activity has received much attention in both gerontology and general social science, for example, consuming whole books devoted to the attempt to define leisure or distinguish its attributes from the attributes of nonleisure behavior (Iso-Ahola, 1980a; Kaplan, 1975; Neulinger, 1974). Indeed, much of the conceptual base utilized in this chapter has been derived from studies of leisure, rather than activity in general. A model will be described that considers the personal and environmental determinants of objective and subjective activity and the psychological outcomes associated with activities. The chapter will conclude with a brief summary of an empirical test of a portion of the model.

OBJECTIVE AND SUBJECTIVE ASPECTS OF ACTIVITY

Objective Activity

The objective aspects of activity are best portrayed in time-budget data, where the samples of time are totally accounted for in terms of the durations of specific behaviors and the contexts where they occur (Chapin, 1974).

Why do time-budget studies? The rationale may not be obvious, since "activity" may also be called "behavior," a topic that has not been under-researched. Let us think of activities as the components of behavior—what happens from minute to minute. Life consists of minute-to-minute behavior and the decisions about what to do minute by minute. We have usually examined activity in larger units ("typical behavior," "life style") or in only selective fashion. For example, when one's spouse asks what one has done today, the answer is usually to describe a high point, a low point, or something unusual, but very little of most days consists of such underlined activities. A great deal of activity is routine, externally programmed, and instrumental to the attainment of some distant goal. Yet each minute of such time is experienced cognitively and sometimes affectively as it goes by. If we are to understand the person in his or her total environmental context, it is necessary to know how the elements are related to the larger pattern (specific versus general behaviors) and how the activities themselves are construed by the person.

It is important to note that while gerontological research often reports data on the activities of older people, these activities are usually selected behaviors singled out for inquiry and aggregated over relatively extended periods of time by estimates from the subject. Social interaction, participation in "leisure" activities, and organizational participation, for example, are usually handled by asking the person to estimate frequency of participation. Instrumental behaviors, such as shopping or housework, are less frequently asked about in similar fashion or in terms of overall time expenditure estimates (Beyer & Woods, 1963). There have been very few time-budget studies of older people. Neither the major cross-national study of 30,000 people in 12 countries (Szalai, 1972) nor its American component (a national sample and an urban sample, Robinson, 1977) included people over 65. Chapin's (1974) large urban sample did include older people, but few analyses by age were reported. In the gerontological literature we have only the work of Carp (1978–1979) and Stephens and Willems (1979), both of which were focused on people living in public housing, and the incomplete and secondary source information from 20 to 25 years ago reviewed by DeGrazia (1961).

Time-budget information is obtained either from diaries kept by a person instructed to write down behavior as it occurs or from an interview in which an entire day (usually the preceding 24 hours) is reconstructed. The activities reported must be classified into categories, which have been purely descriptive in most time-budget studies. The cross-national study (Szalai, 1972) used 99 fairly specific categories, which were reduced to 37 or, for some purposes, to 9 highly aggregated categories (examples of the latter are housework, study and participation, leisure). Chapin's (1974) system as it evolved include a very detailed code (225 categories), a medium level of aggregation (40 categories), and a basic code (12 categories); some of the latter, for example, are main job, eating, and socializing.

Subjective Activity

Constructs that may enable us to understand better the subjective aspects of activity are needs, the meaning of activities, activity satisfaction, and activity preferences. Since most research relevant to these constructs has been done within the framework of leisure research, the applicability of this knowledge to activities in general remains to be demonstrated.

NEEDS

Needs in Murray's (1938) sense were suggested by Tinsley, Barrett, and Kass (1973) and Tinsley and Kass (1978) as capable of being satisfied to different extents by different types of leisure activity. As a demonstration of this need specificity, Tinsley and Kass assembled a list of 45 needs (e.g., abasement, ability-confirmation, achievement) and found that 27 of them varied significantly in terms of their rated function in providing satisfaction to people who were high participants in 10 different activities. Factoring of mean activity-specific scores for these need satisfiers revealed eight factors: self-actualization, companionship, power, compensation, security, social service, intellectual–esthetic, and autonomy. Thus, beginning with the intrapersonal construct "need," they established a link between the need and the actual participation in a particular activity. They concluded that the activity must act to satisfy that need.

Press (Murray, 1938) is a quality of a situation that, when paired with an analogous personal need, elicits behavior designed to meet that need. Neulinger (1974) thus suggested that leisure activities could be characterized in terms of their press toward understanding, sentience, autonomy, achievement, sex, affiliation, order, nurturance, and activity. Here the focus is on the activity, rather than the person, but the press quality of the activity exists only because it is paired with the intrapersonal need. The need and press constructs of Tinsley *et al.* and Neulinger represent attempts to account for the motivation leading people to engage in an activity.

MEANING

The "meaning" of an activity is a difficult concept to define, but it may be seen as a person's characterization of an activity in personally relevant terms. Thus a first characteristic of meaning is that it represents one person's cognition of an activity. Enough persons' cognitions may agree so that a "consensual meaning" can be established for some attributes of some activities.

The literature on "leisure activities" shows an almost infinite variety of dimensions by which subjective activity has been classified. Relatively few empirical studies of the meaning of activities have been done with older people. Even in the research done with people of all ages, the bases for classifying meaning tend to be rather chaotic, reflecting no doubt the general conceptual disarray of our ability to understand subjective processes.

A number of a priori categories by which leisure activity meaning might be characterized have been suggested. An active–passive dimension has been used by many (e.g., deGrazia, 1961), whereas Gordon, Gaitz, and Scott (1976) suggested a single dimension with many defined points—the "degree of expressive involvement." A more elaborate set of attributes was suggested by Dumazedier (1974): relaxation, diversion, knowledge, social participation, and creativity. Meyersohn (1972) suggested rest–respite, entertainment, self-realization, and spiritual renewal as basic meanings by which *leisure* could be defined. Iso-Ahola (1980b) saw dimensions of leisure as described by a set of dialetic dimensions. Within this space people seek an optimal level of arousal: stability–change, structure–variety, familiarity–novelty, social–seclusive, and simple–complex.

There have been some empirical approaches to the study of meaning. One method for mapping cognitive activity space required the person to judge the amount of similarity and difference between a pair of activities and to state the basis for the difference (Ritchie, 1975). The most frequently appearing subjective dimensions describing the reasons for the choice were activity–passivity, individual–group, mental involvement–nonmental involvement, indoor–outdoor, skill–nonskill, and involving–time-filling. Among a sample of older people in Kansas City, the most frequently named meanings of favorite activities were pleasure in the act of itself, a change from work, the newness of the experience, contact with friends, a chance to achieve something, passing the time, and a chance to be creative (Donald & Havighurst, 1959); some of these dimensions also appeared in later research to characterize the meaning of voluntary association participation by older people (Ward, 1979).

Yet another approach to determining meaning derives from the empirical clustering of objective leisure activities. The presumed common quality represented factorially is seen as the connotative meaning of the activity that causes people to make choices of favorite, satisfying, or frequently performed activities. Thus McKechnie (1974) named factors based on correlations among frequency of performance of various activities: mechanics, crafts, intellectual, slow-living, neighborhood sports, glamour sports, and fast-living. Using a similar approach Bishop and Witt (1970) found factors that they named active versus diversionary, potency, and status. Although these approaches do suggest hypotheses about the implicit bases for people's choices, one still needs to marshal evidence that these dimensions are those determining the person's choice, as opposed to those simply supplied by the researcher. Ragheb and Beard (1980) focused their attention on the "sources of satisfaction" associated with leisure activities and found separate dimensions representing psychological, educational, social, relaxation–relief, physiological, and aesthetic satisfaction.

Clearly, these and other dimensions might be called by names other than *meaning*. Dumazedier's dimensions, for example, could be thought of as "functions" of leisure—what the activity does *for* the person—or alternatively, "goals" of leisure. It this the same as *meaning?* Certainly in a semantic sense it is not the same. Dumazedier's dimensions imply universal functions that exist regardless of whether their meanings are apparent to the person. Iso-Ahola's dialectic dimensions may also be thought of as properties of activities themselves rather than subjective aspects of meaning. To my mind, this apparent contradiction stems from the objective–subjective problem. Such dimensions are often asserted to be objective properties of activities. In effect, this assertion was made implicitly by Gordon *et al.* (1976) when they, as researchers, assigned every objective activity to a category falling on their expressive involvement continuum. This assertion is false, since people differ among themselves in whether they experience a particular activity, for example, drinking, as relaxation, diversion, social participation, or even creativity.

Thus, every property of an activity that fails the test of objectivity (can be counted or measured in centimeters/grams/seconds, or is characterized the same way by 100% of observers) belongs somewhere in the realm of a cognition by an individual, that is, a subjective activity. The degree of consensus among individual judgments provides some bridge between the objective and subjective aspects of meaning. If 75% of a set of judges characterize an activity as complex, we know more about the activity than if we had the judgment of only one person, but we should be very clear about stating the quasi-objective nature of any consensually determined property.

ACTIVITY SATISFACTION

Satisfaction is seen as a proximate subjective outcome derived from the person's evaluation of the positive versus negative quality of an experienced activity. Satisfaction, enjoyment, and liking are similar enough to be used interchangeably as affective components of the experience of an activity. A basic distinction was made by Ragheb and Beard (1980) between the satisfaction gained from performing an activity and the satisfaction gained from the consequences of having performed the activity; Neulinger (1974) terms this duality the "final versus instrumental" attribute of an activity. Empirically the two attributes are often impossible to distinguish. If people are asked simply to indicate how much they enjoy an activity, the evaluation may reflect the affect experienced in the doing, the immediate postactivity evaluation, and/or a more cognitively determined evaluation of that activity in terms of its instrumental value in attaining some more distal goal. For some purposes it may be sufficient to determine an overall judgment. When utilized in association with the time budget an enjoyment rating of each activity sequence allows such ratings to be aggregated over all activities of the same type or for activities of all kinds.

For other purposes it may be essential to determine the amount of satisfaction obtained from the actual performance of the activity— "intrinsic satisfaction." Although Mannell (1980) places intrinsic satisfaction within the framework of what he terms the "leisure experience," it could apply equally well to any activity: "a transient psychological state, easily interrupted, and characterized by a decreased awareness of the passage of time, decreased awareness of the incidental features of physical and social surroundings and accompanied by positive affect [p. 76]." Csikszentmihalyi's (1975) concept of "flow," by adding richer perception to this definition (forgetting the self and disorientation in time and space), appears to represent a very intense form of enjoyment of the experience of performing an activity.

A more general indicator of activity satisfaction may be determined from questions regarding the way time is spent, rather than from ratings that apply to a specific activity sequence. This aspect of activity satisfaction constitutes one of the several domains of perceived quality of life. For example, Campbell, Converse, and Rodgers (1976) used such a domain entitled "what I do in my spare time" as one of the 12 domains whose contribution to general life satisfaction was determined. This approach is, of course, not expected to be a substitute for aggregated satisfaction ratings over a set of specific activity sequences. The generalized ratings allow the respondent to weigh activities and time subjectively. The time expanse to which such questions apply is also ambiguous. The aggregated specific activity satisfactions gained from time-budget ratings may, in some ways, be more reliable than generalized ratings because they focus on specific activities: in any case they are an effective way to represent evaluations of particular activities over a short time period.

ACTIVITY PREFERENCE

A great deal of attention has been devoted to "leisure attitudes" (Crandall & Slivken, 1980; Neulinger, 1974; Neulinger & Breit, 1971). This research has dealt with beliefs and values regarding work and leisure as classes, rather than with specific work or leisure activities. Upon examination of one of the classical definitions of attitude—a readiness to put a belief into action—the preference for a particular activity would seem to be a good concretization of attitude. Many attempts have been made to determine simple preferences of older people for leisure activity. Somewhat more meaningful program-relevant information was obtained by McGuire (1980), who compared present participation, wish to participate, and wish to increase participation in 49 leisure activities. What a person is communicating when he or she says "I would like to engage in . . ." is often ambiguous. Nonetheless, conceptually there is clearly a place for activity preference based on past learning, assessment of the present situation, and estimated outcomes of engaging in the behavior.

Few attempts have been made, however, to deal with preference conceptually, that is, to determine how preference fits in with other elements in the behavioral system. The gap between attitude and behavior is well recognized. In program planning for services to older people, the hazards of designing a package of services or an activity program on the basis of simple expressed preference prior to direct experience with the program are proverbial (see Lawton, 1977, for a discussion of preferences in housing research). Nonetheless, I suggest that room must be left for the concept of preference as a determinant of choice of activity. The contribution of preference can be understood only when other factors such as external constraints, personal experience, response styles, and other processes that condition the predictive value of overtly expressed preferences have been jointly considered.

MODELS OF ACTIVITY AND WELL-BEING

Two models by which the antecedents of activity might be predicted have been suggested. Robinson (1977) in a national study of time budgets of people aged 18–64 suggested that time allocation could be viewed as a function of environmental factors, resource factors, and intrapersonal factors. Environmental factors (e.g., day of week, location, weather) are primarily constraining forces, by contrast with resources (e.g., income, appliances, automobiles), which are facilitating opportunities. Two subsets of activity antecedents lie within the person: personal factors (e.g., sex, age, education) and role factors (e.g., employment, marriage, parenthood). Reciprocal relationships are seen between all sets as they affect time use. Most analyses predicting time allocation were performed with multivariate control over 28 separate independent variables representing the four domains. Robinson did not attempt to treat the independent variables as sets or to test any causal hypotheses.

Chapin (1974) developed an elegant theoretical rationale to account for activities on both an individual and aggregate level. *Personal* "energizing" (needs) and "constraining" factors (roles and other personal characteristics) combine to produce a "propensity to engage in the activity [p. 33]." *Societal* factors (that is, influences emanating from aggregates of individuals) are "perceived availability" and "perceived quality" of resources, resulting in an opportunity to engage in the activity. Chapin's empirical test (which, incidentally, did not consider age as an independent variable, but, rather as a "stage in life cycle," a combination of age of self and presence of children) was a test of only the personal portion of the model. Only energizing and constraining factors were used as predictors, and each predictor variable was again treated separately rather than by set. It is of interest to note that for four separate activities and for discretionary activity time as a whole, the proportions of variance accounted for by eight variables in the two categories ranged from 4% to 24%.

For "leisure activities," Mannell (1980) suggested a grouping of antecedents into internal and external determinants of the "leisure experience." Internal factors include attitudes, beliefs, motives, emotions, and past experiences. External factors include other people, groups, social structures, and the environment. The dimensions of the leisure experience were characterized in terms of meaning, quality, duration, intensity, and memorability. He did not attempt to test these classifications or their relationships empirically. None of these models made any formal attempt to link activity variables with any consequences.

The Present Model

The model proposed here and shown in Figure 4.1 links activity with both its determinants and outcomes. This model is meant to indicate *how* a system works, but in itself it affords relatively little understanding of *why* the system works; it is not meant to be a theoretical statement. Its value is seen as helping differentiate one element from another, in suggesting to other researchers what classes of phenomena might be included in future research, and in clarifying which of the many possible interrelationships are particularly worth examining.

As a beginning point, sets of personal and environmental "givens" are seen as joint conditioners of all that follows. Although these factors may be thought of as limiting the kinds of activities that occur, they may also be thought of as enabling or facilitating some activities. Therefore, I prefer to characterize these factors in both ways, that is, as constraints and "affordances" (Gibson, 1979). Clearly, some of these conditioning factors are more fixed than others, but this part of the causal sequence is not the subject of this chapter.

The second domain of antecedents is within the person and consists, first, of what I have called "basic competence" (Lawton, 1979). Although these attributes are not fixed in any absolute sense, they show enough stability to be seen as relatively enduring factors that directly determine activity outcome: physical health, functional health (activities of daily living), and cognitive status. The second constituent of the intrapersonal antecedent domain is "need," conditioned by both constraints and affordances and by basic competence. Need is viewed in Murray's (1938) need–press terms, that is, an internal motivation to seek certain goals. The research cited earlier suggests that needs of this type can be related to activities as such (direct path to activity).

Activity, that is, the occurrence if a specified objectively measurable behavior, is the central member of this model, being directly determined by those constructs mentioned thus far: constraints–affordances, competence, and needs.

A set of intrapsychic processes that collectively may be thought of as

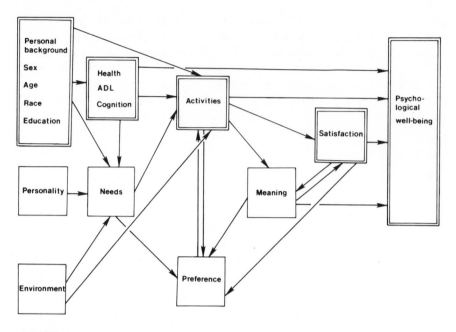

FIGURE 4.1. Conceptual model of the antecedents and consequences of activity. Double-outlined elements represent those used in an empirical test (ADL = activities of daily living.)

"subjective activity" form a complex loop that further affects the occurrence of activity. The cognitive meaning of an activity to the person is multidimensional, as discussed previously, and in turn affects both satisfaction and preference. The direct path from activity to satisfaction represents the affect associated with performing an activity, whereas the indirect path through meaning denotes the instrumental satisfaction derived from performing an activity. Feedback from the affective experience of satisfaction further conditions both meaning and preference. Although the energizing effect, in Chapin's terms, for the initiation of an activity comes from learned preferences (and from needs through preferences), a reciprocal effect from activity to preference indicates the effect of familiarity: Having performed an activity may increase one's preference for performing the activity again. The model emphasizes the central position of preference in determining activity and in being determined by meaning and satisfaction. At the same time it states clearly the conditionality of preference with respect to affordances and constraints.

The proximate consequence of performing an activity is the experience of satisfaction (or disatisfaction) with the activity, whether as a final or instrumental act. The distal effect of an activity contributes to generalized psychological well-being, another multidimensional construct (Lawton, 1979) whose varieties will not be discussed here. Two paths from activity to well-being are affective, through satisfaction, and cognitive, either direct from the performance of the activity or through meaning. The affective path reflects the quantitative balance of positive and negative individual experiences associated with specific activity sequences; the more satisfactions, the greater will be overall psychological well-being as an extended state. The cognitive path emphasizes the confirmation (or disconfirmation) of personal competence, usually through meaning, but possibly also a direct fashion.

The model is complex, and the nonrecursive nature of many of the effects makes it unfeasible to test in its entirety. However, research done at the Philadelphia Geriatric Center did allow a test of a portion of the model. The elements of Figure 4.1 that were used in this empirical test are shown in double outline.

TESTING A PORTION OF THE MODEL

This test dealt with the effect of some affordances and constraints on activity patterns and the direct effects of activity patterns on psychological well-being, as well as their indirect effects on well-being through activity satisfaction. In more concrete terms, the following purposes were served:

1. Descriptive information was obtained through time-budget data on the composition of the day, in terms of time spent in activities, where the activities took place, and with whom they were performed.
2. The variability in activity patterns explainable by social position and personal competences was determined.
3. The relative contributions of personal factors and amount of time devoted to an activity, or in an environmental context, to satisfaction with that activity pattern were ascertained.
4. The joint contributions of personal factors, time per activity or context, and satisfaction with that activity to psychological well-being were determined, in the order and structure portrayed by the portion of the model that includes these constructs.

It should be noted that this operationalization of the model is the first in either gerontological or general time-budget research that includes both objective and subjective activity as intervening variables, that is, as explained by personal factors but in turn acting as statistical explanations for the distal criterion of psychological well-being. The early time-budget research projects and the more recent large-scale efforts reported by Chapin (1974) and Szalai (1972) concentrated on determining which variations in activity pattern were attributable to social status characteristics, including to some extent geography (national differences in the Szalai report and location with respect to the central city as in Chapin & Brail, 1969). Michelson (1973) went one step further in focusing on a natural experiment, residential relocation, in its effect on time expenditures. A few such results did demonstrate some realignment of time as a function of housing-related variables of clustering and location. Among older people, Carp (1978–1979) demonstrated the impact of improving housing on time use over both a short term and a long term. By comparison to nonmovers, those who relocated spent more time in meetings but less time resting and watching television and showed less time that was unaccounted for.

Our research represented older people over a wide range of physical and mental capabilities and thus was able to add indicators of basic behavioral competence to the predictive equation: multi-item indices of physical health, functional health, and cognitive performance.

This attempt to add the subjective aspect of activity to the model, while being the first to do so systematically, encountered many problems. The major difficulty was the limitation of degrees and distinctions in preference, meaning, and sastifaction to a single rating in the full model: For example, how much did you like... (activity): a lot, somewhat, neither liked nor disliked, did not like. The multidimensional aspect of preference and meaning, the distinction between intrinsic and extrinsic satisfactions, and the interesting web of mutual interrelationships among these facets of subjective activity were thus not included in this study. However, by asking even one "like–dislike" question about every activity that occurred during the day and aggregating them over time, a usable index of satisfaction was created against which actual time expenditure could be gauged. This independent look at objective and subjective activity seemed to us the single most important goal of the research.

The details of the research are being reported more completely elsewhere (Lawton, Moss & Fulcomer, 1981; Moss & Lawton, 1980; Moss & Lawton, 1982). Very briefly, complete one-day "yesterday" interviews recreating the preceding 24 hours' activities were obtained from 535 older people representing target groups in presumed descending order of competence: Residents living in independent households, community residents receiving in-home services, and community residents who had been accepted for and were awaiting admission to nursing homes. They were interviewed in their homes with a schedule that included the

Philadelphia Geriatric Center Multilevel Assessment Instrument (MAI, Lawton, Moss, Fulcomer, & Kleban, 1982), a set of composite indices measuring health, functional health, cognition, time use, social interaction, psychological well-being and perceived environmental quality.

Our major set of analyses reported here examined separately each of 13 activity categories, 5 social contexts, and 3 locational contexts, within the path-analytic framework portrayed in Figure 4.1. That is, 5 background characteristics were used as control variables, and health, functional health, and cognition as exogenous variables. Causal hypotheses were tested using as successive dependent variables time per activity, average liking per activity, and psychological well-being, in that order.

In general, the major amount of predictable variation in time expenditure, satisfaction, and psychological well-being was attributable to basic competence. As one might expect, the amounts of time spent in the more active obligatory activities, with friends, in recreation, and away from home were greater for the more competent. The least competent spent more time in personal care, rest and relaxation, with radio and television, and within the dwelling unit.

The assertions made over the years by students of time allocation regarding some implications of the obligatory–discretionary activity distinction were nicely upheld (Chapin, 1974). For four discretionary activities (interaction with friends, reading, watching television, and recreation), the more time spent, the greater the liking ratings. For one discretionary activity, rest and relaxation, the more time spent, the *less* the liking rating. For no obligatory activity was there any relationship between amount of time spent and amount of liking; most interestingly this same lack of relationship was observed for time interacting with family members.

For the critical set of paths relating time allocation and liking ratings to psychological well-being, there was a general tendency for people who liked any activity more to be higher in psychological well-being. In contrast, by either direct or indirect paths, there were few associations between the sheer time spent in any activity or context and personal adjustment. Those who spent more time alone were lower in personal adjustment, and somewhat paradoxically the same was true for those who spent more time cooking.

Of course no activity type occurs in isolation, and one needs to examine how the *relative* allocations among the diverse groupings of activities affect liking and psychological well-being. Major statistical problems intrude at this point; since everyone's day adds up to 24 hours, the resulting "ipsative" effect prevents one from considering all activities simultaneously. If we sacrifice the variation in distribution of time between obligatory and discretionary activity and use only the time spent in one or the other of these sets as predictor variables, the problem can be dealt with partially.

For this test, we asked which activities' time allocations contributed to a single overall liking score (i.e., a liking score computed across all activities, rather than for a specific activity) and in turn, how the time allocations and the overall liking score contributed to psychological well-being. These questions were asked separately for discretionary and obligatory activities.

By this yardstick the investment of more time in some activities did seem to result in higher overall liking scores than did others. Among obligatory activities the few who spent some time doing paid work were measurably more likely to express higher overall liking for their whole day's activities, independently of the increment in health implied by being able to work. Among the discretionary activities, those spending more time with family members, reading, watching television, and engaging in recreation showed overall greater liking for their activities. Direct links between differential time allocation and psychological well-being were smaller but still indicated that spending relatively greater amounts with family, listening to radio, watching television, and in recreation contributed to a better inner psychological state. (This aggregate analysis included all cases, including those who *never* saw family members. It may be that well-being is relatively strongly affected by the presence of *any* family contact, whereas, given some contact, the actual amount of contact may be unrelated to well-being.) Spending less time shopping, and again, curiously, spending *less* time cooking, were associated with higher well-being, alone among the obligatory activities. Finally, an expected substantial link between the overall aggregate liking score and psychological well-being was seen (beta = .228).

The meaning of the high points of these results can be indicated only in very cursory fashion. First, personal competence influences strongly the way a day is spent. Lesser competence means filling the day with inactivity and spending more time on basic self-maintaining activities at the expense of the more strenuous instrumental and social behavior.

Second, people find ways of doing more of what they like to do among discretionary activities (or do they turn out to like better what they do more of?). There is, by contrast, enough demand quality and lack of choice among the obligatory activities to obliterate any direct association between the amount of enjoyment of them and how much time one spends doing them. Different people and different situations seem to require different allocations of time to obligatory activities; we infer that the greatest portion of this time is accepted as necessary and does not evoke either strong satisfaction or dissatisfaction.

Third, liking any particular activity, and liking for the aggregate of one's activities, is one of the major contributors to psychological well-being. However, the concordance is *very* imperfect. Indeed, considering the amount of artifactually shared variance between liking and well-being due to intrapersonal response style, it is perhaps surprising that liking and psychological well-being are not more highly related than they are. Nonetheless, it is clear that there is more to psychological well-being than liking for a single day, a single category of activities, or an aggregate of activities.

Fourth, judging these results at face value, one would guess the activity of a single day to be akin to the swallow that never made a summer, if our index is the absolute amount of time devoted to any single activity. These data show clearly that it is not *what* you do but your *construction* of what you do that attributes to generalized life satisfaction.

These conclusions require many qualifications and point to the need for considerable additional research. For example, Carp and Carp (1981) have presented data calling into legitimate question the reliability of single-day time-budget information. We may counter that as the number of subjects increases, the representativeness of the single-day estimates in the aggregate increase. Nonetheless, the size of potential relationships between psychological well-being and time spent in liked activities were, to be sure, limited by the error inherent in the one-day data and must be viewed as minimal estimates of the relationships.

Another limit to our enthusiasm about the "it's-not-what-you-do" conclusion is that the subjective element in time use is related to psychological well-being through an unknown amount of source variance. The same model needs to be tested using a totally external measure of psychological well-being as the criterion, in order to set a lower limit to the subjective time use–psychological well-being relationship.

CONCLUSION

The overarching impression from these findings, however, is their reminder of the significant independence of how time is spent from the other sectors of the personal system. Being physically or cognitively impaired is the major determinant of how time is spent. Some variation in time allocation is associated with demographic statuses (Moss & Lawton, 1982) and with living arrangement (Moss & Lawton, 1980), but it is small by comparison to that associated with health. The implication of the small but significant relationships between objective and subjective activity is that where people are free to exercise choice, they better enjoy what they do, while accepting the necessity of most mandated activity. The amount of independence between the time budget and the distal outcome—psychological well-being—is particularly impressive. Although we might expect the strength of this link to increase somewhat with more reliable measurement, the fact is that people find ways of being happy or satisfied with life, or unhappy or dissatisfied, in ways that depend on many factors in addition to how they actually spend their day.

The search for the subjective aspects of activity patterns is thus given further urgency by the present findings. The state of the art in gerontology is relatively rich in researcher-generated constructs that impose some useful structure on subjective activity patterns, but the literature is sparse in constructs generated by the older person. The most glaring lack is the area of linkage between the meaning, preferences, and satisfactions associated with specific activities and overt behavior, that is, the time actually spent in these activities.

It is highly likely that further exploration of the meaning of activities will lead us back to personal constructs dealing with time in the abstract, with the very large chunks of time that have been called "stages of life," and with sector-spanning concepts like Rowles's (1978) "environmental fantasy" where space and time become linked. Whether such investigations will validate the suggestion that "time" in these terms is, in fact, subjective activity patterns arranged on a scale from the instant to the life span remains to be determined.

A final thought concerns objective activity patterns. If they are so tenuously related to psychological well-being, are they worth studying? I have argued this same point in my discussion of "the good life" as being composed of behavioral competence, perceived quality of life, objective environment, and psychological well-being (Lawton, 1979). Although well-being in one of these sectors may be reflected in well-being in another sector, the test of the personal or social desirability of one apsect of well-being must not lie in the demonstration of such a correlation with a different sector of the good life. If we see people straining toward competent behavior, toward satisfaction in the separate domains of lifestyle, or for high-quality housing and neighborhoods, these goals are seen as autonomously defensible: They do not have to result in higher morale to be viewed as social goals.

In the case of how one spends time, it may be that the total amount of time spent in peak experiences, in novel behaviors, or in activities with apparent long-range rewards is limited. Even if the ultimate effect of many activities on well-being is small, the fact is that people do work so as to be able to control how they spend their time and they are vehement in liking some activities and disliking others. It thus is important to discover how people can control their time use, how they can maximize the number of minutes in liked or otherwise meaningful activity, or even how nonliked activity can be made to pass more quickly (in a subjective sense). The relationship of these subjective aspects of activity or objective time-budget data must be known if people are to be aided in controlling their time allocations or to increase their proportion of liked activities. If we focus only on subjective experience we lose the possibility of affording better control by either the doer, the planner, or the service provider. Therefore, I suggest that it is most appropriate to seek ways of bringing actual objective time use into better congruence with subjective patterns, that is, increasing the activities that are preferred, satisfying, or otherwise personally meaningful. Also more should be learned about the ultimate pathways by which objective and subjective activity patterns may be associated with psychological well-being, but this task should not be construed as necessary in order to validate the search for daily objective activity patterns that are viewed as meaningful. To be able to do what is meaningful is a goal that requires no external validation.

REFERENCES

Altman, I., & Gauvain, M. A cross-cultural and dialectic analysis of homes. In L. S. Liben, A. H. Patterson, & N. Newcombe (Eds.), *Spatial representation and behavior across the life span.* New York: Academic Press, 1981.

Altman, I., Nelson, P., & Lett, E. E. *The ecology of home environments.* Mimeographed report, Project OEG-8-70-0202 (503). Department of Psychology, University of Utah, Salt Lake City, 1972.

Beyer, G., & Woods, M. E. *Living and activity patterns of the aged.* Ithaca, N. Y.: Cornell University Center for Housing and Environmental Studies, 1963.

Bishop, D. W., & Witt, P. A. Sources of behavioral variance during leisure time. *Journal of Personality and Social Psychology,* 1970, *16,* 352–360.

Campbell, A., Converse, P. E., & Rodgers, W. L. *The quality of American life: Perceptions, evaluations, and satisfactions.* New York: Russell Sage Foundation, 1976.

Carp, F. M. Effects of the living environment on activity and the use of time. *International Journal of Aging and Human Development,* 1978–1979, *9,* 75–91.

Carp, F. M., & Carp, A. *The validity, reliability, and generalizability of diary data. Experimental Aging Research,* 1981, *7,* 281–292.

Chapin, F. S., Jr. *Human activity patterns in the city.* New York: Wiley, 1974.

Chapin, F. W., & Brail, R. K. Human activity systems in the metropolitan United States. *Environment and Behavior,* 1969, *1,* 107–130.

Crandall, R., & Slivken, K. Leisure attitudes and their measurement. In S. E. Iso-Ahlo (Ed.), *Social psychological perspectives on leisure and recreation.* Springfield, Ill.: Charles C Thomas, 1980.

Csikszentmihalyi, M. *Beyond boredom and anxiety.* San Francisco: Jossey–Bass, 1975.

de Grazia, S. The uses of time. In R. W. Kleemeier (Ed.), *Aging and leisure.* New York: Oxford University Press, 1961.

DeLong, A. J. The microspatial structure of the older person. In L. A. Pastalan & D. H. Carson (Eds.), *Spatial behavior of older people.* Ann Arbor: University of Michigan–Wayne State University, Institute of Gerontology, 1970.

Donald, M. N., & Havighurst, R. J. The meanings of leisure. *Social Forces,* 1959, *37,* 355–360.

Dumazedier, J. *Sociology of leisure.* New York: Elsevier, 1974.

Gibson, J. J. *The ecological approach to visual perception.* Boston: Houghton Mifflin, 1979.

Golant, S. M. (Ed.). *Location and environment of elderly population.* New York: Wiley–Winston, 1979.

Gordon, C., Gaitz, C. M., & Scott, J. Leisure and lives: Personal expressivity across the life span. In R. H. Binstock & E. Shanas (Eds.), *Handbook of aging and the social sciences.* New York: Van Nostrand Reinhold, 1976.

Hendricks, C. D., & Hendricks, J. Concepts of time and temporal construction among the aged, with implications for research. In J. F. Gubrium (Ed.), *Time, roles, and the self in old age.* New York: Human Sciences Press, 1976.

Iso-Ahola, S. E. (Ed.), *Social psychological perspectives on leisure and recreation.* Springfield, Ill.: Charles C Thomas, 1980. (a)

Iso-Ahola, S. E. Toward a dialectical social psychology of leisure and recreation. In S. E. Iso-Ahola (Ed.), *Social psychological perspectives on leisure and recreation.* Springfield, Ill.: Charles C Thomas, 1980. (b)

Kaplan, M. *Leisure: Theory and policy.* New York: Wiley, 1975.

Kastenbaum, R. On the meaning of time in later life. *Journal of Genetic Psychology,* 1966, *109,* 9–25.

Lawton, M. P. Public behavior of older people in congregate housing. In J. Archea & C. Eastman (Eds.), *Environmental design research association* (Vol. II). Pittsburgh: Carnegie–Mellon University Press, 1970.

Lawton, M. P. Methodologies for evaluation in environment and aging. In P. Suedfeld, J. A. Russell, L. M. Ward, F. Szigeti, & G. Davis (Eds.), *The behavioral basis of design* (Vol. 2). Stroudsburg, Pa.: Dowden, Hutchinson, & Ross, 1977.

Lawton, M. P. Leisure activities for the aged. *The Annals,* 1978, *438,* 71–80.

Lawton, M. P. *What is the good life for the aging?* Philadelphia: Philadelphia Geriatric Center, 1979. (duplicated report)

Lawton, M. P. Sensory deprivation and the effect of the environment on management of the senile dementia patient. In N. Miller & G. Cohen (Eds.), *Clinical studies of Alzheimers disease and senile dementia.* New York: Raven Press, 1981.

Lawton, M. P., Moss, M., & Fulcomer, M. *Determinants of the activity patterns of older people.* Philadelphia: Philadelphia Geriatric Center, 1981. (duplicated report.)

Lawton, M. P., Moss, M., Fulcomer, M., & Kleban, M. H. A research and service-oriented Multilevel Assessment Instrument. *Journal of Gerontology,* 1982, *37,* 91–99.

McClannahan, L. E., & Risley, T. R. *The organization of group care environments: Living environments for nusing home residents.* Paper presented at the annual meeting of the American Psychological Association, Honolulu, September 1972.

McGuire, F. A. The incongruence between actual and desired leisure involvement in advanced adulthood. *Activities, Adaptation, and Aging,* 1980, *1,* 77–89.

McKechnie, G. E. The psychological structure of leisure: Past behavior. *Journal of Leisure Research,* 1974, *6,* 27–45.

Mannell, R. C. Social psychological techniques and strategies for studying leisure experiences. In S. E. Iso-Ahola (Ed.), *Social psychological perspectives on leisure and recreation.* Springfield, Ill.: Charles C Thomas, 1980.

Meyersohn, R. Leisure. In A. Campbell & P. E. Converse (Eds.), *The human meaning of social change.* New York: Russell Sage Foundation, 1972.

Michelson, W. Discretionary and nondiscretionary aspects of activity in social contact in residential selection. *Society and Leisure,* 1973, *6,* 29–54.

Moss, M., & Lawton, M. P. *Use of time in different types of households.* Paper presented at the annual meeting of the Gerontological Society, San Diego, Calif., November 1980.

Moss, M., & Lawton, M. P. Time budgets: A window on four lifestyles. *Journal of Gerontology,* 1982, *37,* 115–123.

Murray, H. A. *Explorations in personality.* New York: Oxford University Press, 1938.

Neulinger, J. *The psychology of leisure.* Springfield, Ill.: Charles C Thomas, 1974.

Neulinger, J., & Breit, M. Attitude dimensions of leisure: A replication study. *Journal of Leisure Research,* 1971, *3,* 108–115.

Ragheb, M. G., & Beard, J. G. Leisure satisfaction: Concept, theory and measurement. In S. E. Iso-Ahola (Ed.), *Social psychological perspectives on leisure and recreation.* Springfield, Ill.: Charles C Thomas, 1980.

Regnier, V. A. Neighborhoods as service systems. In M. P. Lawton, R. J. Newcomer, & T. O. Byerts (Eds.), *Community planning for an aging society,* Stroudsburg, Pa.: Dowden, Hutchinson, & Ross, 1976.

Ritchie, J. R. On the derivation of leisure activity types—a perceptual mapping approach. *Journal of Leisure Research,* 1975, *7,* 128–140.

Robinson, J. P. *How Americans use time.* New York: Praeger, 1977.

Rowles, G. D. *Prisoners of space?* Boulder, Colo.: Westview Press, 1978.

Stephens, M. A. P., & Willems, E. P. *Daily behavior of older persons in minimal-care housing.* Paper presented at the annual meeting of the Gerontological Society, Washington, D.C., November 1979.

Szalai, A. (Ed.), *The use of time.* The Hague: Mouton, 1972.

Tinsley, H., Barrett, T. C., & Kass, R. A. Leisure activities and need satisfaction. *Journal of Leisure Research,* 1973, *5,* 67–73.

Tinsley, H., & Kass, R. A. Leisure activities and need satisfaction: A replication and extension. *Journal of Leisure Research,* 1978, *10,* 191–202.

Walsh, D. A., Krauss, I. K., & Regnier, V. A. Spatial ability, environmental knowledge, and environmental use: The elderly. In L. S. Liben, A. H. Patterson, & N. Newcombe (Eds.), *Spatial representation and behavior across the life span.* New York: Academic Press, 1981.

Ward, R. A. The meaning of voluntary association participation to older people. *Journal of Gerontology,* 1979, *34,* 438–445.

5

Urban Neighborhood Cognition: Relationships between Functional and Symbolic Community Elements

VICTOR REGNIER

City and neighborhood visual assessment techniques pioneered by Kevin Lynch and his associates have been the primary analysis mechanisms utilized by city planners and researchers to better understand the special qualities of city environments that make them "imageable" or "legible." The assumption underlying their work is that a more legible or imageable city is one that promotes orientation, navigation, and way finding. This chapter investigates the criteria utilized to establish this city design method and introduces case study data. The case study provides evidence that community resources such as retail facilities are more salient to older residents than the symbolic, large scale, or natural features city planners assume to be important in way finding and navigation.

LYNCHIAN ANALYSIS

The work of Lynch (1960) in *The Image of the City* brought about a radical change in the analysis of large-scale urban form. Prior to Lynch's book the city design movement had utilized traditional architectural principles to measure the success or failure of urban design projects. Lynch provided a new vocabulary based on perception of the environment, rather than relegating analysis to a strict set of aesthetic or visual criteria.

In his classic study he elicited from design professionals and community residents sketch maps which were defined as "a rapid description of the

AGING AND MILIEU:
ENVIRONMENTAL PERSPECTIVES
ON GROWING OLD

city (as if) to a stranger, covering all the main features [p. 141]." These sketch maps were collected along with verbal descriptive data regarding the city and a list of the city elements and features considered distinctive. Lynch also directed his staff to conduct a careful field analysis of each area and to abstractly diagram the visual structure of that setting. The diagrammatic language the trained staff person used was Lynch's notation system of nodes (centers), landmarks, paths, edges, and districts. Comparisons of the professionally developed image maps were made with a consensus configuration of individual sketch maps, verbal descriptions, and distinctive elements.

These comparisons revealed that the field map created by city planners was surprisingly similar to the verbal interviews and consensus sketch maps of community residents. Although the level of detail in the sketch maps was somewhat less than the verbal elicitations, this was considered a positive attribute. The map elicitation was thought to capture a simpler expression of the essence of the urban form. Figure 5.1 is the visual form of Boston developed by field observers.This illustration from *The Image of the City* demonstrates the rich detail that characterized the visual form of this varied and fascinating urban environment.

A review of the outcome of this research is warranted because of the subsequent impact it had on urban design theory. The strong link that Lynch demonstrated between professional elicitations and consensus image maps helped to promote the method. City planning departments did not need to commission expensive research to develop an image map, because trained planners and architects could do as good a job in less time. Lynch continued to develop new techniques and to synthesize the work of others. In another more recent book, *Managing the Sense of a Region* (1976), he introduces 52 projects that utilize dozens of techniques for describing, recording, and analyzing the form of large scale environments.

Los Angeles Image Map

Lynch's work sparked the creative imaginations of many city planners. The most interesting and potentially the most policy-related application of his image analysis method took place in Los Angeles in 1971. In this study residents of five very different neighborhoods were asked to sketch a map of Los Angeles. Individual sketch maps were combined from the residents of each neighborhood. The same consensus notation was used with the boldness of the drawing based on the number of individuals that jointly identified certain community attributes. Again, the Lynchian notation system was used. The most startling finding of this research was the radical difference in the scale, depth, detail, and grasp of the city image by

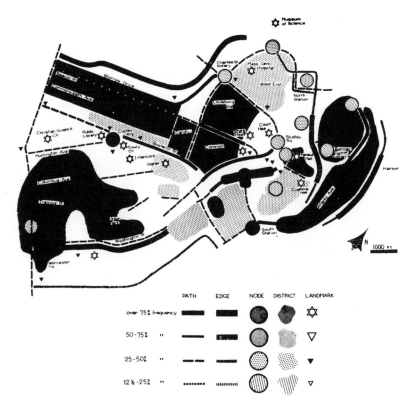

FIGURE 5.1. The visual form of Boston as seen from the field (Reprinted from The Image of the City by K. Lynch by permission of the MIT Press, Cambridge, Massachusetts. Copyright ©1960, p. 145.)

residents living in different neighborhoods. These findings underscored the paucity of information used to describe the city by residents of lower-income minority communities and the rich grasp of detail available to those with higher incomes and greater physical mobility. This was the first evidence of the tremendous variability in the depth and amount of information that residents might be expected to have regarding city structure. Although analyses were not conducted regarding age differences, one may logically deduce that the older, transit dependent, lower-income, physically limited individual may suffer from similar city image deprivations. Having a poorly developed or conditioned city image is not a serious problem by itself, however, since it does suggest that a local neighborhood setting may substitute for the lack of interest, knowledge, and information in the larger city scale environment.

Problems and Limitations of the City Image Method

One particularly important attribute of the work of Lynch and his associates is the implied scale of most of their analyses. Although many of the studies have components that address specific neighborhood concerns, most focus on the structure of the city or the region. This orientation gives some visual-form work a bias toward the measurement of larger scale phenomena. This bias has been misinterpreted by some planners who have attempted to utilize city images and concepts for neighborhood planning projects.

Another problem of Lynch's work has been the translation of findings to policies and programs. Partial success can be claimed in effecting the urban design plans for San Francisco (1971), Minneapolis (1965), and Los Angeles (1971). However, in many cases considerable translation, augmentation, and interpretation of Lynch's original method was required. In most cases the image map has been an interesting and thought-provoking exercise with at best a weak tether to action or program implementation. These two problems, the scale of application and link to program policy change, have limited the utility of Lynch's image mapping in city design.

Sensory and Behavioral Aspects of Urban Form Analysis

A most interesting quality of the work which followed the *Image of the City* study was the concern and interest for other attributes of the environment beyond visual legibililty. Southworth (1969) developed a soundscape of central Boston and Lynch (1972) continued his fascination with time and its impact on the perception of the environment by writing *What Time is This Place?* Of greatest significance, however, was the integration of methods regarding spatial behavior and their effects on the use and perception of various places. Clay (1973) published a noteworthy accounting of this phenomena in *Close Up: How to Read the American City.* This book introduced hundreds of examples of physical settings throughout the United States that had been given symbolic or perceived meaning by the people who used them. Clay's observations were classified into chapters with flashy titles such as "Sinks, Stacks, Beats, and Fronts." Although his presentation of these phenomena was more anecdotal than representative of a new method for analyzing city environments, he nonetheless dramatized the important role of human behavior in altering our perception of the built environment. The Lynchian analyses of built form are attuned to the "sensory" aspects of the environment and concentrate on the visual, aural, and tactile stimuli which affect our understanding and appreciation of a landscape or cityscape.

These sensory aspects are also relevant to the older person who may have limitations in sensory ability. With older people certain aspects of the sensory environment may take on increased importance because the information from these cues may affect the ability to maintain independence.

In addition to the special sensory impairments which may place the older person at risk in the neighborhood, other features, such as stores and services, may also take on special meaning or importance. The older low-income person who has suffered a reduction in mobility may use or relate to various neighborhood elements (stores, services, houses, streets) with greater frequency or interest.

IMPORTANCE OF NEIGHBORHOOD RESOURCES FOR THE ELDERLY

The issue of the relevance of various aspects of the neighborhood environment has been addressed most clearly by Lawton (1977). He has chosen to label the collection of life-supporting, life-enriching, cultural, and social opportunities available outside the immediate dwelling unit as the "resource environment." Further differentiation of this concept reveals four domains: the physical resource environment, the functional resource environment, the perceived resource environment, and the salient resource environment.

Four Resource Environments

The physical resource environment consists of all resources available within a physically bounded area regardless of their relevance or access to the older community resident. The functional resource environment consists of those facilities, services, and elements *used* by the older person. The perceived resource environment is that collection of resources which are thought of as having meaning to the older person. These facilities may be symbolic, functional, or physical aspects of the neighborhood. Finally, the salient resource environment consists of those elements which are considered to be of great value, either because of need or affective attachment.

Physical and Functional Resource Environments

This conceptualization reveals the specific and often overlapping role these resources can play in providing physical as well as psychological support. The physical and functional resource environments are perhaps the easiest to understand and record. These are the services and resources which exist and can be measured, counted, and evaluated.

Salient Resource Environment

The salient resource environment involves a personal interpretation of the resource base. The church or synagogue for a deeply religious individual or the location of a close friend or relative may be the best example of a salient resource. Salient resources vary from one person to the next and may be tempered by one's personal values, affective ties, and individual needs. Although these may vary with the individual, they are likely to be of major importance and are therefore reasonably easy to elicit.

Perceived Resource Environment

The most difficult domain to define is that of the perceived resource environment. Like the salient resource environment it may vary from one individual to the next. Like the functional and physical environment it may include common elements. However, this resource setting is created and nurtured by the mind and, as such, it may be modified, distorted, or augmented from objective reality. The importance placed on various elements, their location, and necessity may differ as new information is processed. These environmental perceptions can also be related to incorrect information, memory loss, or strong emotional influences. Within this domain lies perhaps the most accurate but yet elusive assessment of the utility of surrounding resources—a utility based on the perceived value and accessibility of a resource rather than an objective measure or assessment. For example, a strong argument can be made that a six-block walk to a neighborhood "resource" is not only influenced by the perceived importance of the destination but also by the perceived distance and the perceived safety of the route. The special psychological backdrop of the perceived resource environment is a phenomena which has received little formal attention but is of considerable value.

Emotional and Affective Ties to the Perceived Environment

Graham Rowles (1978) in *Prisoners of Space?* raises another important dimension of the perceived environment, that of association and memory. The older person who has lived the greater part of his or her life in a familiar neighborhood may have strong associations with the past which affect perceptions and assessments of the present.

A story regarding a respondent from a recent research study provides a curious example of this phenomena. Asked to produce a map of her neighborhood, she chose to include elements such as a trolley car line which had been missing for 20 years. Although aware that the line no longer existed, she nonetheless felt her perceived or imagined environment would always contain this element.

Other subjects distressed about changes in a local neighborhood over-emphasized the perceived danger of a nearby park, partly because of the contrast between its current state and their recollection of what it was like 20 years ago. A potential neighborhood trouble area had been introduced and access to a salient, memory-filled neighborhood resource was terminated. This double loss is obviously more serious for the older neighborhood resident who has lived in the area long enough to have created a strong salient association with the park earlier in life. Our objective evaluations of various neighborhood resources must be tempered by an understanding of how these neighborhood elements are viewed in the mind as well as how they have changed over time.

RESEARCH QUESTIONS REGARDING URBAN FORM ANALYSES

Several questions have been raised in this introductory review which deserve closer attention. In order to accomplish this, research conducted in a neighborhood in Los Angeles will be introduced. Three questions follow from the preceding discussion and are addressed by the case study presented:

1. Are the city image maps constructed by planners following the guidelines established by Lynch similar to or different from sketch maps elicited from older community residents? Are the symbolic and larger city form elements used to describe the visual form of the neighborhood the same as those chosen by older residents to describe the neighborhood?

2. What relationships exist between the consensus image maps of older community residents (perceived resource environment) and the facilities and services that are frequently used by older residents (functional resource environment)? Do these maps reflect the same elements? Do they represent symbolic, functional, or civic influences? What parallels or similarities can be drawn between a map of commonly visited neighborhood destinations and the consensus of neighborhood sketch maps from older subjects?

3. What policy or design implications can be drawn from this research? Lynch's analysis of city form had significant impacts on the way in which city planners viewed preservation, height and bulk restrictions, navigation,

orientation, and city form. What policy and planning concerns for older adults are suggested by the research findings?

Answers to these questions, although not fully resolved by the data presented, suggest older people may develop stronger attachments to functional than symbolic resources in the environment.

CASE STUDY REVIEW

Neighborhood Description

The case study was conducted in a downtown neighborhood located within the city of Los Angeles. Westlake is an old neighborhood by Los Angeles standards, having been developed around the turn of the century. The neighborhood was selected after an extensive review of 1970 census data revealed that it contained the largest, densest cluster of lower-income older people in the city.

The neighborhood is approximately 1000 acres in size and is located directly west of the downtown district near the geographic center of Los Angeles County. The land uses which characterize the neighborhood are a mixture of unreinforced masonry hotels and apartments, office and commercial buildings, and newer stucco-and-wood construction apartments. On occasion, adjacent to a 20-story office tower, there is a large single-family dwelling which has long been recycled into multifamily use. It is a neighborhood rich in diversity, with an appearance that resembles more an older eastern city than the broad, low-density expanses generally characteristic of Southern California.

The neighborhood is bisected by Wilshire Boulevard, referred to by city planners as a corridor. The corridor designation seems to fit not only because the high rise buildings on each side of Wilshire create a visual corridor, but also because the boulevard imposes strong influences on adjacent land.

The original housing stock consisted of a large number of residential hotel and single-room accommodations, created to cater to vacationeers visiting Southern California in the 1920s. Replacement stock has been primarily studio and one-bedroom accommodations targeted toward single office workers. The limited size of the overwhelming majority of the housing stock has greatly influenced the way the neighborhood has matured. Families with children have always found it a difficult place to secure housing. In contrast, older people relocated from other neighborhoods or in search of small-sized accommodations have found it inexpensive and convenient. The neighborhood has the highest residential density of any area in the city of Los Angeles and also has the highest percentage of deteriorated or substandard housing. The mixed land use, high development density, convenient and frequent public transportation, and special services for senior citizens have attracted older populations and encouraged present residents to continue to live there. The neighborhood structure and ecology make it a supportive setting for the lower-income older person. Mixed commercial and residential land uses place numerous retail facilities within easy walking distance. The high development density supports numerous retail stores as well as the most convenient public transportation service outside of downtown Los Angeles. The high percentage of older residents has also attracted a comprehensive range of publicly subsided senior citizen services. A large centrally located park is available for passive observation and relaxation.

Although it may sound ideal, the neighborhood is not without problems. A rising crime rate has frightened many older residents who now limit their use of services and facilities. Furthermore, the available low-cost housing stock has been popular with recent groups of oriental and Hispanic immigrants. Increased demand has brought about competition between older residents and minority families. Small apartments which formerly were only acceptable to one-person households now increasingly house larger families. This competition has resulted in overcrowding and escalating rents.

Finally, expansion pressures from office and business use have forced the removal of older residential buildings which have been replaced with parking lots and high-rise commercial towers. This trend has increased traffic congestion and further limited the pool of available housing. The Westlake neighborhood is experiencing change which has affected the comfort of its older population.

The Neighborhood Environment

A map of the Westlake neighborhood is shown in Figure 5.2. The Harbor Freeway forms a strong eastern boundary separating Westlake from the Downtown District. Hoover Boulevard forms the western boundary where the city grid changes orientation. Third street, the northern boundary, runs near the ridge of a gentle hill, creating a visual edge to the neighborhood. The southern boundary, although physically less distinctive, forms a strong social boundary to an adjacent, well-defined Hispanic neighborhood.

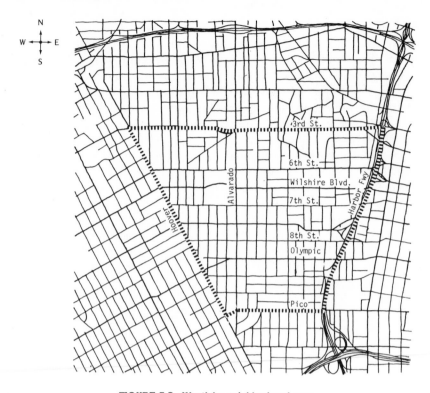

FIGURE 5.2. Westlake neighborhood map.

MacArthur Park is a large, centrally located city park with a lake. It contains a card-playing area, a boat dock, and a children's playground. Park benches are placed along the walking paths that link various recreational features. Lafayette Park is located near the western edge of the neighborhood. It contains a branch library as well as a senior citizens center. Facilities for tennis and basketball are also provided within this park. An elegant old hotel and a new attractively designed modern office tower are adjacent to the park and temper the park's use by introducing office workers, tourists, and visitors.

General land uses are schematically represented in Figure 5.3. Four zones are apparent: a mixed commercial and institutional (strip commercial) area of considerable density; an apartment–commercial zone of medium density; a primarily residential zone of low density; and large park areas.

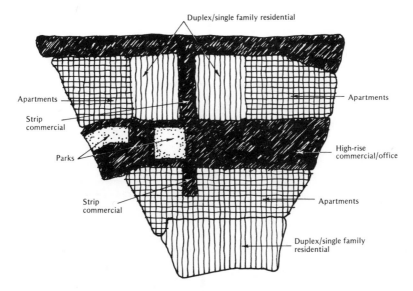

FIGURE 5.3. Schematic land use distribution.

Analysis of the Los Angeles City Planning Department Image of the Neighborhood

Figure 5.4 is reprinted from a Los Angeles City Planning analysis document describing the Westlake district. The notation system devised by Lynch was employed to create this map. The major paths include the east–west streets of Wilshire and Olympic and the north–south street, Alvarado. Minor east–west paths include 3rd, 6th, 7th, and Pico. Ten major landmarks are noted. Many of the major landmarks are tall buildings or structures located near the tops of hilly areas. The minor landmarks are a mixture of large-scale building complexes and tall buildings.Lafayette Park, MacArthur Park, and the Otis Art Institute are considered major and minor activity centers because they are visually dominant places that attract community residents.

The Pico–Union district located on the southern edge of the neighborhood has a distinctly different Hispanic character, and the Lafayette Park apartment area near the north edge of the district contains nicely manicured lawns and has a distinctive middle-class character. The dotted areas adjacent to several of the major arterials contain concentrations of retail uses. Changes in topography which create visual edges are shown by short parallel lines.

FIGURE 5.4. Westlake community image map. (Source: Department of City Planning, Westlake Community Plan: Socio-Economic Analysis. Los Angeles: The Department, 1971. Reprinted with permission.)

Sample Selection

The sample universe from which the 100 respondents were selected was developed from an extensive field survey of eligible residents. A building-by-building survey identified approximately 5000 neighborhood residents over the age of 60 who had lived in the neighborhood for more than one year.

The sample had an average age of 71.3 years and was in reasonably good physical condition. The average number of years spent in the neighborhood was 17.2. Slightly less than half (47%) were males, and the average single-person income in 1977 was between $250 and $333 per month.

Data-Gathering Techniques

Respondents were asked a number of questions regarding their perceptions and uses of the neighborhood. This chapter compares, contrasts, and analyzes relationships between landmarks and streets defined by hand-drawn maps of the neighborhood and the most frequently visited destinations of community residents.

Respondents were given a blank sheet of paper approximately 17½ inches square and were instructed "to draw a map of your neighborhood, that is, the area where you live, are familiar with and know well." Each map was a unique representation and included a combination of place (stores, houses, etc.) and path (streets, highways, etc.) elements. It was our belief that sketch maps would provide good information about the perceived neighborhood. The procedure for map drawing followed that used by Lynch (1960) and other city planners. The result was expected to provide information about valuable city or neighborhood characteristics from the older resident's perspective.

A retrospective recall technique was used to elicit data regarding trips to common community destinations. Subjects were asked to report the number of trips they made to a list of 32 retail and service destinations. This list was compiled from previous origin–destination research which had identified the most frequently visited businesses, personal service, recreational, and shopping destinations.

DATA ANALYSIS

A single consensus map similar to that developed by Lynch was composed from 95 usable, hand-drawn maps. An interim process "translated" each hand-drawn map into a standardized map before they were all combined. This step was necessary because hand-drawn maps were often distorted and, in some cases, contained errors that made simple comparisons difficult.

Consensus of Hand-Drawn Maps

Figure 5.5 illustrates the final consensus representation. A total of 22 places were located on hand-drawn maps by a consensus of at least five respondents. MacArthur Park was by far the most popular single element. Nearly half of the subjects (45) included the park on their hand-drawn

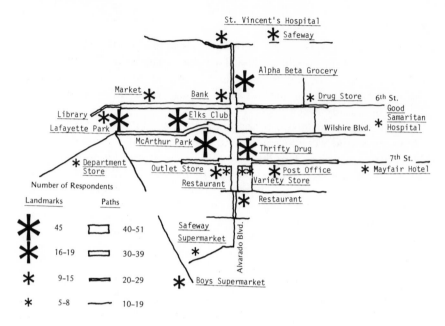

FIGURE 5.5. Hand-drawn consensus map.

maps. This was to be expected because the park is a dominant land use, centrally located, and used by many of the respondents. The next level of consensus (16–19) included 4 places: the Thrifty drug store, Alpha Beta supermarket, the Elks Club, and Lafayette Park. Of these 4 places, 3 were located adjacent to or within one block of MacArthur Park. Lafayette Park, although located on the western edge of the neighborhood, is a large open space with facilities for senior citizens. The third level of consensus (9–15) includes 9 places: two supermarkets, a grocery store, the branch library, the district post office, a restaurant, a bank, a hospital, and a discount clothing store. Although 4 are located on the edge of the neighborhood, 3 are situated adjacent to or within one block of MacArthur Park. The fourth level of consensus (5–8) includes 8 places: two restaurants, a variety store, a hotel, a hospital, a drug store, a grocery store, and a department store. Half of these are located on, near, or outside the boundary of the neighborhood, whereas 3 are located adjacent to or within one block of the park.

Several attributes of these consensus landmarks deserve comment. First, the overwhelming majority of the places selected by respondents are important "functional" resources. The strongest symbolic, aesthetic, or visual elements (as viewed by city planners) were not included on consensus maps. Second, there seem to be two major spatial locations for elements: those clustered near MacArthur Park and those located near the edge of the district. Only 3 of the 22 places are located in the neighborhood area further than one block from the park and less than one block from the edge of the district. It seems as though a system of tightly clustered elements near the park has been produced with outlying functional landmarks that serve to orient the respondent and thus define the outer edge of the neighborhood. The vast array of retail shops, restaurants, and traditional landmarks located between the park and these outlying elements are virtually ignored.

The consensus of paths (streets) reinforce the basic importance of the central park element. The most popular path is Alvarado Boulevard near the eastern edge of the park. The next level of path consensus (30–39) occurs on the north, south, and east edges of the park and extends no further than one block from the edge of the park. The third consensus level (20–29) extends along the major arterials of Alvarado, 6th, Wilshire and 7th, whereas the fourth consensus level (10–19) introduces more cartographic detail. At the fourth level a greater number of shared pathways common to respondents living in various sectors of the district are introduced.

The consensus path map creates a pattern that is concentric in nature. The paths of highest consensus are centrally located, major intersecting arterials. The agreement regarding shared paths lessens as they diverge from the center of the neighborhood. Of additional interest is the relationship between landmarks and paths. Each landmark seems to be coupled to the pathway system.

Frequently Visited Destinations

Figure 5.6 displays the 22 most frequently visited locations in the neighborhood. The size of the symbol represents the total number of trips taken to each destination by all respondents during a typical month. The number of individual trips taken by each respondent to each destination is summed to arrive at this figure. A predominant element in Figure 5.6 is the small groceries and supermarkets. Of the 22 most frequently visited destinations, 12 are food stores. The most frequently visited destinations include MacArthur and LaFayette parks, 3 supermarkets, 9 grocery stores, the discount clothing store, a drug store, 4 restaurants, the branch library, and a bar.

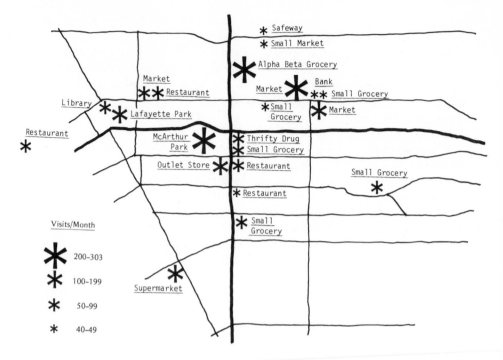

FIGURE 5.6. Number of monthly trips to specific destinations.

Comparisons of Hand-Drawn Consensus Maps and Most Frequently Visited Destinations

Of the 14 landmarks identified by at least nine or more respondents, only 3 were not included in the most frequently visited destination map: the bank, the hospital, and the Elks building.[1] These landmarks are located on Figure 5.7. Twelve respondents said they used the bank, but only 22 total trips were generated during a typical month. The Elks building and St. Vincent's hospital seem to be the most "symbolic" elements. Neither of these two buildings are visited by respondents, although both appeared in the consensus of hand-drawn maps. However, senior nutrition and recreation services are available at the Elks building, and St. Vincent's Hospital has the only publicly accessible emergency room in the district. Therefore, although the use of these two resources may be limited, they still have

---

[1]The post office destinations category was not included as a service destination category.

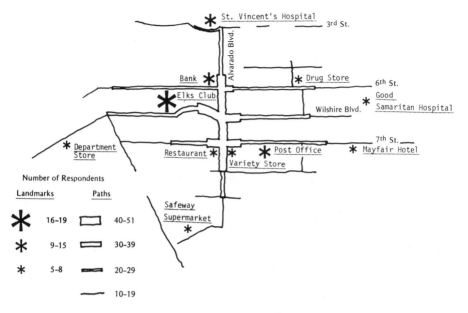

FIGURE 5.7. Resident landmarks not frequently visited.

broad relevance to older people in the commmunity. No original trip destination information was gathered regarding the post office.

The landmarks from the third level of consensus (5–8) are less popular destinations. Only one of these seven places is frequently visited. Three of the five destinations located on the edge of the district (a hospital, drug store, and department store) attract a handful of infrequent visitors. A supermarket near the edge of the district was closed and moved just prior to our interviews; no trips were taken to this location, but it still appeared in the image map. In this consensus category, the Mayfair Hotel was the most symbolic element, similar to the Elks club. No respondents claimed to visit this destination. The hotel, however, is a venerable neighborhood landmark with a large sign which is visible from downtown and various locations east along 7th Street. The remaining two places are nondescript buildings—a variety store and a restaurant located near the intersections of 7th Street and Alvarado Boulevard.

The relationship between hand-drawn map elements and popular, salient destinations is clear. Respondents have predominantly chosen, in their neighborhood hand-drawn maps, landmarks that have direct relevance to them.

Comparison of the Los Angeles City Planning Department Westlake Image Map and the Hand-Drawn Consensus Map

The city planning department image map reproduced in Figure 5.4 also demonstrates an interesting contrast to the hand-drawn consensus map. The concepts developed by Lynch (1960) reviewed early in this chapter were used to create the Los Angeles City Planning Department image map. The district, landmark, activity concentration (node), and street (path) designations are similar to those devised by Lynch. The city planning department Westlake image map contains 10 major and 3 minor landmarks within the boundaries of the neighborhood study. It also defines one major and two minor north–south pathways and three major and five minor east–west pathways.

Of the 14 major landmarks on the elderly resident-created consensus map only 3 are common to the 13 major and minor landmark features in the city planning Westlake image map. These three features—MacArthur Park, Layfayette Park, and St. Vincent's Hospital—are displayed in Figure 5.8. The elements which are missing from the older people's hand-drawn

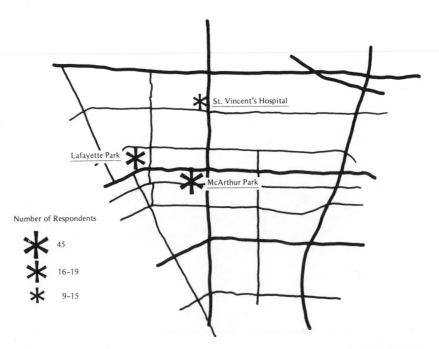

FIGURE 5.8. Landmarks common to resident hand-drawn consensus map and city planning image map.

maps are the large high-rise office and commercial structures. The elements missing from the city planner's Westlake image map are those that represent important neighborhood resources like grocery stores. In an attempt to create an image map which represents important and salient elements of the district, city planners limited their perceptions to the most visually dominant neighborhood elements. Thus, a landmark such as the Otis Art Institute, which appeals to a larger more sophisticated city-wide audience, was selected in place of the Elks lodge, which is located next to the Institute and appeals to local citizens. This exercise in mistaken images is of interest particularly when one considers the implications this type of analysis can have on the policies and programs that specify important historic elements or encourage neighborhood revitalization and change.

CONCLUSIONS

The research has illustrated several examples of how differently city planners and older residents may view neighborhood environments. First, the hand-drawn consensus map data suggest that, for older people, salient resources which represent important and necessary community supports may play an important role in their image of the neighborhood. Not that other less utilitarian elements of a neighborhood environment are ignored—it simply underscores the concern that older community dwellers may share for maintaining and preserving access to various retail, service, and recreational destinations. The significance of a symbolic community design feature, such as a gothic revival church, may pale in comparison to the closing and relocation of a convenient supermarket with low prices.

Second, the procedure and product of the community image map developed by Lynch is of immense value in providing community planners with important information about how people perceive city environments. Data from an analysis such as this can provide information about how to correct confusing street patterns or introduce effective and clear directional graphics. However, it is important to recognize that the image map is a selectively perceived experience for different community residents. Older community respondents in this research did not identify the same buildings and amenities as city planners who studied what they considered to be significant features of the neighborhood. Although some elements such as the two parks and the local hospital were included in both representations, older residents were more likely to identify salient resources in their neighborhood maps. Their "neighborhood" was more likely to be defined by elements which affect them rather than by symbolic or figurative resources. This definition may also lend a new interpretation to the search for a shared "community or public" image. A landmark to an older community dweller may be a local grocery store rather than a tall building. We should seek to recognize that a "public" image is constituted by the perceptions of many different audiences. For the older person this image may be tied less to the visual structure of the environment and more to the social and interactive processes which define neighborhood life.

Finally, in reaffirming the logistic and perceived importance of practical neighborhood resources such as grocery stores and retail services, it should be mentioned that planning which takes place in neighborhoods with high concentrations of lower-income older people should be concerned with the preservation of current access to these resources. Transportation planning, economic development activities, pedestrian improvements, and the construction and location of housing or health and social services should consider access to residential concentrations of older people as paramount. Planned change in a neighborhood that erodes the retail and service base or locates new housing or services in areas of poor accessibility is destined to create problems.

REFERENCES

City Planning Commission. *The visual environment of Los Angeles.* Los Angeles: The Commission, April 1971.

Clay, G. *Close up: How to read the American city.* New York: Praeger, 1973.

Department of City Planning. *Westlake community plan: Socio-economic analysis.* Los Angeles: The Department, 1971.

Lawton, M. P. The impact of the environment on aging and behavior. In J. E. Birren & K. W. Schaie (Eds.), *Handbook of the psychology of aging.* New York: Van Nostrand Reinhold, 1977.

Lynch, K. *The image of the city.* Cambridge, Mass.: MIT Press, 1960.

Lynch, K. *What time is this place?* Cambridge, Mass.: MIT Press, 1972.

Lynch, K. *Managing the sense of a region.* Cambridge, Mass.: MIT Press, 1976.

Minneapolis Planning Commission. *Toward a new city CRP.* Minneapolis: The Commission, 1965.

Rowles, G. *Prisoners of space?* Boulder, Colo.: Westview Press, 1978.

San Francisco Department of City Planning. *San Francisco urban design plan.* San Francisco: The Department, 1971.

Southworth, M. The sonic environment of cities. *Environment and Behavior,* 1969, *1,* 49–70.

6

The Investigation of Environmental Learning in the Elderly

RUSSELL J. OHTA   KATHLEEN C. KIRASIC[1]

How successful are elderly individuals in situations which require the learning of new environments? There are some indications, based on earlier research, that the older adult experiences particular difficulty in these situations. At the same time, there is more recent evidence which challenges such a belief. This chapter will trace the development of this research and describe the accompanying evolution of ideas on the topic. The chapter itself, then, represents a journey, one in which knowledge about environmental learning in the adult increases as the journey progresses.

Without a doubt, one of the most robust phenomena in aging research related to environmental learning has been the observation of an age-related decrement in memory for spatial information. This age difference has been demonstrated repeatedly in studies involving memory for geometric patterns and designs, with both recall and recognition procedures, and in both cross-sectional and longitudinal research designs. Such an age-related decrement has been demonstrated with the use of the Memory-for-Designs Test (Davies, 1967; Heron & Chown, 1967), the Benton Visual Retention Test (Arenberg, 1978), and other similar tests (Arochova & Kostolansky, 1974).

The observation of an age-related difference in spatial memory, however, is not restricted to the use of geometric patterns and designs as stimuli. In a study conducted by Ohta (1979), subjects were presented

[1] The contribution of the second author has been sponsored by a grant from the National Science Foundation, DAR 8011000.

83

AGING AND MILIEU:
ENVIRONMENTAL PERSPECTIVES
ON GROWING OLD

with a street map containing 12 landmarks. After four minutes of studying the map, subjects were given a similar map (without the landmarks) and were instructed to indicate where each of the landmarks had been located on the original map. This procedure was repeated with a second map and new landmarks. Analysis of the number of landmarks correctly located revealed that elderly subjects performed more poorly on this task than young subjects. Similar results were also reported by Perlmutter, Metzger, Nezworski, and Miller (1981) using three maps containing only 8 landmarks each and a self-paced experimental procedure. The results of these studies indicate that the age-related decrement in spatial memory, previously demonstrated in memory for geometric patterns and designs, is general enough to also include memory for locations of landmarks on street maps.

Finally, the presence of an age-related decrement in spatial memory has been observed in a study that even further approximated the everyday situations of individuals. Ohta (1981a) describes a study in which subjects viewed either (a) a model of a 9-block city; or (b) a videotaped simulated "tour" through the streets of that model. The city was designed to depict a typical urban environment and included miniature office buildings, high-rise apartments, streets, a park, and so on. After viewing either the model or the videotape, the subject's task was to indicate where each of 12 prominent landmarks was located in the city, using replicas of these landmarks and an outline of the city street pattern. Analysis of the mean error distance for the landmarks showed that elderly subjects performed more poorly than young subjects in both viewing conditions. Hence, an age-related decrement in spatial memory has been demonstrated in a study which utilizes stimuli closely resembling those encountered in everyday activities (i.e., miniatures of elements found in cities) and presents them in a manner which closely approximates the way in which people normally experience them (i.e., a simulated tour). In short, the evidence from previous studies appears to point to the existence of a highly reliable and extremely generalized age-related decrement in spatial memory.

In addition to remembering spatial information, the learning of an environment also requires the organization and integration of information which is spatially disjointed and temporally separated. Consequently, the impact of aging on spatial and temporal closure is another line of research which is relevant to the topic of environmental learning in the elderly. In an investigation of spatial closure, Basowitz and Korchin (1957) found that elderly subjects were less successful than young subjects in identifying fragmented pictures of persons, objects, and situations. Of particular interest in this study was a tendency for elderly subjects to fixate on details and to treat individual elements separately rather than integrating them into a cohesive whole. Wallace (1956), in a study examining temporal closure, found elderly subjects to be less successful than young subjects in identifying complex designs and pictures that were presented segment by segment over a period of time. On the basis of these studies, it would seem reasonable to assume that the integration of environmental information would also be especially problematic for elderly individuals since such information is, of necessity, spatially dispersed and temporally perceived.

The preceding assumption, however, does not appear to be valid. In the study described earlier (Ohta, 1981a), subjects were exposed to either a model of a city (which suggests an organization of environmental information by city blocks) or a videotaped simulated tour through the streets of the model (which requires integration of continuously changing environmental information). Although both age groups performed more accurately after viewing the model itself as opposed to the simulated tour, this effect was constant for both age groups. In other words, the elderly subjects were not especially disadvantaged by the method of presenting environmental information which placed much heavier demands on the integrative ability of the viewer. Thus, although the literature on spatial and temporal closure may suggest otherwise, the integration of environmental information does not appear to be uniquely problematic for elderly adults.

In summarizing the literature just reviewed, it is clear that the presence of an age-related decrement in spatial memory has been a ubiquitous finding. Such decrements have been observed in studies which range from the rather abstract memory for patterns and designs to the more concrete memory for elements in a model of a city. Consequently, it would appear that elderly adults would also be poorer than younger adults in remembering the environmental information present in real, everyday physical environments. The ability to integrate environmental information, however, does not appear to be age-sensitive. Although age-related decrements have been observed in studies on spatial and temporal closure, the integration of environmental information has not been found to be disproportionately more difficult for elderly adults when the experimental task has approximated the situations normally encountered by individuals. Thus, it does not appear that elderly adults would be poorer than younger adults in integrating the environmental information present in real, everyday physical environments.

With these conclusions in mind, an additional factor crucial to the evaluation of elderly adults' learning capabilities must be considered. Recent studies have suggested an important distinction between elderly subjects' performances on cognitive tasks involving abstract materials in the laboratory and their performances on very similar tasks using materials with direct relevance to their lives outside the laboratory setting (Demming & Pressey, 1973; Lachman & Lachman, 1979; Kirasic, 1981). These findings indicate that a valid assessment of environmental learning must include consideration of results from ecological studies of spatial cognition and spatial behavior in elderly individuals. To date there have been few studies of this type. Only recently has research been directed at delineating the relationship between spatial cognitive abilities and actual environmental use on the part of elderly adults (Walsh, Krauss, & Regnier, 1981). This research has indicated significant relationship between these factors, and future studies must be focused on the delineation of this relationship. These studies will optimally include observational and experimental effects in real-world settings.

THE CURRENT STATE OF ENVIRONMENTAL LEARNING RESEARCH

As has already been stated, previous research dealing with the spatial abilities of older adults has not been focused on typical spatial behavior in typical spatial settings. Consequently, it is not clear what special problems this population encounters in the course of adapting to and navigating in new environments. In many instances, speculations about spatial ability have been based on nonspatial data (Wallace, 1956; Basowitz & Korchin, 1957). Only recently have researchers begun to complement laboratory investigations with behavioral–observational studies of spatial ability in environments actually frequented by older adults. In the remainder of this chapter, three such studies will be described in some detail.

The Medical Center

In the course of daily transactions with the environment, people occasionally must make detours. For example, a road could be closed for repairs, or a hallway could be barricaded during waxing. In such cases, the traveler is forced to reach his or her destination by way of a different route, perhaps never before encountered. The obstructed pathway presents the traveler with a classic spatial problem-solving task. How do people decide which one of a number of alternate routes to take their destination? In a recent investigation, Ohta (1981b) examined the performance of older and younger adults faced with this spatial problem. In this study, route choice was regarded as a special case of response selection in a problem-solving task.

The most relevant literature that addresses the issue of response selection has been the work of Botwinick (1966). From studies in which subjects were presented with a series of hypothetical "life situations," Botwinick found that elderly subjects were more likely than young subjects to choose a moderately rewarding alternative with an *assured* outcome rather than a highly rewarding but risky outcome. Ohta (1981b) investigated similar response-selection tendencies in both a hypothetical spatial problem-solving situation modeled after Botwinick's (1966) procedure and a decision-making situation in an actual environment.

The participants in this investigation were 15 West Virginia University undergraduate students ($\bar{X}$ age = 19.9 years, range = 18–25 years; $\bar{X}$ education = 14.0 years) and 15 elderly community residents ($\bar{X}$ age = 71.6 years, range = 60–81 years; $\bar{X}$ education = 12.7 years).

After arriving at the outpatients' lobby of the West Virginia University Medical Center, the subject first answered the following question:

How good is your sense of direction?
Check the appropriate answer below.

Poor _ _ _ _ _ _ _ _ _ Good
-4 -3 -2 -1 0 $+1$ $+2$ $+3$ $+4$

The subject then completed the following hypothetical spatial "life situation"[2] (Ohta, 1981b) modeled after Botwinick's (1966) "life situations":

> You arrive in a neighboring city for the first time to attend a meeting just outside the central business district. You arrive early, however, since you wish to do some shopping before the meeting. You park your car in a parking structure in the central business district. After 2 hours of shopping, you suddenly realize that the meeting will begin in 5 minutes. You look down a street that seems as though it may lead directly to the parking structure. Realizing that returning to the parking structure by "backtracking" the original route will certainly make you late for the meeting, you must decide whether to take the familiar original route or the alternate route which is unfamiliar, but may be a short-cut to the parking structure.
>
> Imagine that you are making this decision. Listed below are several probabilities or odds that the alternate route will be a short-cut to the parking structure.
>
> Please check the lowest probability that you would consider acceptable to make it worthwhile for you to take the alternate route.
>
> The chances are 1 in 10 that the alternate route will be a short-cut.

---

[2]The hypothetical spatial "life situation" was taken from *Experimental Aging Research*, 1981, 7(1), 81–84. Copyright Beech Hill Enterprises, Inc., 1981.

The chances are 3 in 10 that the alternate route will be a short-cut.
The chances are 5 in 10 that the alternate route will be a short-cut.
The chances are 7 in 10 that the alternate route will be a short-cut.
The chances are 9 in 10 that the alternate route will be a short-cut.
Place a check here if you would *not* take the alternate route no matter
what the probabilities [pp. 81–82].

The subject was then familiarized with a particular section of the highly
complex medical facility, namely, the area between the outpatients' lobby
and the emergency room (see Figure 6.1). The subject and the experimenter walked from the outpatients' lobby to the emergency room
along a specific route (the original route) and returned to the outpatients'
lobby along a different route (the return route). The subject was instructed to pay close attention to the route traveled in getting from the
outpatients' lobby to the emergency room, that is, the original route. The
subject was not instructed to pay attention to the return route. Four walks
were conducted. After each walk, the subject drew a map of the route
between the outpatients' lobby and the emergency room (i.e., the original
route) on a sheet of paper which showed the first segment of the route
(thus providing a scale for the map). Subjects were not informed in
advance about the number of walks which were to be conducted.

The subject was then taken to a point along the original route (the
impasse point) and told, "Imagine that it is vital for you to get to the
emergency room but, for some reason, this hallway is impassable at this
point. Show me how you would get to the emergency room [Ohta, 1981b,
p. 82]." The experimenter followed the subject and recorded the route
traveled. In this actual spatial problem-solving situation, the subject could
have selected either of two different approaches (see Figure 6.1): (*a*)
backtrack along the original route and then over what was previously the
return route; or (*b*) proceed along an alternate route, *never before
traversed by the subject*, which proves to be a shortcut to the emergency
room.

Finally, the subject and the experimenter proceeded to a classroom in
the Medical Center. There, the Road-Map Test of Direction Sense
(Money, 1965) was administered. Visual acuity was then measured using a
Snellen chart, and color perception was assessed using pseudoisochro-
matic plates of the American Optical Corporation.

Results from the perceptual tests indicate that the visual acuity of the
elderly subjects was somewhat poorer than that of the young subjects for
both the left eye [$t(28) = 4.32, p < .01$] and the right eye [$t(28) = 3.04$,
$p < .01$]. The visual acuity of the young subjects was 20/15 (left) and 20/17
(right), whereas for the elderly subjects it was 20/27 (left) and 20/28
(right). The elderly subjects also performed more poorly than the young

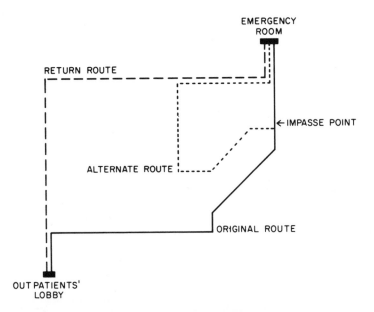

FIGURE 6.1. The relevant section of the West Virginia University Medical Center. [Taken from Experimental Aging Research, 1981, 7(1), 81–84. Copyright Beech Hill Enterprises Inc., 1981].

subjects on the color perception test [$t(28) = 5.49, p < .01$]. Out of 14 items, young subjects responded correctly to 13.1 items, whereas elderly subjects did so to 10.7 items. The score of the elderly subjects indicates that their color vision was on the borderline between "normal" and "defective."

In the clinical test of "Direction Sense," the elderly subjects performed more poorly than young subjects on the Road-Map Test of Direction Sense [$t(28) = 4.84, p < .01$]. The young subjects commited only 2.13 errors, comparable to the 12th graders (and optimally performing group) in Money's normative study. On the other hand, the elderly subjects committed 9.53 errors, comparable to the sixth graders in Money's study and a group of adult patients with Turner's syndrome (Alexander, Walker, & Money, 1964).

For the self-reported "Sense of Direction" measure, the two age groups did *not* differ in their evaluation of their own sense of direction [$t(28) = .27, p > .05$]. Young subjects rated themselves a 0.67, whereas the elderly subjects rated themselves a 0.47. Thus, both age groups evaluated their sense of direction as being midway between poor (−4) and good (+4).

The environmental learning measure was divided into two phases: (a) sketch mapping; and (b) way finding.

SKETCH MAPPING

In an accurate sketch map of the the route between the outpatients' lobby and the emergency room (drawn on the sheet of paper showing the first segment of the route), the angle between the outpatients' lobby and the emergency room would be 43°, the total distance would be 22.3 cm, and the sequence of turns would be right–left–right–left.

Repeated measures analyses of variance revealed that the elderly subjects were consistently less accurate than the young subjects on all three measures of accuracy. Elderly subjects were less accurate than young subjects in estimating the angle between the outpatients' lobby and the emergency room [$F(1, 28) = 12.70, p < .01$]. The mean error for the young subjects was 9.38°, whereas for the elderly subjects it was 24.85°. Elderly subjects were also less accurate than young subjects in estimating the distance between the outpatients' lobby and the emergency room [$F(1, 28) = 7.23, p < .02$]. For young subjects, the mean error was 4.16 cm, while for the elderly subjects it was 7.93 cm. Finally, elderly subjects were also less accurate than young subjects in sequencing the turns (correct sequence = 1, incorrect sequence = 0) involved in getting from the outpatients' lobby to the emergency room [$F(1, 28) = 19.32, p < .01$]. For young subjects, the mean score was .73, whereas for the elderly subjects it was .27.

WAY FINDING

Despite the presence of age differences in all three accuracy measures derived from the sketch maps of the route between the outpatients' lobby and the emergency room, *all* subjects were successful in finding the emergency room by some route other than the original route when presented with the spatial problem-solving situation.

The analysis of the hypothetical spatial "life situation" indicated that young and elderly subjects differed in their choice of acceptable probability levels for the alternate route: 3/10 (young = 7%, elderly = 0%), 5/10 (young = 33%, elderly = 7%), 7/10 (young = 27%, elderly = 0%), 9/10 (young = 13%, elderly = 7%), and avoid the alternate route altogether (young = 20%, elderly = 87%). No subject from either age group chose 1/10 as acceptable. As can be seen, there was a pronounced tendency for elderly subjects, as opposed to young subjects, to choose to avoid the alternate route no matter what its probability of being successful. These results clearly replicate the findings of Botwinick (1966).

In the actual spatial problem-solving situation, however, young and elderly subjects did *not* differ in their selection of approaches. Two-thirds of the young subjects and one-third of the elderly subjects chose to backtrack along the original route and then over what was previously the return route, whereas one-third of the young subjects and two-thirds of the elderly chose to proceed along the alternate route.

In certain ways, the elderly subjects in the study appeared to be at a distinct disadvantage, relative to the young subjects, in their capacity for environmental learning. For one thing, the elderly subjects possessed poorer visual acuity and color perception, characteristics which may interfere with the processing of critical environmental information (Ohta, 1981a; Pastalan, 1973). Furthermore, the elderly subjects were poorer in manipulating spatial information as required by the clinical test of "direction sense," manipulations which may also be involved in environmental learning. Some evidence confirming the potentially negative impact of these characteristics on environmental learning can be found in the less accurate sketch maps drawn by the elderly subjects, and in their preference for an assured course of action in the hypothetical spatial "life situation."

However, there is even stronger evidence which argues against the notion of impaired environmental learning in the elderly. To begin with, the elderly subjects did not, on the basis of their own subjective experience, evaluate their "sense of direction" as being any different from that of the young subjects. In addition, when confronted with an actual spatial problem-solving task in a real physical environment, elderly subjects were just as successful as young subjects in their way-finding endeavors. Finally, the elderly subjects showed no more of a preference for an assured course of action than the young subjects in their approach to the actual spatial problem-solving task.

Taken together, the results of the present study suggest that elderly adults, while performing less well on isolated perceptual tasks and "paper and pencil" spatial tasks, are in fact equally as effective as younger adults in dealing with the environmental learning demands posed by real physical environments.

The Hometown

In two different research efforts Kirasic (1980, 1981) further demonstrated the importance of ecological validity in assessing the spatial competence of elderly adults. The first series of studies (Kirasic, 1980) focused on young, middle-aged, and elderly adults' abilities to solve problems involving spatial relationships by cognitively manipulating spatial arrays. Subjects inferred the location of various target sites within a novel, laboratory-learned spatial array and within their hometown using two cognitive manipulations, referred to as imagined self-movement and imagined array-movement (Huttenlocher & Presson, 1979).

In both studies, subjects made distance and directional estimates to target locations under both sets of cognitive manipulation instructions. In the study involving the novel spatial array, analysis of direction estimates revealed that elderly adults were less accurate under both manipulation conditions than were middle-aged or young adults, who did not differ from one another. Furthermore, elderly adults performed with less accuracy under imagined array-movement instructions than under self-movement instructions. A corresponding difference was not found for the other age groups. Distance estimation analyses revealed that the elderly were less accurate than either the young or middle-aged adults.

These findings could be taken as additional support for the proposition that perspective-taking and/or mental rotation abilities are diminished in elderly adults (e.g., Herman & Coyne, 1980). Had the experimentation stopped here, a general statement of declining spatial competence would have been made. However, a parallel study was conducted involving the same generic procedure and the same subjects as those in the study just described. However, a different spatial array, the subject's hometown, was used in the second study. Analysis of direction estimates from this study revealed no significant effects or interactions. The same was true for the analysis of distance estimates.

The results of these studies suggest that the accuracy of elderly adults' performance on spatial cognitive tasks is directly affected by the context in which the task is presented. Thus, it appears that age-related decrements on some spatial tasks are due to ecologically based performance factors rather than to differences in general cognitive competence per se.

The Supermarket

In response to the need for additional information about older individuals' spatial cognition and spatial behavior in real-world settings, Kirasic (1981) initiated a research project focusing on the ecologically valid context of the supermarket. This ongoing project is aimed at delineating the relationships among psychometric measures of spatial abilities (including the factors of spatial visualization, spatial orientation, and visual memory), behavioral measures in a simulated shopping trip through familiar and unfamiliar supermarkets, and experimental measures involving scene recognition, route planning, and place knowledge within the two supermarket settings.

Thus far, data have been collected from 30 female subjects. The 15 young subjects ($\bar{X}$ age = 25.3) were recruited from undergraduate classes, while the 15 elderly subjects ($\bar{X}$ age = 69.5) were recruited from a senior citizen center. These data have not been analyzed completely. However, preliminary examination of the data revealed some pertinent trends.

Preliminary results from the experimental tasks indicated that both young and elderly adults' accuracy in recognizing scenes, planning routes, and locating items on maps was lower in the novel supermarket than in the familiar setting. In the unfamiliar setting, significant age-related decrement was found only on the recognition test, but other differences were in this same direction.

Behavior during the simulated shopping tasks is being examined in terms of (*a*) efficiency, that is, how far the subject traveled in locating seven shopping items compared to the minimum distance that had to be traveled in order to locate these items; and (*b*) the frequency of four types of behavior, namely standing–scanning, walking–scanning, standing, and walking. Preliminary results indicated that, not surprisingly, more efficient travel was accomplished in the familiar store for both age groups. No age differences have been observed between age groups on the efficiency measure, but behavioral differences were apparent during a familiarization period during which subjects quickly scanned the novel supermarket prior to the shopping tasks and during the shopping tasks themselves. In the familiar store, subjects in both age groups spend most of their time walking to the series of locations, with little time required for scanning that environment. During the familiarization period in the novel store, however, the elderly adults exhibited more standing–scanning and standing and less walking–scanning than did the younger adults. These differences appeared again during the shopping task itself in the novel supermarket.

It would compound the misdemeanor of reporting results from an incomplete study to discuss these preliminary findings at length. At this point, it seems reasonable to suggest that, when completed, this study will show either little or no age-related decrements in experimental task performance and in efficiency of travel on the one hand, and very significant differences in specific spatial behaviors on the other. One of the major objectives of this and future studies will be determining the relationship between types of behavior in the environment and the acquisition of spatial knowledge regarding that environment. Clearly, it is not yet possible to specify changes in the dynamics of this relationship that may be associated with the aging process.

CONCLUSION

The picture which emerges from the research described in this chapter is that of an *environmentally competent* elderly individual. It appears that age-related decrements in spatial cognition and spatial behavior may not be as pervasive or as obvious as previous research and cultural stereotypes would suggest. Specifically, it has been demonstrated that elderly adults' approach to solving spatial problems is more exploration-oriented and more risky than laboratory studies have suggested. Furthermore, it has been shown that elderly individuals' performance in complex tasks requiring the processing of spatial information is strongly influenced by the familiarity of the spatial context involved. Finally, it has been suggested that, although elderly adults apportion their effort differently than young adults in their environmental transactions, their resulting knowledge of the environment and the efficiency of their movement therein may not differ substantially, if at all, from that of young adults.

Taken together, these findings suggest that future research focusing on the spatial competencies of older adults consider performance on spatial tasks in the context of ecological factors. The authors are *not* advocating the abolition of traditional laboratory studies of spatial cognition but instead are arguing in favor of complementing the laboratory approach with studies of spatial cognition and spatial behavior in real environments. Results from both types of studies are necessary in order to achieve a better understanding of age-related changes in environmental learning.

ACKNOWLEDGMENTS

The first author would like to express a special "thank you" to Brenda M. Lubozynski for her assistance in the preparation of this chapter.

REFERENCES

Alexander, D., Walker, H., & Money, J. Studies in direction sense, I. Turner's Syndrome. *Archives of General Psychiatry*, 1964, *10*, 337–339.

Arenberg, D. Differences and changes with age in the Benton Visual Retention Test. *Journal of Gerontology*, 1978, *33*, 534–540.

Arochova, I., & Kostolansky, R. Developmental trends in a short term visual task. *Studia Psychologica*, 1974, *16*, 293–296.

Basowitz, H., & Korchin, S. J. Age differences in the perception of closure. *Journal of Abnormal and Social Psychology*, 1957, *54*, 93–97.

Botwinick, J. Cautiousness in advanced age. *Journal of Gerontology*, 1966, *21*, 347–353.

Davies, A. D. M. Age and the Memory-for-Designs Test. *British Journal of Social and Clinical Psychology*, 1967, *6*, 228–233.

Demming, J. A., & Pressey, S. L. Tests indigenous to the adult in older years. *Journal of Consulting Psychology*, 1973, *4*, 144–148.

Herman, J. F., & Coyne, A. C. Mental manipulation of spatial information in young and elderly adults. *Developmental Psychology*, 1980, *16*, 537–538.

Heron, A., & Chown, S. *Age and function*. Boston: Little Brown, 1967.

Huttenlocher, J. E., & Presson, C. C. The coding and transformation of spatial information. *Cognitive Psychology*, 1979, *11*, 375–394.

Kirasic, K. C. *Spatial problem solving in elderly adults: Evidence of a hometown advantage*. Paper presented at the annual meetings of the Gerontological Society of America, San Diego, November 1980.

Kirasic, K. C. *The elusive concept of cognitive competence in aging research: The case of spatial cognition*. Paper presented at a symposium entitled "New Directions in Gero-psychology" at the meetings of the Midwestern Psychological Association, Detroit, May 1981.

Lachman, J. L., & Lachman, R. Age and the actualization of world knowledge. In L. W. Poon, J. L. Fozard, L. S. Cermak, D. Arenberg, & L. W. Thompson (Eds.), *New directions in memory and aging: Proceedings of the George Tolland Memorial Conference*. Hillsdale, N.J.: Lawrence Erlbaum Associates, 1979.

Money, J. *A standardized road-map test of direction sense*. Baltimore, Md.: Johns Hopkins University Press, 1965.

Ohta, R. J. *Spatial cognition and the relative effectiveness of two methods of presenting spatial information in young and elderly adults*. Unpublished doctoral dissertation, University of Southern California, Los Angeles, 1979.

Ohta, R. J. Spatial orientation in the elderly: The current status of understanding. In H. L. Pick, Jr., & L. P. Acredolo (Eds.), *Spatial orientation: Theory, research, and application*. New York: Plenum, 1981. (a)

Ohta, R. J. Spatial problem solving: The response selection tendencies of young and elderly adults. *Experimental Aging Research*, 1981, *7*, 81–84. (b)

Pastalan, L. A. How the elderly negotiate their environment. *Housing and environment for the elderly*. Washington, D.C.: Gerontological Society, 1973.

Perlmutter, M., Metzger, R., Nezworski, T., & Miller, K. Spatial and temporal memory in 20 and 60 year olds. *Journal of Gerontology*, 1981, *36*, 59–65.

Wallace, J. G. Some studies of perception in relation to age. *British Journal of Psychology*, 1956, *47*, 283–297.

Walsh, D. A., Krauss, I. K., & Regnier, V. A. Spatial ability, environmental knowledge, and environmental use: The elderly. In L. S. Liben, A. H. Patterson, & N. Newcombe (Eds.), *Spatial representation and behavior across the life span*. New York: Academic Press, 1981.

7

The Meaning of Place in Old Age

SANDRA C. HOWELL

The 1972 Life Span Developmental Psychology Conference in West Virginia dealt with personality and socialization. I was asked to generate discussion on the contribution of environments across the life cycle. I did not accept that invitation, as I did not at that time feel that I or anyone else knew much about the roles environments might be playing in the later life development of human behavior or identity. After 10 years and a number of research efforts, collaborations, and readings of the literature in human development, cognition, perception, and environmental behavior, I am still unsure that there is much known, theoretically or methodologically, on this topic, but the most thoughtful contributions to date are coming from this assembled group. I am more than intuitively sure that designed environments are of considerable importance to the shaping and mainte-nance of personal identity and social relationships. I have become equally convinced that present paradigms employed to tease out intrapsychic and interpersonal factors in human behavior are ineffective in isolating or identifying what the physical environment *means* to human beings across the life cycle. The 1972 conference papers have been a particularly important body of source material for me, since I view place and place making as an integral part of personality development and social learning. The chapter on environment, prepared by Klausner (1973), organizes the epistemological problem we have when we attempt to deal with one thought structure which appears to be in the domain of physical science (our senses in the built environment) and another which is clearly humanistic or at least mentalistic. Transformations and mediators are

AGING AND MILIEU:
ENVIRONMENTAL PERSPECTIVES
ON GROWING OLD

surely required as we now become convinced that direct correlations and regressions provide impotent explanations.

In keeping with Klausner's (and Looft's) 1973 admonition that we need to tighten up our commonly used definitions, it seems to me that we must clearly designate what we think we are exploring and agree on what we mean by the *Meaning of Place*:

1. How is a place sensed, perceived, recorded (i.e., what attributes are selected to experience and remember)?
2. How is a place understood or known? To somehow know a place is preliminary to giving it meaning but *not equivalent to its meaning.*
3. What is the *history* of the individual's experiences with a place? What transactions with or actions on the place have actually occurred or are perceived by the individual to have occurred?
4. How has a place related to domains of the individual's life—family, work, social–educational, cultural–political experiences?
5. What has the individual learned from others in the society about the particular place or this category of places (i.e., what are the rules, attitudes, norms, values related to the places)?
6. What *changes* have occurred to the place *and* in the individual's transactions with it? How does the individual perceive and interpret these changes?

In the 1972 conference, great emphasis was placed on antecedent–consequent models for research in development; but is antecedent–consequent analysis appropriate to the study of the meaning of place, as it is purported to be for all other types of developmental studies? The antecedent–consequent approach seems to assume some stability in the definition of the variables across time. In the case of person–place relationships, the salience and valence (and these may not be equivalent) of a particular event in place to the individual may vary over time, that is, a particular consequence may be the result of a different reading of the same antecedent events in place at time 3 rather than at time 2 or than at the original time 1.

The problem seems to be that attributes or elements of the built environment which might be classed as antecedents for one or many individuals appear, themselves, to be manipulated and modified *by the individual* over time and thus to vary, in inexplicable ways, in consequences. I previously referred to this form of perception as hypothetical constructions and suggested that, as such, an individual's psychoenvironmental experiences were unlikely to be elicited by a single-point verbal stimulus nor to be easily interpreted from prestructured response alternatives (Howell, 1980).

For some years now I have been straining to understand "attachments to home." As can be inferred from the preceding enumeration of questions about "place meaning" I am not yet even sure of the relationship between how and why a place has *meaning* to an individual and the individual's attachment to that place. Attachment is often operationally defined as some version of staying in or going back to place (Stueve, Gerson, & Fischer, 1975). Can a place have "detached" meaning? Can its valence remain but its salience be split between action and intrapsychic worth? According to Graham Rowles (1978) and a few others, it can.

The physical environment may turn out to be the true holistic variable. We encode this cardinal dynamic stimulus set in multisensory and multiexperiential fashion, using its many cue values (meanings) idiosyncratically (and what else is personality?) in a range of operations across the course of life: in infancy and childhood, to sense and classify the spaces, shapes, and textures of our species, culture, and family (and that is where some language gets attached); in adolescence to challenge and manipulate (if you have given a teenager a room of her or his own, you know what I mean). Hansen and Altman (1976) speak about the latter relative to college students and their personalization of dormitory rooms. They speculate that students who do not manipulate their private space are dealing with so serious an identity crisis that they can be predicted to do badly and even drop out academically. But what of the meaning of place in mid-adulthood and aging?

Here I would like to propose a few tentative general principles:

1. The attachment of meaning to life, to self in relation to events, people, and place is a *continuous reweaving process*. For example, analyses by Siegler and George at Duke University in studies of adaptation to perceived life events evidence the distinction made between positive and and negative perceptions of happenings in life. In the narratives, place showed varied emphases. Since the internal process is continuous, study approaches which focus on *discrete* place or event variables probably miss, entirely, measures of meaning (Palmore, Cleveland, Nowlin, Ramm, & Siegler, 1979).

2. Places are affectively *redefined* in the course of utilizing them in reminiscence, self-concept reviews, problem solving, social rule maintenance, and other operations. Thus, the relative importance of any attribute of place may appear, disappear, and re-emerge in varied form and with associational differences. It might be said that "schema" for utilizing

place–images are highly "fluid." Not so the linguistic attributes of place, which are essentially "fixed" and limited by a language community and individual experience in labeling and attributing across life.

3. A way of conceptualizing the meaning of place would be to attempt to evaluate the roles of place in self- or identity reconstructions. If, as Kelly (1955), Clark (1976), and Pierce and Chiriboga (1979) all affirm from their research, the "structure or meaning-of-self changes over time" and shows great interindividual variation, then such a dimension of self-meaning as place must also be very dynamic and quite contextual. A person may, for example, see in a shop window a vintage table lamp and laughingly say to a companion, "We had a lamp like that when I was a kid," which in turn initiates a flood of place–event–people memories, some of which are allowed to emerge as verbal reminiscence, some as fleeting imagery, but all contextually selective. The affective meaning may begin as positive associations and weave, in and out, through a range of emotions. In looking at our national neighborhood land use data in 1975 for the settings and services surrounding elderly housing projects, Lawton commented to me about the relative absence of places for elderly to window-shop. One of my students, revisiting a New Jersey site in 1979 heard tenants quote Gertrude Stein (about their neighborhood): "There's no there, there!"

4. Is there any reason to believe that the individual reinforces place imagery by recurrent experiences (intermittant reinforcements) so that the same attributes of place are recurringly evoked? Does all environmental learning and memory behave as we think other types of learning do? It is not clear to me that this is so, but rather, in environmental memory and the meaning attributed to place, much more of *self* is invested than with other forms of memory, and place elements get unevenly (and at this juncture unpredictably) attached to other selective self-in-time and space components of recall. On the other hand, if cues to past meanings recur frequently in the existing environment, some images must attain more prominence than others. Parenthetically, it seems so with elderly women and their retention of china cabinets, from our research on what was preferentially moved to small elderly housing units (Howell, 1980b).

5. Attributes of self-concept may psychodynamically function *parallel* to attributes of place, and thus we should consider that the meaning of a place attribute may, for the individual, change over time or be different from one group of people to the other (depending on how the group is defined). For example, consider the much used environmental attribute of *private* and the meanings of spatial privacy. When I was in Tokyo recently, a Japanese grandmother said to me, "There are two things good about having your grandchildren living nearby: One is when they come into your

house; the other is when they leave and go back to their own house!"
There are several dimensions of both self-and-place (or self-in-place?)
that are represented.

In terms of identity (self-concept), the ability to control, temporally and
physically, intrusions into private space (Altman, 1975) is for this Japanese
woman, a salient issue. In terms of *place*, important dimensions appear to
be residential separateness, residential proximity, and an untapped collection of built spaces and objects of meaning identified as part of her
experiential world as separate from those of her children and grandchildren. Furthermore, it is not a discrete (daily) life event that is being
reflected but a repetitive "occasion" and a continuous probability that
reinforces place identity. Scheidt and Schaie (1978) attempted to draw
such contextual saliences out in the development of a "situation taxonomy" thought to be useful in the assessment of competence in the aged.
The authors themselves acknowledge that although the situations vali-
dated by their sample may apply to other segments of American urban,
well elderly, the appearance of situations common across age cohorts may
be deceptive, since different or younger populations may give the apparently same situation a different attributive classification. In fact, Wolfe and
Laufer (1974) found distinct and varied meanings of privacy across
children by ages. "Traveling around looking for a new residence," which
was classified as "supportive" and "social" by the Scheidt and Schaie
sample, might well, in another sample, be classified as "depriving" and
"nonsocial" (their categories). In any case, the research strategy is worthy
of further exploration, since it implies place as well as situational meaning,
if only for issues of the present.
Cole and Scribner in *Culture and Thought* (1974) have discussed how
people remember place–events as a culture specific (social leaning) issue
and propose fashioning experiments in place–memory to determine
consistency (or inconsistency) of a particular individual's memory habits.
Defining *cognition* as those processes by which information about the
world is acquired, transformed, and used, these authors comment on the
questionable validity of using linguistic evidence (e.g., semantic differ-
entials) to make inferences about perception and thought (a particular
problem in inquiries about the meanings of place). They argue that simply
showing a relation between some aspect of place and some individual
behavior or attitude does not tell us much about the cognitive nature of
the connection. We need to find a way to understand the interweaving
between individual processes (cognition, perception, learning, and memory) and characteristics of place as an interactive developmental process

within a particular culture and for a particular age cohort (Shaw & Bransford, 1977).

WORDS, MEANING, AND VALUE (VALENCE)

Wohlwill (1976) also comments on verbal response modes in environmental cognition research. He argues that the absence of explicit references to an object (or its attributes) in choice items of such instruments as the Repertory Grid of Personal Construct Theory or the Semantic Differential can be interpreted as a positive attempt at subjectifying (i.e., making meaningful?) the cognition of place. On the other hand, such paradigms can also be seen as only reflecting the limitations of a language and/or the contraints of language use resulting from individual differences in experience (with either language or environment).

The presumptions are, of course, that (a) there is consistency of meaning of words across members of the same language community; (b) the same word in a language is used by an individual consistently and knowingly across all its applications; (c) a given word (representation of an abstract construct) or a set of opposites is meaningfully relevant to all referents (particularly environmental); (d) for all referents (and particularly environmental referents) a *set of opposites* is an appropriate symbol or sign (e.g., hot–cold is a silly evaluative alternative for a building or the concept of privacy); and (e) language use remains the same over time (e.g., the influence of colloquial and slang uses of *hot, cool,* and *baad* may readily seep into response selections).

What Wohlwill is calling for is the development of objective environmental referents that have a verified experimental commonality to the individuals in a particular sample [Rowles' communities of Lanchester (urban) and Colton (rural) elderly appear to have this capability]. He is also arguing for inclusion of measures of individual saliency as attempted by Scheidt and Schaie (1978). Most of all, Wohlwill is urging the refinement of multiple methods in search of environmental cognition and meaning, wherein verbal response modes are only one of many approaches.

I am not arguing that the language of environmental (place) meaning is not somehow and partly expressed in linguistic vocabularies. Rather, I am extending Wohlwill's discussion and criticism of the assumption that there is a necessary and *sufficient* correlation between words in a language and the ways in which particular environments are construed, cognitively and affectively (Wohlwill, 1976). A recent gift from my own parents illustrates this point. An oriental rug on which my brother and I pranced-to-pattern and a chinoiserie cabinet at which I idled childhood time fingering the carving requires language to describe to readers, but does not require language, rather visual and tactile reminiscence, to make them affectively meaningful to me.

As Wohlwill (1976) comments: "Words are no more than overt responses of a particular sort, and cannot always be accorded the privileged status of revealing directly the form or content (and we may add affect) of mental images or contructs at least in the absence of some determination of their reliability and, above all their external validity [p. 390]." As an illustration, Wohlwill humorously refers to Hamlet's taunt of Polonius in which a cloud is sequentially a camel, a weasel, and a whale. In a later footnote he chastises the tendency to "reify the results of unbridled open-ended verbal responses" by suggesting this to be "like pulling *ha*bits out of a rat [p. 392]."

I am now informed that it is possible to extract a single word, one representative of an abstract concept such as "privacy," from a total text by computer and then to analyze all the varied ways in which that word is used in the text. If done in the case of a philosopher (e.g., Descartes) or a sociologist (e.g., Weber), the issue is "what did he mean?" The test is of application consistency and linguistic constancy. If, on the other hand, we are dealing with the popular use of language to connote relationships, test of consistency and constancy may be quite contra-indicated. Semantic analysis of how and where language elements are used may play a very small part in the comprehension of the meaning of place.

RELATIVE DEPRIVATION

Several authors have used the concept of "relative deprivation" in describing individual behaviors of old people in environmental (social) situations. The idea is that older people perceive their situation in comparison to situations either of their earlier life or of people somehow similar to themselves (perhaps even both strategies). Thus, a change in the individual's health, socioeconomic state, or environment may produce a self-image of deprivation or of satisfaction. In discussing the perception of financial adequacy among the aged, Liang and Fairchild (1979) explored the subjective meanings which older people attach to their personal economic situation and attempted to relate this subjectivity to objective economic conditions. As a mediation paradigm, the reflective deprivation hypothesis may be very fruitful in explorations of the meaning of place. The argument goes that objective impoverishment or affluence are not always perceived as a deprivation or advantage, nor are they truly reflected in satisfaction–dissatisfaction reports (Lawton, Kleban, & Carlson, 1973). The issue of "definition of the situation" is related to the perceptual theories of selective attention wherein reactions to a stimulus field are purported to be selectively mediated by an individual's interpretation of the situation.

While we, in gerontology, have given limited attention to this issue, there is a strong theoretically based literature in sociology that recommends it (Davis, 1959). The theory is in the form of a reference group analysis, only both behavior of like-persons and referent values or standards (expectations) are included. As applied to perceptions of financial adequacy, the researchers using this theory argue that individual reference points may include the perceived situation of younger cohorts, their own cohort at earlier stages, and a preceding cohort (parents). Relative deprivation, when applied to place meaning, thus becomes a complex jigsaw to be explored.

Ideographically, Tobin and Lieberman (1976) attribute the coping capacities, reactive depressions, and withdrawals of residents of nursing homes they studied in terms of perceived deprivations ("environmental discontinuities [p. 19]"). It might also be argued that the attachment which sometimes appears as the irrational unwillingness of older people to move from either an inappropriate neighborhood or an outsized home is a form of defense against self-deprivation (Lawton, Kleban, & Carlson, 1973). In the Tobin and Lieberman (1976) study, amount of deprivation was related in the total sample to reminiscence qualities and these, in turn, to coping behaviors (p. 181). The difference between community residences and institutional environments appeared to have been appraised (objectively) independent of the perceptions or expectations of the respondent (p. 20). In fact, the absence of anticipatory anxiety, given a discontinuity or disparity, was postulated as a major factor in maladaptations to the institutional environment, implying that the individual did not force out a conscious comparison and resolve the discontinuities.

We are increasingly using the term *saliency*. What is *saliency* relative to attention and cognition of environment among the aging? What a person has been taught to attend to, that is, repertoires of attention? What is relevant to the situation at hand in terms of socially learned appropriateness, priorities, or problem solving? What is particularly important to the individual for intrapsychic reasons? In most of our research salience appears, in operational definition, as either a point on a rating scale or a trade-off selection. It seems time to explore this construct in greater depth. Is it, for example, equivalent to our construct of "contextual relevance?"

REMINISCENCE AND MAINTENANCE OF IDENTITY

I am what I remember about myself. I choose to remember certain aspects of myself in relation to my *current* mental, physical, and social state. I reject (deny?) alternative readings of myself which other people may perceive, including interpretations of my recall of and behavior in places. In all of these acts, the natural (including built) environments remind me of what I choose or reject about myself. Since I am a member of a society, major segments of how I choose to know me are dictated by social learning. In those societies dominated by consistent behavioral, spatial, and building rules, which are strongly reinforced over long periods of time, there is probably little conflict or difficulty in establishing and continuously reconfirming personal identity. If my society, including its built environment, changes very slowly, my *adaptation* (for the sake of maintaining identity) will be to remold or transfer pieces of the past into a new habitat, so that enough objects and allowable spatial behaviors continue to remind me of where I have been, with whom, and how this connects to where I am. If, on the other hand, my society or proximate environment, including their built aspects, changes rapidly and I am not a participant in the change decisions, I must surely lose or have great difficulty in placing myself in space, time, and society. I will likely survive such disruptions, but the required adjustments may have major intra-psychic costs—I fear the disintegration of myself. Place is necessary to identity.

SCENARIO FOR A WORLD WITHOUT PLACE

The importance of exploring the complex interrelationships among the themes I have discussed is highlighted if, in concluding, we consider the implications of a placeless world.

There is *no memory* of self, event, or relationship. No durable element of past experience for the individual.

There is *uniformity of objects* in daily use and of spaces within which to move and to be.

There is *neutrality* of spaces, an absence of distinguishing character-istics by which one area can be responded to differently from another.

Rules disallow modification and personalization of spaces and elements or features within spaces.

Spaces are *defined only by collective activities* performed within them—and these remain constant or out of the individual's control.

There are *neither cohort nor culture symbols* in the environment, nothing to support recall of the collective history of the generation or the group.

In order to understand a world without place it is necessary to understand what humans, across the life cycle and across cultures, do *within* and *to* place. Place elements which are affectively salient to an age cohort need to be identified, if not reified in the preservation of meaning. Dreams, photographs and reminiscence of ceremony, and active retracings of behaviors in space with objects, all become part of our understanding of the meaning of place in aging. Can we reverse the developmental research paradigm and exploit the reminiscences of the aging in order to discover the essences or meaning of environment, thereby to better direct policy and program planning in the built environment?

DEDICATION

This chapter is dedicated to Flo Berkowitz Livson who, literally, could have been my sister or myself. Following our communications during the West Virginia Conference, and according to my parents, my great aunt had tried to make a *shitak* ("a match") between her father and my mother many years ago in Los Angeles. Our paths overlapped, but did not converge, through close associates and experiences, as graduate students in Berkeley, California, in the 1940–1950 period. As a teenager, Flo desired the fancy Beverly Hills clothes in my father's store, which her mother bought, and I, as a teenager, stupidly rejected, although I sometimes helped decorate the shop windows that Flo said she relished. I feel such an enormous loss in her senseless death; a truly potential intimate has been taken away. But, notice, what I reminisce on includes Place.

REFERENCES

Altman, I. *The environment and social behavior.* Monterey, Calif.: Brooks/Cole, 1975.

Clark, M. The anthropology of aging. *The Gerontologist,* 1976, 7, 55–64.

Cole, M., & Scribner, S. *Culture and thought.* New York: Wiley, 1974.

Davis, J. A. A formal interpretation of the theory of relative deprivation. *Sociometry,* 1959, 22, 282–298.

Hansen, W. B., & Altman, I. Decorating personal places. *Environment and Behavior,* 1976, 8, 491–504.

Howell, S. C. Environments as hypotheses in human aging research. In L. W. Poon (Ed.), *Aging in the 1980s.* Washington, D.C.: American Psychological Association, 1980. (a)

Howell, S. C. *Designing for aging: Patterns of use.* Cambridge, Mass.: MIT Press, 1980. (b)

Kelly, E. L. Consistency of the adult personality. *American Psychologist,* 1955, 10, 659–681.

Klausner, S. Z. Life-span environmental psychology: Methodological issues. In P. B. Baltes &

K. W. Schaie (Eds.), *Life-span developmental psychology*. New York: Academic Press, 1973.

Lawton, M. P., Kleban, M. H., & Carlson, D. A. The inner-city resident: To move or not to move. *The Gerontologist*, 1973, *13*, 443–448.

Liang, J., & Fairchild, T. Relative deprivation and perception of financial adequacy among aged. *Journal of Gerontology*, 1979, *34*, 736–745.

Looft, W. R. Socialization and personality throughout the life span. In P. B. Baltes & K. W. Schaie (Eds.), *Life-span developmental psychology*. New York: Academic Press, 1973.

Palmore, E., Cleveland, W. P., Nowlin, J. B., Ramm, D., & Siegler, I. C. Stress and adaptation in later life. *Journal of Gerontology*, 1979, *34*, 841–851.

Pierce, R. C., & Chiriboga, D. A. Dimensions of adult self-concept. *Journal of Gerontology*, 1979, *34*, 80–85.

Rowles, G. D. *Prisoners of space?* Boulder, Colo.: Westview Press, 1978.

Scheidt, R. J., & Schaie, K. W. A taxonomy of situations for an elderly population: Generating situational criteria. *Journal of Gerontology*, 1978, *33*, 848–857.

Shaw, R., & Bransford, J. (Eds.). *Perceiving, acting and knowing*. Hillsdale, N. J.: Lawrence Erlbaum Associates, 1977.

Stueve, A., Gerson, K., & Fischer, C. *The structure and determinants of attachment to place*. University of California, Berkeley: Institute of Urban & Regional Development, 1975, Working Paper #255.

Tobin, S. S., & Lieberman, M. A. *Last home for the aged*. San Francisco: Jossey–Bass, 1976.

Wohlwill, J. F. Searching for the environment in environmental cognition research: A commentary on research strategy. In G. T. Moore & R. G. Golledge (Eds.), *Environmental knowing*. Stroudsburg, Pa.: Dowden, Hutchinson, & Ross, 1976.

Wolfe, M., & Laufer, R. The concept of privacy in childhood and adolescence. *Proceedings of EDRA-5*, 1974, 29–54.

III

SOCIAL PERSPECTIVES ON MILIEU

8

Geographical Dimensions of Social Support in Rural Appalachia[1]

GRAHAM D. ROWLES

Over the past few years there has been a burgeoning of research on the rural elderly (Ansello & Cipolla, 1980; Atchley & Byerts, 1975; Lee & Lassey, 1980; Wilkinson, 1978; and Wilkinson, Rowles, & Maxwell, 1982). One outcome of this activity has been the recognition of the need for critical appraisal of the appropriateness of urban designed programs as models for service provision in rural areas (Ansello, 1980; Lohmann & Lohmann, 1977). Indeed, many expensive programs, including the heavily funded Transportation Remuneration Incentive Program (TRIP) in West Virginia, have had marginal impact in improving the quality of life of the rural elderly (Office of Research and Development, 1977). In part, this is a result of poor planning and inherent logistic and cost difficulties of servicing geographically dispersed populations. However, the ineffectiveness of many programs can also be attributed to limited understanding of both the individual experience and the culture of aging in a rural environment. Policymakers seem to have ignored the role of "natural" support systems as a feature of rural life and, until recently, have been selectively myopic in considering the implications of evidence that many old people solve their problems without the benefit of social service intervention (Gottlieb, 1975). Indeed, the entire superstructure of services for the rural aged may be based on erroneous assumptions regarding

[1]The research reported in this chapter is supported by a grant from the National Institute on Aging—AG00862.

AGING AND MILIEU:
ENVIRONMENTAL PERSPECTIVES
ON GROWING OLD

the relationship between rural environments and the well-being of the elderly.

Foremost among these assumptions has been an uncritical acceptance of the premise that there is a direct relationship between "objective" indicators of quality of life—such as income status, housing quality, transportation availability, and health status—and life satisfaction. Recent studies investigating rural–urban differences among the elderly have revealed that the poorer "objective" conditions of rural residence are not necessarily associated with lower levels of subjective well-being (Lee & Lassey, 1980). This paradox is significant for two reasons. First, it suggests that the measures of "objective" conditions may be inappropriate—dollar income may be a poor indicator of available resources; physical indices of a house's quality may provide a poor reflection of its ability to provide a home; car ownership and public transit may be poor indicators of potential mobility; and clinical measures of health may be less significant than self-perceived health status. Second, and perhaps more important, the paradox suggests there are aspects of rural residence that compensate for poorer objective conditions. Lee and Lassey conjecture that such features include higher levels of social participation, reduced fear of crime, and a culture allowing a more gradual process of retirement and transition to aged status (Lee & Lassey, 1980, pp. 68–70). To these themes may be added a slower place of life, lower levels of cognitive complexity, more gradual processes of change within the physical environment, and the smaller scale of rural life—all features conducive to coping with the transitions of aging.

In this chapter I wish to move beyond such general hypotheses and to build on an emergent literature on natural support networks in rural areas (Hooyman, 1980; Wang, 1979). My intention is to explore geographical dimensions of social support that have hitherto been given minimal attention. These dimensions may be summarized within the twin themes of space (the role of distance and relative location) and place (the subjective meanings of individual locations that serve to bring them to life and provide their identity) (Buttimer & Seamon, 1980; Tuan, 1975, 1977). Using an in-depth case study, I will argue that indigenous support resources identified in many rural areas have distinctive spatial manifestations and are inextricably intertwined with important nuances of place identification and attachment. In conjunction, these geographical considerations make possible a more sophisticated understanding of the way a rural milieu nurtures a variety of sociospatial support systems that can sustain the old person.

GROWING OLD "INSIDE": A CASE STUDY

The empirical basis for my observations is a 3-year intensive participant observation study of elderly residents of Colton, a declining northern Appalachian mountain community.[2] Colton was once a thriving small town with an economy based on coal mining and a railroad which bisected the community. At its peak in 1920 the population exceeded 850 persons, and there was even talk of Colton being named the county seat. However, the demise of the local railroad "shops," the sagging fortunes of the mines, and the impact of the depression initiated a process of decline which continues even today. The characteristic Appalachian scenario of out-migration of the young and able-bodied, coupled with the "aging in place" of those who remained behind has transformed the demographic structure of the community. According to preliminary tabulations of the 1980 United States census, approximately 400 people now reside in Colton. A significant proportion of this population (approximately 20%) is over 60 years of age.

During three summers' residence in the community and frequent visits during the remainder of each year, I have come to develop a close relationship with Colton's elderly community. I have focused on a panel of 12 old people that, over the course of the study (due to processes of attrition and replacement), has included a total of 15 individuals. Members of the study panel, ranging in age at the initiation of the research from 62 to 91 years, have lived in the locality most of their lives. Several of them have never resided outside Colton.

Close interpersonal relationships have been established with these old people in order to develop a climate of mutual rapport enabling them to reveal and articulate dimensions of experience that are normally taken for granted and thus remain inaccessible to traditional social–scientific inquiry. The philosophy and practical implications of this approach, building on a lengthy tradition of anthropological and sociological research, have been explained in detail elsewhere (Blumer, 1969; Glaser & Strauss, 1967; Rowles, 1978b; Von Eckartsberg, 1971). Here it is necessary merely to point out that the approach involves a combination of critical observation, unconstrained interpersonal dialogue, and measurement procedures emerging as relevant during the course of the research. In this study over 500 hours of tape-recorded interviews were supplemented by simple questionnaires, time–space activity diaries, several cognitive mapping

---

[2]Colton is a pseudonym as are all proper names in this chapter.

tasks, measures of social support networks, photography (including aerial photography), and seven measures of life satisfaction (Rowles, 1981b). The primary purpose was to develop holistic understanding of the environmental experience of the Colton elderly, utilizing the perspective of humanistic social geography (Buttimer, 1976; Entrikin, 1976; Gregory, 1981; Ley & Samuels, 1978).

The contribution of geographical considerations in conditioning the participants' social support resources emerged as an important component of this understanding. Early in the fieldwork it became apparent that the key to understanding the Colton elderly lay in framing their experience against the backdrop of an intimate immersion within the local milieu. The old people of Colton, almost without exception, consider themselves to be "inside" this place (Rowles, 1980). A *physical insideness* emanates from familiarity with the contours of the physical setting. Repeated use of the same route in the journey to the store, or to church, over a period of several decades means that these paths become ingrained within the participants' inherent awareness of the setting. They become part of what Seamon has termed *body subject* (Seamon, 1979). An implicit awareness of cracks in the sidewalk, steps, changes in slope, and other features of environmental configuration enables the "automatic pilot" of routine to take over at a level that becomes subconscious. The old person comes to wear the setting like a glove.

Such affinity for place is supplemented by a sense of *social insideness* stemming from integration within the social fabric of the community. To live in Colton as an elderly person is to have the option of becoming part of an age peer group culture, a "society of the old," with its own values, accepted norms of conduct, mutual obligations, and rewards. Social insideness centers on a "community of concern" melded by involvement in the church and the senior center and by participation in an extensive telephone network. In addition to reinforcing an aura of belonging, membership within such a "community of concern" conveys both identity and status. As 84-year-old Beatrice, a respected member of the society of the old observes, "If I lived anywhere else, I'd be a nobody. I wouldn't have the position I do."

Finally, a sense of *autobiographical insideness* stems from the temporal legacy of having lived one's life in this environment. Colton and its surroundings are known as the arena of personal history. Each location lives as an "incident place"—where a child was born, a husband was met, or a first job was obtained. Place becomes a landscape of memories, providing a sense of identity, and an ever present source of reinforcement for a biography interpreted from the retrospective vista of life review (Butler, 1963).

In concert, physical, social, and autobiographical insideness express a relationship with the setting that distinguishes Colton from spaces that, moving away from the core of the community, become increasingly viewed as "outside." This relationship forms the backdrop for an array of social supports harnessed by the Colton elderly.

SOURCES OF SUPPORT

Social support resources include an array of both *explicit* (overt) and *implicit* (taken-for-granted) forms. Explicit support is traditionally differentiated as either "formal" or "informal," although the distinction is often blurred (Longino, 1979). Formal support in Colton is provided primarily through the church and a senior center that is well utilized by a more active, primarily female, young-old subgroup within the society of the old. In addition, there are a variety of social service programs, including a Title III-C Nutrition Program (located at the senior center), a rural health clinic, and a limited rural transit system. These resources I have discovered are used but not relied upon (see also Rodeheaver, 1981).

Far more important are indigenous informal support networks involving family members, neighbors and confidants, and fellow members of the society of the old. There is a voluminous literature on the role of family in supporting old people (Treas, 1975; Troll, 1980; Sussman, 1976), but relatively few studies focus on old people within rural families (Powers, Keith, & Goudy, 1975). In Colton, as in many rural communities, there has been considerable spatial dispersion of families. Only 24 of the study panel's 60 living children reside within 25 miles. These children tend to become primary sources of everyday practical assistance and social support. Asel, now 93 years old, is able to remain in his tiny cottage as one of his daughters, who lives in the house behind his home, is close enough to bring over his meals each day. She provides for his service needs, ensures that he takes his medicine, and constitutes an important source of everyday social contact. Another daughter who lives in the community visits frequently to play dominoes and provide companionship. As Asel has grown more vulnerable, geographically proximate family members have provided increasing levels of support. During the past winter the family decided he should no longer be left alone at night. A schedule was developed whereby, each night, a family member now "stays over" to sleep in his spare room.

Considerable support is also received by many of the Colton elderly from neighbors. This is especially the case for those who are childless or do not have family living nearby. Neighbors not only provide concrete forms of support such as bringing in the mail from the roadside mailbox, cutting the grass, running errands, or providing assistance with home maintenance chores, but also often become close friends and confidants. The social relationships that evolve from such support reflect an assumed responsibility by those who live close to the old person's home. Neighbors may come to assume "surrogate family" status.

Finally, there is the mutual support that stems from participation within the society of the old. Such support is harnessed in a variety of ways. First, there is the support that derives from involvement in community level activities. The senior center provides an important focus here, for this is the setting of the bake sales, the dinners, and other activities that provide a sense of coherence within the society of the old. The focus of these activities is often upon raising money to support the center and pay its bills. Considerable social and emotional effort is invested. For several weeks before each "event," it provides the focus for planning and discussion. This legitimizes an extensive communication network that functions through the telephone as the details are worked out. Through such activities, a "community of concern" evolves and is maintained. Its coherence is illustrated in the routine sending of "get well" cards to members who fall ill and by the manner in which snippets of news and gossip are rapidly diffused via the telephone network.

Participation in certain subgroups within the society of the old also provides an important nexus of social support for the Colton elderly. There exist a number of smaller more intensive telephone networks within which five or six elderly women support each other through the frequent exchange of telephone calls. Over time these social clusters develop into supportive networks in which each participant knows about the status and troubles of his or her peers in intimate detail. The old men of the community represent another subgroup. This group does not utilize the telephone. Rather, it is focused on the exchange of news and information through daily discussions each morning outside the post office and the Colton store, as the elderly men linger after collecting their mail.

A final component of the supportive social fabric of the society of the old is provided by numerous dyadic relationships within the total network. Lucinda, now 65 years old, exchanges telephone calls each morning with 76-year-old Nakoma who frequently receives no other contacts during the day. Audrey spends an hour on the phone every evening sharing the news of the day with 71-year-old Jennifer Rose. Indeed, throughout the Colton area pairs of old people maintain linkages that are valued sources of support. Such dyads do not function independently of the society of the old. Instead, they are part of a total system that functions through the exchange of information about its members—information that provides the social currency of an age peer group society.

It would be erroneous to conclude that the society of the old is entirely age exclusive. Several younger people, mainly in their 40s and 50s, provide important assistance to elderly people and hence become embraced as "caretakers" within the society of the old. These individuals are often to be found visiting the Colton elderly in their homes. They will fix a leaky faucet, wallpaper a room, or provide help with cleaning. Over a number of years these caretakers become known by the society of the old and their services are frequently in demand. Mary McKenzie, a woman in her 30s who works part-time at the senior center, is known as a person who will assist with wallpapering. Betsy Hart provides help with house cleaning and redecorating. Often the assistance provided is voluntary. On other occasions the informal exchange of money for services and the associated social contact is mutually beneficial.

Much of the social support provided by the Colton milieu is, however, far more *implicit* than the formal and informal sources, considered by sociologists and social gerontologists, that I have outlined. Implicit support is provided to the Colton elderly through being a part of the social identity of this place. This has two components. First, there is the reassurance that stems from awareness that this is a place in which one knows and is known by others. Such support is clearly revealed by data on the age peer group social awareness network of the study panel (Figure 8.1). Each participant identified individuals he or she knew "well," "well enough to talk to," or "by sight or reputation," from a list of all the old people living in the Colton area.[3] In addition, participants were asked to identify persons on the list they had seen in the previous month. What emerges is that, with few exceptions, these old people are not as socially isolated as the public stereotype would suggest. Moreover, there is a large pool of age peers who, although infrequently seen or contacted, provide a sense of belonging by virtue of their mere existence.

A second aspect of implicit support is more subtle. A social affinity with place stems from autobiographical insideness. Although her husband is dead and her two children now live far away, Jennifer Rose derives comfort from the aura of her home, because this is where they lived. She can visualize her children as they played in the yard. The rooms are still, in a sense, "inhabited" by people who years ago made them important social

---

[3]This list was derived from a membership roster of the Colton Senior Citizens Club and supplemented by information I gained on the existence of other old persons in the community during the 3 years of field research. The list was also verified by consultation with a number of community residents who were not in the study panel.

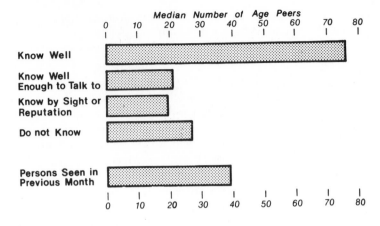

FIGURE 8.1. Implicit peer group social support network.

spaces. Like many of her peers, Jennifer Rose finds it difficult to explain this historical meaning of her home as an experienced social ambience. It is something she takes for granted. Yet the ability of a place to act as a cue and to trigger the resurrection through reminiscence of the social auras that once pervaded it may contribute to a sense of identity which enhances well-being. Indeed, the implicit social support of place may contribute to explaining the sense of alienation and stress often associated with relocation (Tobin & Lieberman, 1976).

As we begin to explore these less concrete sources of support, the environmental context begins to assume a significance far beyond its customary role as a passive backdrop to experience—merely the stage upon which lives are played out. Places become "fields of care" imbued with distinctive social meanings by those who inhabit them (Ley, 1977; Tuan, 1975). We begin to understand how people, for example Jennifer Rose's husband and children, may become a part of a place, and how the social meaning of an environment may provide a source of support to an old person.

To summarize, it is possible to identify an array of both explicit and implicit sources of support for old people within the Colton milieu. However, more important than identification of these sources, is the finding that each has distinctive geographical manifestations. There exist in the participants' worlds a series of zones of space, focused on each individual's home but extending "outside" Colton. *Different types and intensities of both explicit and implicit support are derived from different spatial zones.* It is helpful to identify a general hierarchy of environmental spaces and to consider the different kinds of support provided within each zone (Figure 8.2).

A HIERARCHY OF SPACES

Clearly, the most intensive manifestations of social support are available within the *home.* There is no substitute for living with a companion in terms of around-the-clock availability of practical assistance and compan-

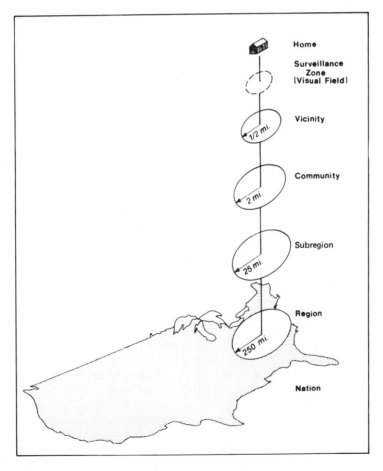

FIGURE 8.2. A hierarchy of environmental spaces.

ionship. Beatrice and Walter, a married couple in the study, exchange the kind of support that enables them to remain independent at 84 years of age and provides for mutual assistance during temporary crises such as illness. However, the majority of the Colton elderly live alone. Many, like Jennifer Rose, cherish their independence. They are reluctant to live with relatives or companions, so this option is avoided.The home is also a place providing important emotional support through both the personal and social meanings with which it is imbued (Bachelard, 1969; Loyd, 1975; Porteous, 1976).

As people grow older and spend more time at home the *surveillance zone*, space within the visual field of home, may become an increasingly significant source of support (Rowles, 1981a). As has already been noted, there often develops a strong functional relationship between the old people of Colton and their neighbors. Within the surveillance zone a watchful reciprocity is apparent, particularly among elderly neighbors, which frequently includes the scheduled exchange of visual signals—such as drawing the curtain or switching on the porch light to indicate that all is well. In times of crisis support from within this zone is particularly important. Neighbors often act as intermediaries between the old person and his or her children who may live far away, as a collaborative strategy is evolved for assisting the old person (Lowenthal & Robinson, 1976). The surveillance zone also furnishes other forms of social support. This is space that can be monitored from the window; a zone in which certain supportive, if transitory, relationships develop. Observing the daily routine of neighbors, chastizing the children for overly zealous play on the path outside, and watching those who regularly pass by, provides support through a sense of ongoing social involvement. Finally, the space of the surveillance zone may harbor cherished social meanings. As the old person gazes out of the window, memories of events that transpired in this arena many years ago may be evoked. For the long-time resident, a sense of belonging to this place, of having its history closely intertwined with ones own provides an important sense of identity.

The *vicinity* is a very important space for the old people of Colton as it harbors relationships that may provide critical support as the individual becomes more vulnerable. The size of this zone may vary considerably depending upon topography (and hence potential for interaction) and population density. For the study participants living in the more densely populated areas of Colton, this zone may be quite small, ranging from the outer limits of the surveillance zone to a distance of 800 feet or less. For others, this zone may extend in some directions, to a distance of over one-half a mile. Within the vicinity, family members and close friends provide frequent functional support. They purchase the groceries, provide a ride to church, and fix the door. A supportive social network emerges as a result of geographical proximity. Old people may find that a younger caretaker assumes a prominent role. Thus Audrey is accustomed to the visits, practical assistance, and social support of Betsy Hart who lives in her vicinity. More important in this context, is the way in which elderly peers within each others' vicinity, drawn together by the chance of proximate location, coalesce into a mutually supportive subgroup within the society of the old. Supportive relationships evolve from lengthy habitation of a common space—the legacy of having brought up families together, having watched over each other's children, and having shared in local crises and events that make up the history of a locale. Most individuals know the family history, life-style, state of health, and other more intimate details of the lives of their peers in the vicinity. Interaction through lengthy telephone conversations becomes increasingly significant as face-to-face contact decreases. The importance of such linkages is well illustrated by Audrey (Figure 8.3). In a sample week during which she kept a record of all her telephone calls, with the exception of her daily calls to Jennifer

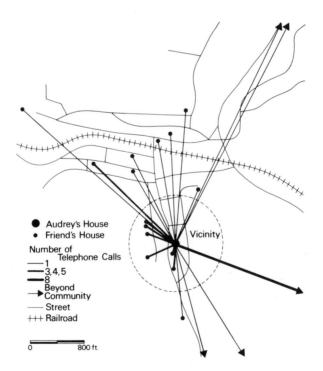

FIGURE 8.3. Audrey's telephone network within the community (January 5–11, 1980).

Rose, most of her telephone conversations involved age peers in the vicinity.

At its outer limits, the vicinity merges into the Colton *community*, the primary domain of the society of the old. The precise definition of this zone is difficult because its inner bounds represent a transition rather than an abrupt change in the nature of social support relationships. Moreover, toward the periphery of this zone there tends to be overlap with other communities, particularly for those elderly like Jennifer Rose who happen to reside on the outskirts of Colton and hence maintain multiple community affiliations. However, most of the linkages and relationships among the society of the old are confined within a radius of 2 miles from the center of the community (see also Wang, 1979). The community is important within the Colton elderly's support systems as it is the scale upon which formal support is available. A considerable degree of functional support is also provided by family members. Those children who still reside in Colton tend to visit several times a week. Several study participants also receive a daily telephone call from a son or daughter living in the community. However, it is the society of the old that provides the most pervasive focus of support on the community level. An extensive telephone network provides an indigenous information and reassurance service. This network also acts as a medium for mutual decision making. When Jennifer Rose was in the hospital, arrangements for her convalescence—where she would stay and who would stay with her—were a major topic of conversation. The resources of the society of the old were evaluated through numerous telephone conversations. This activity was complemented by face-to-face discussions among members of the society of the old who attended lunch at the senior center.

Outside Colton, the *subregion* (approximately a 25-mile radius), embraces the spatial limit of resources utilized by the study panel. This zone contains the larger communities in which are located the hospitals to which they are transported when they fall ill, the doctors they visit, the supermarkets they patronize,their banks, and other resources they may have utilized throughout their lives (Figure 8.4).[4] Direct contact through visits from children and siblings who live within this zone is less frequent (perhaps once or twice a month), but this seems to be compensated for in part through telephone calls. Friends become far less important within this zone. Indeed, few of the Colton elderly are in frequent contact with age peers outside the community. The subregion defines the spatial extent of an environment known in detail through personal experience. It

---

[4]This map was compiled from a questionnaire which sought information concerning each participants service network including physicians, banks, stores, personal services, recreational opportunities, and other services utilized.

harbors an array of historical social meanings as the space where events of significance within autobiography transpired. Continuing involvement is often more vicarious than physical. It involves ongoing concern, through the local newspaper and radio stations, with events (a political confrontation, controversy over the schools, the fortunes of the local basketball teams) within a "community of interest." On occasion, support from this zone for the more active Colton elderly assumes a more direct form. An annual vacation bus trip is cooperatively sponsored by all the senior citizen organizations in the county. This offers an opportunity to spend time with age peer group friends from the past.

In moving to the *region* (an approximately 250-mile radius), there is a major transition. Support from this zone is far less frequent and almost exclusively derived from family, particularly children who have relocated one or two states away. Geographical distance is reflected in different manifestations of support. Letters and postcards become increasingly important. Occasional telephone calls assume special significance. More tangible forms of assistance may also be received from these children. They may send a check to pay for the fuel or for major household repairs. Visits become events rather than routine happenings. When children

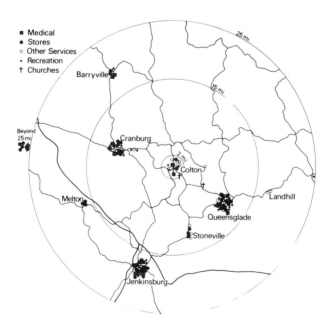

FIGURE 8.4. Resources within 25 miles utilized by the study panel.

"come in" once or twice a year, both their presence and the anticipation of their arrival, provides an important source of personal reinforcement. No less eagerly anticipated are occasional outgoing trips to vacation with these children or, in some cases, to stay with them during the worst winter months—a form of family "snowbirding." Support is also derived through vicarious participation in the ongoing lives of geographically displaced children (Hochschild, 1973; Rowles, 1978a). Although the constraints of distance make family members less viable as providers of everyday practical assistance or as sources of direct support during crisis, there is little evidence that spatial separation is associated with any lessening of emotional and social commitment (Litwak, 1960; Osterreich, 1965; Schwarzweller, 1964). Intergenerational social support merely assumes a different mantle.

Finally, *the nation* (space beyond 250 miles from Colton), is generally beyond the purview of the study panel members. A few have kin living far away. The homes of these relatives are perceived as islands of "known" space in a sea of "no place" beyond the pale. Social contact tends to be primarily through letters and postcards. Visits are viewed as major events due to their rarity. Practical support, even in crisis situations, does not come from this distance, apart from a rare visit precipitated by serious illness.

Clearly, boundaries between the various realms of space are approximate. Neither are they annular. Topography, population density, the orientation of road networks, and other aspects of environmental design result in considerable directional distortion. The intent has been to describe a generic conceptual hierarchy of spaces based on functional transitions in the matrix of support available to the Colton elderly.

SOCIOSPATIAL SUPPORT SYSTEMS

If we now consider this spatial hierarchy in relation to the sources of both explicit and implicit support available to the old person, it is possible to hypothesize a variety of support styles strongly linked to geographic location and to develop the concept of a *sociospatial support system*. Figure 8.5 illustrates sources of explicit support for four members of the study panel for a week in January 1980. These data were derived from a detailed time–space diary maintained by the participants. A diary form was used to record the details of all trips outside the home, all visits received, and all telephone calls made or received. The completed protocols for each day were corroborated and supplemented by a daily interview during which the previous day's activities were confirmed.

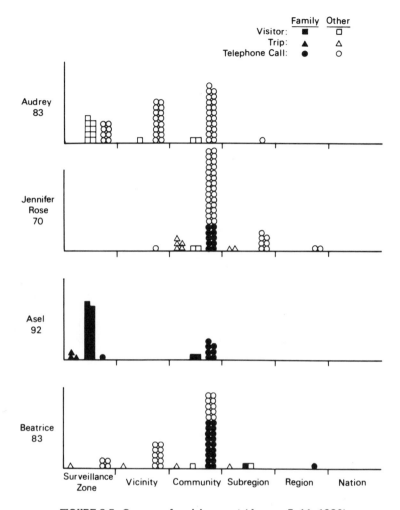

FIGURE 8.5. Sources of social support (January 5–11, 1980).

Considerable variation was apparent in both the sources of support and the zones from which it was derived.

Jennifer Rose lives alone on an isolated stretch of country road. She does not receive support from neighbors within her surveillance zone because there are no people living within visual range. Nor are her children sources of everyday practical or social support because they live far away. Yet, following her husband's death, she has been able to develop a life-style utilizing a variety of supports. A nondriver, she relies heavily on friends within the community for rides. She embraces the telephone network of the society of the old and engages in lengthy conversations with her friend Audrey. Finally, as is indicated by her trips within the community, she is committed to the formal support system provided by her church and the senior center, where she serves on several committees.

Audrey, who is confined to her home but surrounded by houses, has evolved a different support system. She relies almost exclusively on practical and social support from neighbors within the surveillance zone and intensive telephone contact with age peer group friends in the vicinity and community. Audrey has no family in proximate zones. In contrast, Asel relies almost exclusively on family members living nearby. As a result, he has remained very much on the periphery of the society of the old. He does not participate in the activities of the senior center nor involve himself in the telephone network. Finally, Beatrice's profile illustrates the importance of telephone linkages with friends from proximate zones and family support from within the community. In addition, during this week, she received an important telephone call from her son in Ohio. In sum, each old Colton resident is enveloped within a multifaceted sociospatial support system harnessing a combination of resources that are closely linked to personal circumstances and geographical location.

Change is an inherent characteristic of sociospatial support systems. In Colton there are distinctive *seasonal variations*. Family from distant zones of space tend to "come in" during the summer, whereas the reverse "snowbirding" vacation is primarily a winter phenomenon. A lessening of face-to-face contact is apparent during the winter months as the telephone assumes increased importance.

More permanent adjustments may be necessitated by change in *contextual* circumstances. A transportation service may be terminated, a daughter may relocate beyond the community, or a neighbor–confidant may die or move away. Peggy, 71 years old, rarely leaves her house but, until recently, she derived considerable social support through daily telephone conversations with her neighbor Mayella, 84 years old, and with Jenny Calstock, another elderly widow who resided in the house beyond Mayella's. In 1979 Mayella left to live with her daughter in Ohio and, in the spring of 1980, Jenny Calstock died. Peggy has accommodated to these losses by reorienting her telephone network toward other age peers in the vicinity and by placing even greater reliance on her son who lives in the community.

A third dimension of change involves long term *developmental* transitions. As sensory decrements become more limiting and mobility decreases, it can be hypothesized that increasing reliance is placed on geographically proximate sources of support.

The activities, norms of behavior, and values of Colton's society of the old also evolve over the years as the death of senior members and the integration of younger elderly people introduces a *generational* effect. Support systems progressively reflect the changing culture of a more mobile society. It is difficult to disentangle the effects of aging, period, and cohort influences. However, there seems to be a difference in the sociospatial support systems harnessed by Colton's old-old (persons over 75) and young-old (those between 60 and 75). The old-old who have spent all their lives within the community seem to derive more support from the social affinity for place stemming from "autobiographical insideness," than do the young-old who, due to their greater historical mobility, seem more adept at harnessing support from zones beyond the community.

Finally, there are brief but intense episodes of change that occur as the old person's sociospatial support system responds to a *crisis* such as a serious illness.

SOME IMPLICATIONS

This chapter has argued that it is possible to view each old resident of Colton as enveloped within a dynamic sociospatial support system with distinctive geographical characteristics. Publicly supported service programs are only one limited component of these support systems. Very few of the Colton elderly are dependent upon the specific programs available; indeed several participants claim to patronize them primarily out of a sense of obligation to their peers (who might otherwise have to forego the program).

Of course Colton is only one community. It may not be typical. However, data from this in-depth study reinforce and perhaps help to account for the paradox discussed in the opening paragraphs of this chapter. It is necessary to explore alternative means of identifying and helping the needy rural elderly—those not fully sustained by indigenous support systems. Central to the search for alternatives might be the quest for a service delivery model that will supplement rather than supplant the diversity of existing sociospatial support systems. Approaches oriented to encouraging self-help constitute one promising option (Hooyman, 1980). Another would be to harness local "known" people in caretaker roles, or as facilitators, charged with identifying those in need, building functional support networks attuned to specific circumstances, and fostering social integration within existing social support networks (Rowles, 1981b). Such alternatives not only acknowledge the characteristics of the rural milieu, but also are fiscally attractive in an era of retrenchment in federal support for capital intensive service programs. Regardless of the strategy, it seems imperative that future consideration of the rural elderly acknowledge significant geographical dimensions of the support systems they utilize.

ACKNOWLEDGMENTS

Thanks are due to Donna Meadowcroft for her assistance in field work, transcribing tapes, and the preparation of this manuscript.

REFERENCES

Ansello, E. F. Special considerations in rural aging. *Educational Gerontology*, 1980, 5, 343–354.

Ansello, E. F., & Cipolla, C. E. (Eds.). Rural aging and education: Issues, Methods and Models. *Educational Gerontology*, 1980, 5. (Special issue)

Atchley, R. C., & Byerts, T. O. (Eds.). *Rural environments and aging.* Washington, D. C.: Gerontological Society, 1975.

Bachelard, G. *The poetics of space.* Boston: Beacon Press, 1969.

Blumer, H. *Symbolic interactionism: Perspective and method.* Englewood Cliffs, N. J.: Prentice–Hall, 1969.

Butler, R. N. The life review: An interpretation of reminiscence in the aged. *Psychiatry*, 1963, 26, 55–76.

Buttimer, A. Grasping the dynamism of lifeworld. *Annals of the Association of American Geographers*, 1976, 66, 277–292.

Buttimer, A., & Seamon, D. (Eds.). *The human experience of space and place.* London: Croom Helm, 1980.

Entrikin, J. N. Contemporary humanism in geography. *Annals of the Association of American Geographers*, 1976, 66, 615–632.

Glaser, B. G., & Strauss, A. L. *The discovery of grounded theory: Strategies for qualitative research.* Chicago: Aldine, 1967.

Gottlieb, B. H. The primary group as supportive milieu. *American Journal of Community Psychology*, 1975, 7, 469–480.

Gregory, D. Human agency and human geography. *Transactions of the Institute of British Geographers* (New Series), 1981, 6, 1–18.

Hochschild, A. R. *The unexpected community.* Englewood Cliffs, N. J.: Prentice–Hall, 1973.

Hooyman, N. R. Mutual help organizations for rural older women. *Educational Gerontology*, 1980, 5, 429–447.

Lee, G. R., & Lassey, M. L. Rural–urban differences among the elderly: Economic, social, and subjective factors. *Journal of Social Issues*, 1980, 36, 62–74.

Ley, D. Social geography and the taken-for-granted world. *Transactions of the Institute of British Geographers* (New Series), 1977, 2, 498–512.

Ley, D., & Samuels, M. (Eds.). *Humanistic geography: Prospects and problems.* Chicago: Maaroufa Press, 1978.

Litwak, E. Geographical mobility and extended family cohesion. *American Sociological Review*, 1960, 25, 385–394.

Lohmann, N., & Lohmann, R. Urban designed programs for the rural elderly: Are they exportable? In R. K. Green & S. A. Webster (Eds.) *Social work in rural areas: Preparation and practice.* School of Social Work, University of Tennessee: Knoxville, Tennessee, 1977.

Longino, C. F. *The unit of analysis problem and network measures of changing support.* Paper presented at the 32nd Annual Scientific Meeting of the Gerontological Society, Washington, D. C., 1979.

Lowenthal, M. F., & Robinson, B. Social networks and isolation. In R. H. Binstock & E. Shanas (Eds.), *Handbook of aging and the social sciences.* New York: Van Nostrand Reinhold, 1976.

Loyd, B. Woman's place, man's place. *Landscape,* 1975, *20,* 10–13.

Office of Research and Development. *Transportation remuneration incentive program evaluation: Phase III* (Vol. 2). Morgantown, W. V.: Office of Research and Development, West Virginia University, 1977.

Osterreich, H. Geographical mobility and kinship: A Canadian example. In R. Piddington (Ed.), *Kinship and geographical mobility.* Leiden, Holland: E. J. Brill, 1965.

Porteous, J. D. Home: The territorial core. *Geographical Review,* 1976, *66,* 383–390.

Powers, E. A., Keith, P., & Goudy, W. J. Family relationships and friendships. In R. C. Atchley & T. O. Byerts (Eds.), *Rural environments and aging,* Washington, D. C.: Gerontological Society, 1975.

Rodeheaver, D. *Going my way: The social environment of elderly travelers.* Unpublished Master's thesis, West Virginia University, 1981.

Rowles, G. D. *Prisoners of Space? Exploring the geographic experience of older people.* Boulder, Colo.: Westview Press, 1978. (a)

Rowles, G. D. Reflections on experiental fieldwork. In D. Ley & M. Samuels (Eds.), *Humanistic geography: Prospects and problems.* Chicago: Maaroufa Press, 1978. (b)

Rowles, G. D. Growing old "inside": Aging and attachment to place in an Appalachian community. In N. Datan & N. Lohmann (Eds.), *Transitions of aging.* New York: Academic Press, 1980.

Rowles, G. D. The surveillance zone as meaningful space for the aged. *The Gerontologist,* 1981, *21,* 304–311. (a)

Rowles, G. D. *The geographical experience of the elderly.* Final Report, National Institute on Aging, Grant AG00862, 1981. (b)

Schwarzweller, H. K. Parental family ties and social integration of rural to urban migrants. *Journal of Marriage and the Family,* 1964, *26,* 410–416.

Seamon, D. *A geography of the lifeworld: Movement, rest and encounter.* New York: St. Martin's, 1979.

Sussman, M. B. The family life of old people. In R. H. Binstock & E. Shanas (Eds.), *Handbook of aging and the social sciences.* New York: Van Nostrand Reinhold, 1976.

Tobin, S. S., & Lieberman, M. A. *Last home for the aged.* San Francisco: Jossey-Bass, 1976.

Treas, J. Aging and the family. In D. S. Woodruff & J. Birren (Eds.), *Aging: Scientific perspectives and social issues.* New York: Van Nostrand Reinhold, 1975.

Troll, L. E. Intergenerational relations in later life: A family system approach. In N. Datan & N. Lohmann (Eds.), *Transitions of aging.* New York: Academic Press, 1980.

Tuan, Y. E. Space and place: Humanistic perspective. In C. Board, R. J. Chorley, P. Haggett, & D. R. Stoddart (Eds.), *Progress in geography: International reviews of current research* (Vol. 6). London: Edward Arnold, 1975.

Tuan, Y. F. *Space and place: The perspective of experience.* Minneapolis: University of Minnesota Press, 1977.

Von Eckartsberg, R. On experiential methodology. In A. Georgi, W. F. Fischer, & R. Von Eckartsberg (Eds.), *Duquesne studies in phenomenological psychology* (Vol. 1). Pittsburgh: Duquesne University Press/Humanities Press, 1971.

Wang, Y. *Natural support systems and the rural elderly*. Unpublished doctoral dissertation, University of Missouri, Columbia, 1979.

Wilkinson, C. W. *Comprehensive annotated bibliography on the rural aged (1975–1978)*. West Virginia University Gerontology Center, Occasional Papers on the Rural Aged, 1, 1978.

Wilkinson, C. W., Rowles, G. D., & Maxwell, B. *Comprehensive annotated bibliography on the rural aged (1975–1981)*. Morgantown, W. V.: West Virginia University Gerontology Center, 1982.

9

Changing Sex Roles in the Social Environment of Later Life

FLORINE B. LIVSON

THE AGED AND CULTURAL CHANGE

The aged in today's society are, in a sense, strangers in a strange land, immigrants in an alien culture. Today's generation of elderly has witnessed more change than any generation in history. Socialized by parents emerging from the Victorian age, participants in the sexual revolution of the 1920s, witnesses to successive waves of social upheaval, yet rooted in tradition, they are caught in the cracks of cultural change. Major discontinuities separate the worlds of their youth from that of their later years. Not the least of these are in the roles that women and men occupy in the family and the larger society and in the behaviors that are expected of each.

The impact of social change on a given cohort depends on that cohort's cumulative experience in earlier stages of life. The response of today's aged to recent shifts in sex-role norms must be viewed against the backdrop of a lifetime of conditioning to traditional roles for women and men in the family, in the workplace, and in relation to one another. Correspondingly, changes in the economic and family structure over the past few decades have much to do with the blurring of traditional sex roles in today's society.

How do changing sex roles influence adaptation in later life? Are more flexible definitions of maleness and femaleness useful in coping with the challenges of growing old? The convergence of two trends will be

AGING AND MILIEU:
ENVIRONMENTAL PERSPECTIVES
ON GROWING OLD

considered as they influence adaptation in the aged: one social and historical, the other individual and developmental.

THE AGED AND DEMOGRAPHIC CHANGE: SEX DIFFERENCES

Increased longevity along with smaller family size has changed the course of the life cycle in our society and altered the age distribution of the population. People live many decades after children have left the household, surviving loss of their occupational role and ultimately of their marital role. More and more of these people are women.

Outliving men by nearly 8 years, older women are the fastest growing segment of the population. The number of women over 65 has increased from 1.5 million in 1900, or 2% of the population, to 19 million by the year 2000, or roughly 7% of the population. Today there are 13 million women in the United States over 65 (Uhlenberg, 1979). In 1930, the balance of men and women in this country was approximately equal. By 1975, there were 69 men to every 100 women over 65. By 2000, the ratio will increase to 65 men to every 100 women (U.S. Bureau of the Census, 1976). The problems of aging are becoming largely the problems of women.

A major change since 1940 has been a tendency for elderly women to live alone. There has been a steady decline in the numbers of elderly persons who live with children or other kin, reflecting not only the tendency of widows to live alone but also of males to remain married or to remarry. Nearly two-thirds (63%) of women over 65 in 1977 were single as compared with one-fourth of older men (Mindel, 1979). The vast majority of these single women were widows. Nearly half were over 75 (Uhlenberg, 1979). Not surprisingly, 2½ times as many women as men live alone (women, 36%; men, 14.2%) (Mindel, 1979). The population of older women increasingly consists of relatively healthy, educated, native-born women who live alone, are not employed, and are living above the poverty level.

The high proportion of older women who live alone is due to a combination of trends over the past decades (Masnick & Bane, 1980). First, of course, is the greater increase in life expectancy since 1940 for women relative to men. Second, older women tend to have relatively few surviving children as compared to past generations. They are part of the low fertility generation who entered adulthood during the Depression. Substantial numbers of these women remained unmarried and childless. In 1980 44% of women aged 70–74 never had children or had only one child (Masnick & Bane, 1980). A third factor contributing to the higher proportion of older women living alone today is their greater ability to support themselves through survivors' benefits from pensions, social security, or their own employment.

Finally, the age structure of the American household has become more homogenous. Although the nostalgic image of the multigenerational American family of the past has been exposed as myth (Foner, 1978; Mindel, 1979), the nuclear family in the nineteenth century was often supplemented by a shifting variety of people, relatives and strangers of various ages. Old people were not prominent in these families because there were so few of them, but boarders, lodgers, servants, friends, and relatives were likely to come and go in households that expanded and contracted according to economic need (Masnick & Bane, 1980). In nineteenth century urban communities, one-third of men and women in their 20s and 30s boarded with other families (Hareven, 1979). Solitary living was extremely uncommon.

There is an emerging trend today that echoes these communal households of the past, not only among the young, but also in shared living arrangements of the elderly. These pseudofamilies, however, are rarely intergenerational and are still relatively uncommon.

How well equipped is the growing cadre of single, older women to create a reasonably satisfying style of life? The fact that more elderly women live alone does not mean that they suffer from what Brody (1978) calls the "myth of abandonment." Substantial kinship solidarity remains in the American family system (Shanas, 1979). Also, as noted, the economic position of older women has improved somewhat over the past decade as a result of increases in social welfare and retirement benefits. The proportion of older women who were living below poverty level declined by almost 50% between 1967 and 1975 (Uhlenberg, 1979). Older women, however, are likely to have suffered a greater decrease in income with age than men (Bengston, Kasschau, & Ragan, 1977). Over the next several decades, an increasing number of women will have participated in the labor force earlier in life and the length of their employment will have been longer, improving their income position. However, the benefits of improved income and family bonds, though important, may be overshadowed by psychological deficits in the resources of older, single women.

SEX ROLES AND ADAPTATION IN LATER LIFE

It is obvious that women are a critical group in the older population. A national sampling of Americans 60 and over found that the majority of persons classified as enjoying life were men while the majority of those experiencing severe difficulties were women (Aging in America, 1981). Women are likely to experience greater discontinuities than men in later life. Men retire from their jobs, certainly a major disruption, but women retire from their families, largely through widowhood, losing not only their jobs but also their primary support system and source of identity. Recent national surveys have found that widows have more difficulty coping than other groups in the older population and are more unhappy than widowers (Aging in America, 1981; Campbell, 1981). Widowed women confront not only bereavement but also the challenge to function independently: to develop their resources, create new links to society and new sources of identity and self-esteem. Yet most older women today were socialized to traditional patterns of femininity: to nurturing, living vicariously, and depending on spouse or children for emotional support. As Lopata (1973) points out, most widows have not been trained to analyze resources of the environment or to take initiative in assuming social roles. In losing roles that define them and tie them to society, widows are vulnerable to social isolation and ultimately to reactive depression (Lopata, 1975).

A traditional sex-role orientation is no more adaptive for men than women in later life. Retirement, an invention of the twentieth century, has become a significant stage of life in today's society, particularly for men. Yet the traditional masculine role with its emphasis on instrumental competence—assertiveness, independence, achievement—may conflict with the roles and activities open to the retired person. Conversely, traditional feminine qualities—sociability, emotional expressiveness, intimacy—may gain value. Sex-role flexibility—the capacity to call on or integrate qualities conventionally ascribed to both sexes—seems the adaptation of choice for older men as well as women.

A number of studies support this proposition. In a group of over 300 men and women aged 52–90, persons who were psychologically androgynous—who scored high on both masculine and feminine personality traits on a sex-role inventory—adjusted most successfully to aging (Sinnott, Block, Grambs, Gaddy, & Davidson, 1980). A longitudinal study of women and men from ages 30 to 70 suggests that highly feminine women may be at a particular disadvantage in later life. Traditional, family-oriented women in this study were more dependent on the proximity of family members for successful adaptation and presumably more vulnerable to social isolation in widowhood (Maas & Kuypers, 1974). A study of transitions at four life periods ranging from high school graduation to preretirement found an increase with age in the degree to which a feminine self-concept in women is correlated with self-criticism (Lowenthal, Thurnher, & Chiriboga, 1975). An exclusively feminine orientation appears to be increasingly disadvantageous for women as they grow older. Older women today are caught in a cultural gap between traditional models of feminity to which they were socialized earlier and the advantages of developing more autonomous strategies to cope in today's society.

SEX-ROLE NORMS: A HISTORICAL VIEW

Historical periods differ in the degree to which they require conformity to sex-typed roles. Just as societies produce individuals whose modal personalities are peculiarly suited to the economic and social structure of that society—so-called national character—historical periods within a society then generate a succession of cultures, each with a particular economic and social structure and preferred personality type.

The tendency to polarize sex roles—to draw sharp distinctions between feminine and masculine modes of being—was heightened by changes in the family and economic structure brought about by the industrial revolution. In subsistence economies, husbands and wives shared in economic production. Farms, shops, and cottage industries were family operations. The colonial household in this country was a small factory which produced clothing, furniture, bedding, and other accessories (Demos, 1974, p. 430). The female's role was central, though always within the context of the patriarchal family. The two major adult roles, parenthood and work, generally stretched over an entire lifetime for both sexes and provided continuity for older people (Hareven, 1979).

With industrialization, urbanization, and the shift to a money economy, however, the man's economic role shifted to work places outside the home (Bernard, 1981; Hareven, 1979; Lopata, 1975). At the same time, the shift from a rural to an industrial economy led to greater productivity and an economic surplus that made it possible to exempt women and children from economically productive roles. The man was expected to be the only breadwinner supporting the economically dependent wife and children. As a result, families became segregated not only by gender but also by age. Children became students; women became nurturers; and the aged became hobbyists. Bernard (1981) notes that the good-provider role for males emerged in this country roughly in the 1830s and continued to the late 1970s when the 1980 census declared that a male was not automatically assumed to be the head of the household.

Blake (1974) traces the evolution of women's secondary status in industrialized nations:

> The migration of industrializing peoples out of rural settings into urban factories and bureaucracies . . . progressively removed work from the family milieu and put men in jobs away from home. . . . Gradually, both wives and children became economic liabilities to the men. . . . Industrializing societies [developed] all kinds of rationalizations and legitimations for the wrenching change in the position of women that was accompanying the industrial revolution and the demographic transition. In particular they [asserted] that women's personalities and behavior actually conformed by nature to the restrictions of their new way of life [p. 92].

Sex differences and sex-role stereotypes were sharpened by a misleading identification of men with production and women with consumption (Toffler, 1981). As Lopata (1975) points out, though the woman was even more essential to the functioning of the nuclear family than before—she was now solely responsible for the emotional and practical operation of the household—the prestige of her role declined. Many of the instrumental functions of the family—educational, religious, medical, economic—were relinquished to outside institutions, and the home gradually lost its position as the center of family life.

Although women were oppressed before industrialization, the modern stereotype of the dependent woman can be traced to the rise of the good provider role. Discouraged from labor force participation, many women, especially the affluent, were deprived of opportunities to develop strength and competence in a variety of roles (Bernard, 1981). As a result, conflicts and anxieties over assuming adult roles in the larger society could be postponed, sometimes indefinitely. A woman may have resented her dependency while gaining security from it and felt helpless to modify either.

Most importantly, women were socialized to adopt a self-image that fit their secondary economic status. They internalized the social identity they were assigned. As Bernard (1981) points out, the effects of this self-image could be crippling. Viewing themselves as less competent than men in worldly affairs, many women have voluntarily held back from participating in roles outside the home (Lopata, 1975). It is out of this milieu that the current generation of older women emerged. Yet this is a generation of women who are living longer than ever before and are more likely to spend their last years widowed and called upon to develop their own resources.

The change in family life brought on by the industrial revolution had psychological effects on the roles of men as well as women. Maleness came to be identified not only with the job and work site—now removed from the home—but more importantly with the man's success in the work role. Success in the good-provider role came to define masculinity itself

(Bernard, 1981). The role led to an enormous drive to achievement while emotional expressiveness was devalued. The man had to win, dominate, show toughness, endurance, and leadership. Relationships with other men were colored by competition which inhibited expressions of intimacy. Families became showpieces to display the success of the good provider. A wife's earning capacity, for example, diminished a man's prestige as head of household (Gould, 1974). Moreover, as Bernard (1981) comments, when the division of labor removed the man from the family dwelling for most of the day, intimate relationships became less feasible and emotional expressiveness in men less desirable. In sum, the industrial revolution exaggerated status differences between the sexes and polarized social definitions of the masculine and feminine personality.

SEX ROLES: A LIFE-SPAN VIEW

Socialization of the Sexes

Thus has society created different life scripts for women and men. These scripts define what is appropriate and inappropriate in a person's behavior and self-image at successive stages of development. They influence the individual's style of coping and sense of self. Sex roles shape the course of individual development.

Many of the polarities confronting the individual over the life span are subsumed in our culture by gender. I refer to polarities such as those between dependence and independence, attachment and separation, submission and dominance, emotionality and self-control. In each dimension, the more self-oriented, assertive pole belongs to the masculine stereotype, the more person-oriented or expressive, to the feminine. In this section, I will review evidence that suggests that women in our society move more slowly than men into their full adulthood. I will not consider here the influence of biology on sex differences—a complex and controversial issue—but will focus instead on the impact of socialization.

Men are socialized to individuate—to develop a separate and autonomous sense of self—early in life. Women are socialized to affiliate. Thus individuation for women is slower to develop and longer in coming than for men, with advantages and disadvantages for both sexes at different stages of the life cycle.

Girls and boys are socialized to develop qualities that are congruent with their major adult roles as mothers and economic providers and to disown qualities that do not fit these roles (Hoffman, 1977). The socialization of girls reinforces communal qualities—affiliation, nurturance, dependence—and discourages agentive qualities. The woman learns early in life to express herself for and through others and to suppress aspects of herself that are self-oriented or aggressive. Boys are encouraged to develop skills useful in instrumental roles—independence, self-assertion, mastery. In turn, they learn to suppress their emotionality and vulnerability and to tone down affiliative needs.

Both Hoffman (1977) and Block (1976), in their critiques of the literature on sex differences, conclude that girls are given less encouragement by parents in early independence strivings. Girls also have more difficulty than boys establishing a separate sense of self because they are the same sex as the mother with the same role expectations (Chodorow, 1978; Hoffman, 1977). Not surprisingly, girls have been observed to be less confident of their ability and more likely to cope by seeking help or approval from others (Block, 1976).

Traditional wife and mother roles in adulthood perpetuate the woman's affiliative orientation. Pressures to regress in marriage—to retreat into dependency or inhibit individuality—are often greater for women than for men. Wives have been found to make more of the adjustments in marriage and to be more unhappy than husbands (Bernard, 1973). Encouraged to assume a complementary role to their husband's assertiveness, wives often suppress their own ambition and power drives. Many women respond by projecting power and competence onto men. They define themselves through husbands and children and so rely on others for their sense of worth. Women are thus less likely than men to develop confidence in their ability to cope with the complexities of modern society. Nor are they as likely to develop the skills to do so.

Males, by contrast, have to push aside their dependence on the mother in order to establish a masculine identity. The boy needs to separate from his mother earlier than the girl and more fully. To do so, he must develop his competence in the outer world and deny his vulnerability and longings for nurturance. In adult roles as economic provider, the man continues to actualize his sense of self as agent. Though the man may also regress in marriage in the sense of depending on maternal qualities in his wife, he retains his instrumental roles in the outside world and is less likely to borrow his wife's identity as his own. His early (and possibly premature) independence may interfere with his capacity for affection or intimacy later in life or lead to concern about success, but the woman's prolonged dependency may result in chronic vulnerability.

Two forces, however, militate against an overly feminine orientation in older women. Social–historical changes batter from without while developmental forces thrust from within to press women as well as men into more flexible sex-role positions. Women in this sense are late maturers. Their socialization in childhood no less than their roles in early adulthood converge to delay the actualization of a separate sense of identity until well into the adult years. Only in later adulthood when parenting is no longer salient do many women move toward a more autonomous self. Men by contrast are early maturers. Traditional male roles and socialization experiences encourage men to actualize their selfhood much earlier in life. For the man too, however, a narrow sex-role orientation becomes less adaptive at the end of life. Both men and women have been found to shift in their later years toward more androgynous sex-role orientations.

Beyond Socialization: Sex Typing in Later Life

A mounting body of evidence points to an intrinsic or developmental shift in the quality of maleness and femaleness as the individual moves through successive stages of the life cycle. According to Jung (1933), "[The man] discovers his tender feelings and [the woman] her sharpness of mind [p. 108]." Jung regards this shift as generated from within, as a genuine developmental phase in the human life cycle transcending cultures and historic periods. He suggests that the roles we fulfill in the first half of life—usefulness, achievement, nurturing the young—require that we develop selected parts of ourselves at the expense of others that we suppress. In the second half of life the individual turns inward to greater awareness of parts of the self that were suppressed earlier. Jung asserts that the person can achieve true individuation only when she or he actualizes latent sides of the personality—most importantly for the man his feminine side and for the women her masculine side.

This view finds empirical support across a wide range of cultures. Gutmann (1975, 1977) finds that men in preindustrial societies become less power-oriented than when they were younger and women become more so, at least in domestic settings. Older women move out of sub-servient positions in the household to positions of power. Older men replace individual strength as warriors and hunters with strength through magic as priests and shamans. Affiliation with supernatural power replaces individual power. In traditional patriarchal societies, no less than our own, women become more aggressive in later life, less emotional, and more domineering. Men become more receptive and sensual. Gutmann (1975) argues that since these age-related changes occur in predictable sequence across disparate cultures, they can be viewed as developmental in nature.

Studies in our own society reveal similar trends. The comparison of adults at four life transitions found that young men saw themselves as active and energetic while women's self-images lacked energy (Lowenthal *et al.*, 1975). At age 60, women's assertiveness contrasted with the expressiveness of men. Correspondingly, older women saw themselves as less feminine than did younger women. Both men and women in this study agreed that in later life fewer men are "boss" in the family and more women are.

An assessment of sex-role orientation in college students aged 16–54 by means of a self-descriptive personality inventory found that middle-aged students attributed more cross-sex characteristics to themselves than younger students (Fischer & Narus, 1981). These older women and men were more androgynous than those who were younger, despite the fact that they had been exposed to traditional sex-role norms in their youth more than had younger groups. The same sex-role instrument was given to a group of men and women aged 52–90 (Sinnott *et al.*, 1980). Over half of this group of older persons was classified as androgynous, that is, they described themselves as possessing characteristics common to both their own sex and the opposite sex.

Fantasies and dreams reflect less conscious aspects of a person's self-image. A study of women's dreams found that women over 40 depict themselves as more robust and energetic and less concerned with the effects of aggression than adolescent girls or young adults (Brenneis, 1975). Conversely, men's daydreams of heroic action or personal advancement decline steadily with age (Giambra, 1973).

All of these studies draw on cross-sectional age comparisons. However, two studies of my own, using data from the longitudinal studies at the Institute of Human Development, University of California, Berkeley, suggest that the association between increased psychological androgyny and aging is not an artifact of cohort efforts.[1] An analysis of personality change in persons who have been observed periodically from early adolescence through age 50 revealed increasing similarity in the characteristics of men and women as they approached 50, particularly among those who were psychologically healthier at 50 (Livson,-1976b). Women who were psychologically healthier became more assertive and analytic with age while remaining nurturant and open to their feelings. Men became more giving and expressive while they continued to be ambitious

---

[1]Participants in these studies were members of the longitudinal Oakland Growth Study at the Institute of Human Development, University of California, Berkeley. This study was begun in 1932 with over 200 boys and girls entering junior high school. Participants were assessed throughout their adolescent years and again in 1960 and 1970 when they were approximately 40–50 years of age. Close to 80 persons who had participated in all four data collections were included in the preceding analyses. The group is composed of white, primarily middle-class, urban women and men. The data base for the assessment of sex typing was personality evaluations (Q-sorts) based on intensive clinical interviews in adulthood and on interviews and behavior observations in adolescence.

and assertive. The two sexes did not reverse roles. Men remained masculine and women remained feminine. Rather, each moved toward a more androgynous position, allowing qualities conventionally assigned to the opposite sex to emerge. In this sense, each became a little more like the other. Psychologically less healthy men also moved toward a more androgynous balance of personality characteristics by 50. They became more openly dependent and less power-oriented.

Only one group failed to actualize cross-sex characteristics by 50. These were psychologically less healthy women. Dependent and relatively passive in adolescence, these women changed very little by 50. This group, significantly, was the most anxious at 50 and the only group to decline in IQ since adolescence. In sum, all of the men in this study but only those women who assumed active aspects of the feminine role—who were actively nurturant and expressive—became more androgynous by 50. Socialization to dependent aspects of the feminine role seems to inhibit later life development.

In order to assess changes in sex-typing in this group more directly, I constructed personality scales to assess masculine and feminine characteristics from personality profiles of participants at successive age periods (Livson, 1980). The scales provided independent measures of masculinity and femininity for each individual at each age period. Women and men showed a steady increase in same-sex characteristics from adolescence to age 50. Women became increasingly feminine and men increasingly masculine. With respect to cross-sex characteristics, however, the trend was more complex. Both sexes were relatively high in cross-sex characteristics in junior high school, became less so in senior high and early adulthood, and then increased again by age 50. The same persons who were higher in cross-sex characteristics in early adolescence were also higher in middle age. In their late teens and early adulthood, they seemed to suppress these characteristics, but by 50, they revived the flexibility of sex-typed behavior that had belonged to their past and had been put in the closet, so to speak, after puberty.

At the same time, these men and women continued to evolve qualities appropriate to their own sex throughout the adult years. What seems critical in shaping gender identity over the life cycle is the corollary development of cross-sex characteristics. These characteristics modify the form and expression of same-sex typing at successive stages of development. It is the balance between these two vectors—the degree, for instance, to which a woman's nurturance is expressed assertively or submissively or a man's independence is modified by warmth or aloofness—that guides the development of sex-typed behavior.

Gutmann (1975) suggests that sex roles are polarized in early adulthood to meet the universal need to care for the young. He views the shift to more androgynous patterns in middle age as a response to the termination of parenting functions. I suggest more generally that life tasks and roles shape the development of sex typing at successive phases of the life cycle. The central tasks of early adulthood—career building, mating, parenting, consolidating identity—all tend to polarize sex roles. To perform these roles efficiently, individuals may need to disown characteristics conventionally assigned to the opposite sex, but sex roles become less salient when mates have been chosen, children reared, and careers won. The older individual may be able to tolerate more complexity in role behavior and to define the self more flexibly. There may be a general progression from social and role-dictated modes of experiencing to increasingly personalized and integrated styles.

If, however, the person's life structure and social network, particularly family, continue to reinforce earlier personality traits—for example, compliance or self-doubt in overly dependent women—the individual may be trapped in a mutually reinforcing system, a vicious circle. She or he may have litle incentive to expand nor room to do so. A key factor, I suggest, is the fit between an individual's personality and her or his roles and life structure.

This assertion is supported by a more intensive analysis of the Berkeley longitudinal data, this time focusing only on persons who were judged to be psychologically healthy at age 50 (Livson, 1976a, 1978, 1981). Two types of well-functioning persons were identified: traditional women and men whose personalities corresponded to conventional sex-role norms and nontraditional women and men whose personalities were more androgynous. Both groups, regardless of personality, had conformed to traditional gender roles in early adulthood. The men were high achievers, mainly in business and industry; the women were primarily wives and mothers.

Nontraditional women and men suppressed cross-sex characteristics in early adulthood in order to function successfully in these traditional roles. Both paid a price in emotional stress. By age 50, however, these men and women reclaimed the more androgynous identities apparent in adolescence with an upsurge in psychological health. The women had been intellectually oriented, high-achieving adolescents who put these qualities aside during their mothering years. Disengaging from mothering by 50 allowed them to reconnect with their intellectuality and achievement needs. Correspondingly, there was an expansion of emotional life. Nontraditional men were expressive, rather impulsive teenagers whose emotional style was poorly suited to the self-discipline required for occupational advancement. Suppressing their emotionality in early adulthood, these men assumed an exaggerated masculine posture, but with considerable stress. By 50, however, they revived the warmer expressiveness of their youth with improved psychological health.

Traditional women and men, by contrast, had personalities better matched to the roles they occupied in early adulthood. This group did not become more androgynous as they grew older. The women were interpersonally oriented, giving, protective, and sociable. The men were emotionally controlled, rational, and competent. The women as wives and mothers and the men as successful achievers elaborated their natural skills in these roles. Their psychological health remained consistently high. Traditional women and men changed relatively little from adolescence to middle age.

To summarize, studies of age differences in sex typing suggest that most people actualize cross-sex characteristics in the second half of life, at least to some degree, but there are individual differences. When the person's life structure and roles reinforce her or his preferred personality style, there may be little incentive to develop unused parts of the personality in later life. Older women who have been socialized to be dependent adults, to accomodate to the needs of others, may be at a particular disadvantage at the end of life. Reinforced for compliant qualities in their roles as daughters and wives and even as mothers, these women may fail to develop their potential as autonomous adults. Coping with widowhood and aloneness at the last of life may be especially problematic for such women. Similarly, men who have spent their lives suppressing their capacity for intimacy and emotional expressiveness may face occupational loss or widowhood with inappropriate resources. The evidence, however, suggests that women who fail to develop cross-sex characteristics are at greater risk.

Sex Typing and Mental Health in Later Life

More women than men in every population group suffer from depression and anxiety-related disorders (Dohrenwend & Dohrenwend, 1974; Goldman & Ravid, 1980; Gove & Tudor, 1973; Weissman & Klerman, 1977). This trend holds up in community surveys as well as psychiatric treatment centers. It appears to be neither an artifact of help-seeking patterns nor to reflect greater willingness on the part of women to admit symptoms. (Clancy & Gove, 1974). The pattern has been found not only in the United States but also in a wide variety of countries, both industrialized and developing.

It has been argued that high rates of depression and anxiety in women result from internalizing cultural definitions of femininity (Klerman & Weissman, 1980). Stereotyped feminine role expectations may produce in women a cognitive set against assertion, a kind of learned helplessness (Seligman, 1975), which can weaken the sense of control over life and lead to depression. A study of sex differences in coping mechanisms, for example, found that men relied more on mastery and action while women relied on more passive strategies: appeal to others, helplessness, emotional discharge, denial (Pearlin & Schooler, 1978).

However, sex differences in depression and anxiety-linked disorders even out in later life, largely because women improve. A national survey found that women over 55 were less self-critical, relative to men of the same ages, than women under 55 but they were still more self-critical than their male age mates (Gurin, Veroff, & Feld, 1960). Another national survey found that complaints of depression, anxiety, and somatic tension were greater in women than men under 60, but women's complaints declined to the level of men after 60 (Huffine, Note 1). The suicide rate in women declines after age 50 (Breed & Huffine, 1979).

Study after study finds similar trends, especially when life stage is taken into account. The life transitions study found that 60-year-old women were more confident than 50-year-olds, but only after children were launched (Lowenthal et al., 1975). Neugarten (1970) reports that life satisfaction improved for women after children left home. The evidence clearly suggests that depression and anxiety decline in women in the later years of life, particularly when they disengage from mothering.

I suggest that this decline reflects a shift to more autonomous sources of self-esteem. The traditional woman may come fully into her own only when disengaging from mothering allows her to disengage from internalized stereotypes of femininity and actualize the other side of the sex-role polarity: the assertive, agentic side of herself. Less dependent on others to validate her self-esteem, the older woman can assume greater control over her sources of worth.

With some exceptions (Hefner, Rebecca, & Oleshansky, 1975; Livson, Note 2; Sinnott et al., 1980) sex-role theorists focus on gender development in childhood and adolescence but do not address the possibility of continuing gender development in the adult years (e.g., Block, 1973). The studies reviewed earlier suggest that personality continues to develop throughout the life course and that the direction of this development is toward greater flexibility of sex-typed characteristics. The evidence suggests that this developmental shift is more advantageous for women. Today, this shift occurs in the midst of a revolutionary upheaval in traditional sex roles.

SEX ROLES IN TRANSITION

Recently the structure of the American urban family has undergone profound changes which have undermined the division of labor between the sexes and struck at the foundation of traditional sex roles. In the 1960s and 1970s, a single income became inadequate for more and more families (Bernard, 1981). Women began to reenter the labor force at an accelerating rate. The proportion of married women aged 15–54 in the labor force more than doubled between 1950 and 1978 from 25.2% to 55.4%. The proportion for 1990 is estimated to reach 66.7% (Smith, 1979, p. 14).

The move of married women into the labor force had a major impact on both the work and family roles of men and women. As Bernard (1981) observes, it has chipped away at the privileges of the breadwinner and legitimized women's demands that men share their traditional role, not only in child-care and household tasks but also in their age-old function as custodians of domestic intimacy. Men are expected to be more expressive and nurturant, women more assertive and instrumental, at least in those segments of society that are at the frontiers of change. The blurring of traditional sex roles is apparent in the rise of the women's movement, in new forms of family life, and in a general call to equalize sex-role norms and privileges.

Lopata (1975) points out, however, that the main thrust of this assault on traditional sex roles has not been to eliminate discrimination but rather to change the self-concept of increasingly large numbers of women. The new ideology redefines not only which roles are appropriate for men and women but also recasts the images assigned to both. It undermines the assumptions by which women have voluntarily avoided many outside roles. Whether this reconstruction has floated upwards to the older population to any appreciable degree is questionable, although it has affected selected segments of that population.

The cutting edge of the new ideology among older women is in political activist movements such as the Gray Panthers (Bequaert, 1976). Founded in 1970 by their spokeswoman, Maggie Kuhn, the Gray Panthers emphasize that they are a movement, not an organization. They encourage the membership of young persons and project an image of radical militancy. Their accomplishments and goals cover a broad spectrum of social programs for the elderly. Although not a single-sex association, the Gray Panthers encourage women to take assertive roles in both policy planning and social action. Their philosophy and the composition of their leadership have promoted a more androgynous, agentive, and, indeed, militant image of the older woman.

Another activist group for older women is the NOW Task Force on Older Women, an organization begun in 1974. Among its priorities are income maintenance, job opportunities, and job retraining for older women. The Task Force has been active in designing jobs that use the skills women have employed as housewives and mothers or in training women to convert these skills into marketable services. Like the Gray Panthers, this organization encourages older women to move beyond traditional roles and develop the talent and self-confidence to connect with the resources of mass society.

Other political organizations as well as educational institutions are contributing to the transition of older women to more flexible and self-sufficient life styles. A publication called *Prime Time* has become a clearinghouse for information about organizations, opportunities, and resources for older women. This newsletter provides not only information but also an alternative, positive image of the older woman in appearance, strengths and usefulness (Bequaert, 1976).

The vast majority of the current generation of older women, however, remain rooted in the traditional values and life-styles to which they were accustomed earlier in life. Many of these values are particularly maladaptive in later years of life. The retired homemaker, conditioned to live for others, may feel guilt over assuming more self-centered roles. The devoted wife or mother, bonded to husband or children by excessive closeness, may cling to these relationships in an ambivalent, love–hate relationship. If abandoned by either, she may regress into helplessness or depression.

Perhaps the most obvious traditional value that damages a woman's self-esteem in later life is the so-called double standard of aging. Insofar as women are valued for beauty, and feminine beauty is equated with youth, aging robs a woman of a central source of worth. Though this obsolescence occurs later than it used to (with better health, diet, cosmetics), the pattern remains unchanged. Sontag (1972), in a strong polemic against the double standard of aging, points out that men are permitted two standards of physical attractiveness, the youth and the man. Women are permitted only one. A man's sexual attractiveness is enhanced by signs of aging: thickening of the body, lines on the face, graying hair, and his desirability is enhanced by his accomplishments—power, wealth, success—which increase with age. Although older men are admired for attracting younger women, the converse does not hold. Older women are not sought-after sex partners. They do not have the same access to younger partners that males have, an inequity compounded by the imbalance of women in the older population.

Not surprisingly, older men are more sexually active than older women, particularly unmarried women (Ludeman, 1981). Single, older women have been found to engage in very little sexual activity with male partners, whereas single, older men remain relatively active (Christenson & Gagnon, 1965; Pfeiffer, Verwoerdt, & Wang, 1969). Most older persons of both sexes, however, report a decline in sexual activity at older ages, although most continue to be capable of sexual functioning (Ludeman, 1981). It should be noted that these data are based on studies completed in the 1960s. It would be interesting to determine whether sexual patterns in the aged have altered over the past decade with its emphasis on sexual liberation, particularly of women.

Ironically, sexual capacity, at least as defined by frequency of arousal and vigor, declines earlier in men than in women. Kinsey's early findings that male sexuality reaches a peak in the early 20s and declines steadily thereafter have been supported by subsequent investigators (Kaplan, 1974). Physiological changes in older men may include longer refractory periods and greater need for direct stimulation for arousal (Kaplan, 1974; Masters & Johnson, 1970). However, sexual problems in the male are generally reversible (Sviland, 1978). For example, a major psychological basis of impotence in the male is anxiety over sexual failure (Kaplan, 1974).

Female sexuality reaches peak responsiveness in the late 30s and early 40s and can maintain this level into the 60s (Kaplan, 1974). Although postmenopausal women may also experience physiological changes that affect timing and ease of arousal, these rarely interfere with capacity for sexual functioning (Ludeman, 1981; Masters & Johnson, 1970). Following menopause, many women show an increase in sexual interest which concurs with the theoretical increase in libido when androgen action is unopposed by estrogen (Kaplan, 1974; Sviland, 1978).

Sexual activity in older women is impeded largely by cultural and psychological factors. Limited availability of partners, a negative self-image arising from the double standard of aging, and sexual prohibitions internalized earlier in life stand in the way of sexual activity in older, single women. Older women have been found to have more conservative attitudes toward nontraditional sexual behavior than do younger women (Snyder & Spreitze, 1976). Narrow definitions of gender roles in which the man is the prime initiator of sexual contact, whereas the woman remains receptive, in love-making as well as in courting, are clearly disadvantageous in later life.

The extent to which cultural changes have made inroads against traditional sex-role expectations in the older population is uncertain. In more traditional times, the developmental shift toward greater assertiveness in older women found expression primarily in family relations, at times in maladaptive efforts to control and dominate. Today, with the expanding population of older, single women, the emerging assertiveness of older women serves an adaptive function. Contemporary older women are called upon to cultivate their selfhood more fully than ever before. Resourcefulness in the outer world, urged by feminists for young women, is no less essential for those who are old. Similarly, societal permission for men to soften their macho image and open themselves to emotionality, tenderness, and intimacy is even more adaptive for old men than for young.

CONCLUSION

The roles assigned to males and females in a society are shaped by economic and social forces no less than by the biological tasks of bearing and nursing children. Industrialization and urbanization changed the division of labor in the nineteenth century family, polarizing the roles and ultimately the life course of women and men. More recent changes— medical advances that permit freedom of choice with respect to family size and the return of women to economic production—have called traditional sex roles into question. At the same time, they have begun to shape a new kind of person, equally at home with masculine instrumentality and feminine expressiveness, regardless of gender.

I have argued that historical periods, like cultures, create modal character types particularly suited to the adaptive tasks of those periods. Shifts in the major roles of society create shifts in the modal personality which appear first in the young and last in the old in a kind of cultural lag. The androgynous personality has emerged as an increasingly common character-type among the young of our time, but sex-role flexibility, I have suggested, is even more critical for the old in today's society, especially for women.

Although older persons have always had the potential to actualize cross-sex characteristics as part of a natural developmental sequence, many are held back by early socialization patterns. This is particularly true of women who have spent their adult lives in dependent roles. Traditional sex roles and formative experiences have made it difficult for women to actualize their selfhood as early and perhaps as completely as men. The price women have had to pay is reflected in higher rates of depression and anxiety disorders. The older woman who is suddenly widowed and cast on her own is particularly at risk. With increasing numbers of older, single women in the population and even more projected in the future, it is essential that women develop the skills to build lives of their own. To do so, women will have to take hold of their potential to integrate qualities conventionally ascribed to men. They will have to move closer to what Gutmann (1977) calls the normal unisex of later life.

For men, too, an androgynous orientation is advantageous in the later years. With the decline of the breadwinner role and the shrinking demand for labor in our increasingly technological world, retirement or partial retirement might be expected to come earlier in life. The recent trend to raise the compulsory retirement age suggests that retirement may become more voluntary and flexible than in the past. The work ethic and achievement orientation promoted for men in industrializing societies is increasingly incongruent with today's social realities, especially for older men.

Thus, the importance of flexible sex typing for mental health is highlighted for older groups in today's society. It is not surprising that women and men who are more androgynous in personality characteristics have been found to age more successfully.

As Lopata (1975) points out, the current generation of older persons is unique in history. They grew up under conditions not likely to be repeated in future generations, at least in developed countries. They carry with them the traditions of the past. Yet many are influenced by changes in the present. Socialized by younger cohorts, especially children and grandchildren, many older persons have liberated themselves with respect to sex roles and sexual behavior. Some single older women openly enjoy their sexuality and some older couples cohabit without benefit of marriage. Political activist groups urge old women to assert their independence. Some older women launch their selfhood only after they are widowed. Yet many older people, perhaps the majority, remain rooted in traditional behaviors and traditional ways of viewing themselves.

Older cohorts of the future are likely to move more easily and more fully into flexible sex-role styles. Earlier and longer exposure to more equalitarian roles for men and women may produce more androgynous persons earlier in life. Women will have participated longer in the labor force at jobs requiring skill and training. More women will enter old age already divorced and practiced in the skills of singlehood. Men, at least some men, will have participated more actively in childrearing and will have elaborated the softer, communal side of their personalities. Both sexes may be able to profit more fully from the developmental thrust to integrate the masculine and feminine in later life.

REFERENCE NOTES

1. Huffine, C. L. Research undertaken at Institute for Research in Social Behavior, Oakland, California. Personal communication, August, 1980.
2. Livson, F. B. Gender identity: A life span view of sex-role development. In R. Weg (Ed.), *Sexuality in the later years: Roles and behavior*, in preparation.

REFERENCES

Aging in America. *Society*, April 1981, p. 4.

Bengston, V. L., Kasschau, P. L., & Ragan, P. K. The impact of social structure on aging individuals. In J. E. Birren & K. W. Schaie (Eds.), *Handbook of the psychology of aging*. New York: Van Nostrand Reinhold, 1977.

Bequaert, L. H. *Single women alone and together*. Boston: Beacon Press, 1976.

Bernard, J. *The future of marriage*. New York: Bantam, 1973.

Bernard, J. The good-provider role: Its rise and fall. *American Psychologist*, 1981, 36, 1–12.

Blake, J. The changing status of women in developed countries. In *The human population* (A Scientific American Book). San Francisco: W. H. Freeman, 1974.

Block, J. H. Conceptions of sex role: Some cross-cultural and longitudinal perspectives. *American Psychologist*, 1973, 28, 512–526.

Block, J. H. Issues, problems and pitfalls in assessing sex differences. *Merrill–Palmer Quarterly*, 1976, 22, 283–308.

Breed, W., & Huffine, C. L. Sex differences in suicide among older white Americans: A role and developmental approach. In O. J. Kaplan (Ed.), *Psychopathology of aging*. New York: Academic Press, 1979.

Brenneis, C. B. Developmental aspects of aging in women. A comparative study of dreams. *Archives of General Psychiatry*, 1975, 32, 429–435.

Brody, E. The aging of the family. *The Annals of the American Academy of Political Science*, 1978, 438, 13–27.

Campbell, A. *The sense of well-being in America: Recent patterns and trends*. New York: McGraw-Hill, 1981.

Chodorow, N. *The reproduction of mothering: Psychoanalysis and sociology of gender*. Berkeley: University of California Press, 1978.

Christenson, C. B., & Gagnon, J. H. Sexual behavior in a group of older women. *Journal of Gerontology*, 1965, 20, 351–356.

Clancy, K., & Gove, W. Sex differences in mental illness: An analysis of response bias in self-reports. *American Journal of Sociology*, 1974, 80, 205–216.

Demos, J. The American family in past time. *American Scholar*, 1974, 43, 422–446.

Dohrenwend, B. P., & Dohrenwend, B. S. Social and cultural influences on psychopathology. *Annual Review of Psychology*, 1974, 25, 417–452.

Fischer, J. L., & Narus, L. R., Jr. Sex-role development in late adolescence and adulthood. *Sex Roles*, 1981, 7, 97–106.

Foner, A. Age stratification and the changing family. *American Journal of Sociology*, 1978, 5340–5365. 84 (Supplement).

Giambra, L. *Daydreaming in males from seventeen to seventy-seven: A preliminary report*. Paper presented at the meeting of the American Psychological Association, Montreal, September 1973.

Goldman, N., & Ravid, R. Community surveys: Sex differences in mental illness. In M. Guttentag, S. Salasin, & D. Belle (Eds.), *The mental health of women*. New York: Academic Press, 1980.

Gould, R. E. Measuring masculinity by the size of a paycheck. In J. E. Pleck & J. Sawyer (Eds.), *Men and masculinity*. Englewood Cliffs, N. J.: Prentice–Hall, 1974.

Gove, W. R., & Tudor, J. F. Adult sex roles and mental illness. *American Journal of Sociology*, 1973, 78, 812–835.

Gurin, G., Veroff, J., & Feld, S. *Americans view their mental health*. New York: Basic Books, 1960.

Gutmann, D. Parenthood: A key to the comparative study of the life cycle. In N. Datan &

I. H. Ginsberg (Eds.), *Life-span developmental psychology.* New York: Academic Press, 1975.

Gutmann, D. The cross-cultural perspective: Notes toward a comparative psychology of aging. In J. E. Birren & K. W. Schaie (Eds.), *Handbook of the psychology of aging.* New York: Van Nostrand Reinhold, 1977.

Hareven, T. K. The last stage: Historical adulthood and old age. In D. D. Van Tassell (Ed.), *Aging, death, and the completion of being.* Philadelphia: University of Pennsylvania Press, 1979.

Hefner, R., Rebecca, M., & Oleshansky, B. Development of sex role transcendence. *Human Development, 1975, 18,* 143–158.

Hoffman, L. W. Changes in family roles, socialization, and sex differences. *American Psychologist,* 1977, *32,* 644–657.

Jung, C. *Modern man in search of a soul.* New York: Harcourt Brace, 1933.

Kaplan, H. S. *The new sex therapy.* New York: Bruner–Mazel, 1974.

Klerman, G. L., & Weissman, M. M. Depressions among women: Their nature and causes. In M. Guttentag, S. Salasin, & D. Belle (Eds.), *The mental health of women.* New York: Academic Press, 1980.

Livson, F. B. Patterns of personality development in middle-aged women: A longitudinal study. *International Journal of Aging and Human Development,* 1976, *7,* 107–115. (a)

Livson, F. B. *Coming together in the middle years: A longitudinal study of sex role convergence.* Paper presented at the meeting of the Gerontological Society, New York, October 1976. (b)

Livson, F. B. Personality development of men and women in the middle years. In D. Levinson (Chair), *The life cycle: Development in the middle years.* Symposium presented at the meeting of the American Association for the Advancement of Science, Washington, D. C., February 1978.

Livson, F. B. *Sex typing over the life span: His, hers, and theirs.* Paper presented at the meeting of the Gerontological Society of America, San Diego, November 1980.

Livson, F. B. Paths to psychological health in the middle years: Sex differences. In D. H. Eichorn, J. A. Clausen, N. Haan, M. P. Honzik, & P. Mussen (Eds.), *Present and past in middle life.* New York: Academic Press, 1981.

Lopata, H. Z. *Widowhood in an American city.* Cambridge, Mass.: Schenkman, 1973.

Lopata, H. Z. Widowhood: Societal factors in life-span disruptions and alternatives. In N. Datan & L. H. Ginsberg (Eds.), *Life-span developmental psychology.* New York: Academic Press, 1975.

Lowenthal, M. F., Thurnher, M., & Chiriboga, D. *Four stages of life.* San Francisco: Jossey–Bass, 1975.

Ludeman, K. The sexuality of the older person: Review of the literature. *The Gerontologist,* 1981, *21,* 203–208.

Maas, H. S., & Kuypers, J. A. *From thirty to seventy.* San Francisco: Jossey–Bass, 1974.

Masnick, G., & Bane, M. J. *The nation's families: 1960–1990.* Boston: Auburn House, 1980.

Masters, W. H., & Johnson, V. E. *Human sexual inadequacy.* Boston: Little Brown, 1970.

Mindel, C. H. Multigenerational family households: Recent trends and implications for the future. *The Gerontologist,* 1979, *19,* 456–463.

Neugarten, B. L. Adaptation and the life cycle. *Journal of Geriatric Psychiatry,* 1970, *4,* 71–87.

Pearlin, L. I., & Schooler, C. The structure of coping. *Journal of Health and Social Behavior,* 1978, *19,* 2–21.

Pfeiffer, E., Verwoerdt, A., & Wang, H. S. The natural history of sexual behavior in a biologically advantaged group of aged individuals. *Journal of Gerontology,* 1969, *24,* 193–198.

Seligman, M. E. P. *Helplessness: On depression, development, and death.* San Francisco: W. H. Freeman, 1975.

Sinnott, J. D., Block, M. R., Grambs, J. D., Gaddy, C. D., & Davidson, J. C. *Sex roles in mature adults: Antecedents and correlates* (Tech. Rep. NIA-80-1). National Institute on Aging, 1980.

Shanas, E. The family as a social support system in old age. *The Gerontologist,* 1979, *19,* 169–174.

Smith, R. E. (Ed.). *The subtle revolution.* Washington, D. C.: Urban Institute, 1979.

Snyder, E. E., & Spreitze, E. Attitudes of the aged toward nontraditional sexual behavior. *Archives of Sexual Behavior,* 1976, 5(3), 249–254.

Sontag, S. The double standard of aging. *Saturday Review of the Society,* October 1972, 29–38.

Sviland, M. A. P. A program of sexual liberation and growth in the elderly. In R. L. Solnick (Ed.), *Sexuality and aging.* Los Angeles: University of Southern California Press, 1978.

Toffler, A. *The third avenue.* New York: Bantam, 1981.

Uhlenberg, P. Older women: The growing challenge to design constructive roles. *The Gerontologist,* 1979, *19,* 236–241.

U. S. Bureau of the Census. Demographic aspects of aging and the older population in the United States. *Current Population Reports,* Series P-23, No. 59. Washington, D. C.: U. S. Government Printing Office, 1976.

Weissman, M. M., & Klerman, G. L. Sex differences and the epidemiology of depression. *Archives of General Psychiatry,* 1977, *34,* 98–110.

10

Age-Role Stereotyping: Implications for Physical Activity Participation

ANDREW C. OSTROW

The positive relationship across the life cycle between participation in physical activity and physical and mental health is well documented (Johnson & Buskirk, 1974; Ostrow, 1980; Shepard, 1978). It appears that many of the known training effects associated with participation in regular programs of physical activity and exercise can be extrapolated to the older adult—even among individuals who have been inactive for many years (Adams & deVries, 1973; Clarke, 1977; Sidney & Shephard, 1977). Improvements in vital capacity, oxygen pulse, working heart rate, systolic and diastolic blood pressure, blood volume, percentage of body fat, and blood lactate concentrations have been reported among individuals, regardless of age, who engage in regular and vigorous programs of physical activity.

In addition, epidemiologic data obtained on 6928 adults (Belloc, 1973) indicate an inverse relationship between mortality rates and frequency of participation in physical activity. Participation in exercise has been proposed as a means of reversing commonly reported declines in reaction time with increasing age by facilitating stimulation of the central nervous system (Spirduso, 1980; Welford, 1977). Also, research has documented the beneficial role of physical activity in the mental health of the older adult. Reductions in anxiety, depression, and tension and enhancement of the self-concept and body image have been reported among individuals participating in programs of regular physical activity (Cureton, 1963; deVries & Adams, 1972; Olson, 1975; Sidney & Shephard, 1976).

Yet, in spite of the well-documented and publicized benefits of partici-

AGING AND MILIEU:
ENVIRONMENTAL PERSPECTIVES
ON GROWING OLD

pation in physical activity, consistent reports have surfaced indicating a declining involvement in physical activity with increasing age (Gordon, Gaitz, & Scott, 1976; McPherson & Kozlik, 1979; Ostrow, 1980; McPherson, Note 1). Data from the National Adult Fitness Survey (Clarke, 1973) indicated that only 39% of Americans aged 60 or older (N = 979) participated in any systematic exercise (primarily walking), and that there was a sharp decline in *vigorous* physical activity participation with increasing age. Cross-cultural data reviewed by McPherson (Note 1) and data obtained by Robinson (1967) confirm the decline in involvement in physical activity with increasing age. McPherson and Kozlik (1979), in a secondary analysis of data collected on the physical activity patterns of 50,000 Canadians (Table 10.1), concluded that the most dramatic declines in participation occurred after the age of 19 years and after the age of 64 years—two points in the life cycle which mark entry into and exit from the labor force. Although these data indicate that the better educated and more affluent members of each society are more inclined to participate in physical activity, a pattern of disengagement from physical activity as a function of age clearly emerges.

Traditional theoretical perspectives of aging—activity (Bengston, 1973) and disengagement (Cummings & Henry, 1961) theories would appear to be in conflict when attempting to explain the noted decline in physical activity participation with increasing age. Certainly, these data appear to violate the activity theory notion that continued participation in physical activity, particularly as traditional roles are lost, is essential for the life satisfaction, health, and general well-being of the individual. Conversely, however, studies of successful aging persons suggest that these individuals characteristically maintain participation in regular and vigorous physical activity (Palmore, 1979; Teague, 1980). Therefore, successful adjustments to aging, through a mutual and inevitable disassociation (disengagement) of the individual from society, would also seem to be in disrepute.

The disengagement perspective tends to blame the aged for their own condition (Levin & Levin, 1980). Physiological and psychological research tends to characterize the aging process as a period of decline. As Shiver's and Fait (1980) point out, "Older persons are the human signposts that forcefully indicate the imminence of death [p. 43]." As a functionalist theory, the disengagement perspective focuses on the way individuals disengage from societal roles. Disengagement is seen as a means of maintaining the functional equilibrium of the social structure. However, disengagement theorists have failed to examine the role of social systems in creating and maintaining the conditions under which the aged exist (Levin & Levin, 1980).

The basic tenet of this chapter is that to understand why the evidence

TABLE 10.1. Percentage of Participation in Sport and Exercise Programs by Age ($N = 50,000$)[a]

Age	Sport[b]	Exercise[c]	Jogging[c]	Golf[b]	Swimming[b]
15–16	82.0	86.9	53.4	16.9	60.5
17–19	73.3	75.4	34.6	15.3	53.3
20–24	66.3	63.4	19.9	15.0	44.7
25–34	61.3	62.3	12.2	12.9	38.4
35–44	51.2	53.3	9.2	11.1	30.7
45–54	37.2	50.1	5.3	8.9	20.4
55–64	24.5	45.7	2.4	6.7	11.7
65 and over	9.7	37.0	4.0	2.5	3.6

[a]Based on a secondary analysis of data collected in a 1976 Canadian Labour Force Survey as adapted from McPherson, B. D., & Kozlik, C. A. Canadian leisure patterns by age: Disengagement, continuity, or ageism? In V. M. Marshall (Ed.), *Aging in Canada: Social perspectives.* Pickering, Ontario: Fitzhenry & Whiteside, 1979.
[b]Participated at least one in the past year.
[c]Participated at least once in the past month.

points to a declining involvement in physical activity with increasing age, one must understand the underlying dynamic social forces that bring to bear pressures for the individual to disengage from physical activity. Several authors (e.g., McPherson, Note 1; McPherson & Kozlik, 1979; Snyder, Note 2) have alluded to the potential restrictive function of age as a socially constructed category defining appropriate role behaviors, including involvement in physical activity, at specific points in the life cycle. This chapter will present evidence that a blatant system of age grading exists regarding the acceptability of physical activity participation, and that this system may be responsible, in part, for the relinquishment of participation in physical activity with increasing age.

Background information on age stratification systems and the development of age roles and norms will first be reviewed. Data will then be presented describing the age grading of what is viewed as appropriate participation in physical activity across the life cycle. Preliminary data on a proposed conceptual model characterizing the stereotyping of physical activity participation based on age appropriateness will then be reviewed. The chapter will conclude with a set of recommendations for further research on understanding age-role stereotyping as it relates to physical activity participation.

THE AGE GRADING OF HUMAN BEHAVIOR

Socialization is viewed as a lifelong process whereby individuals acquire, through complex interactions with members of society, patterns of socially relevant behaviors and experiences that enable them to become and remain effective participants of that society (Kleiber & Kelley, 1980). Through socialization the individual learns appropriate role behaviors, knowledge, skills, and values. Recent evidence (e.g., Maddox & Wiley, 1976; Neugarten & Hagestad, 1976) indicates that societies tend to be stratified by age and that, through the process of socialization, age norms for a pervasive network of social control, allocation, and reward.

Age Stratification Systems

Riley (1971, 1976) proposed that American society is characterized by distinct age strata that dictate the way people behave, think, and relate to one another. "A person's activities, his attitudes toward life, his relationships to his family or work, his biological capacities, and his physical fitness are all conditioned by his position in the age structure of the particular society in which he lives [Riley, 1976, p. 189]." The study of age stratification systems is viewed as an important and emerging field of sociology.

Each age cohort, then, is seen as exposed to a potentially unique set of socially relevant experiences that dictate many behaviors evident across the life cycle, including participation in physical activity. This can be easily illustrated by the recent upsurge in participation in physical activity by women. Until the early 1970s, participation by the female in sport and physical activity was generally viewed as taboo (i.e., participation was viewed as incompatible with the enhancement of the feminine image). Sports were seen as too strenuous for women, as producing excessive muscular bulk, and as eliciting aggressive and independent behaviors—behaviors traditionally viewed as masculine-based (Harris, 1973). However, the last decade has witnessed the emergence and acceptance of women in sport, concomitant to the emancipation of women, in general, in society. If one supports a continuity perspective on aging (Atchley, 1971), it can be hypothesized that adolescent females who are active in sport today will maintain physically active life-styles throughout their life course, if they view participating in sport as a satisfying and reinforcing role. Clearly, both historical time and lifetime impact on participation by females in sport and physical activity.

The notion of age stratification systems is based on the premise that age functions as a prime criterion in the assignment of people to opportunities and responsibilities in society. Age strata are viewed as dynamic rather than static and are in covariance with the historical events of that time period (Atchley & Seltzer, 1976). Rapid social change can heighten the differences among age strata, contributing to a sense of uniqueness (and perhaps isolation) among members of a given age stratum. Social mobility of individuals from one age stratum to another is universal, unidirectional, and irreversible (Riley, 1971).

Understanding age strata permits us to make tentative hypotheses about the life course of various cohorts. For example, the size of the aged stratum at the turn of the next century should be small, reflecting the low birth rate during the depression; however, during the early decades of the coming century, the size of the aged cohort should markedly increase as a result of a "baby boom" that occurred after World War II (Riley, 1971). If one can project the current emphasis on physical fitness across time, then it can be hypothesized that this baby boom will impose great demands for recreational services and sport facilities during their retirement in the next century.

Clearly, however, the use of chronological age (or lifetime) alone as a predictor of human behavior and events is inadequate. It is naive to make judgments about physical (and mental) functioning on the basis of age without considering the social context in which these judgments are made. It is Neugarten's contention (Neugarten, 1980; Neugarten & Datan, 1973; Neugarten & Hagestad, 1976) that lifetime and historical time must be examined within the framework of social time (i.e., within the context of understanding how age roles, age norms, and age statuses systematically regulate self-perceptions and human behavior).

Age Roles and Age Norms

In West Virginia, the Monongalia County Consolidated Recreation Commission sponsors an "Over the Hump" Basketball League for individuals over 30 years of age. Until 2 years ago, one of the modified basketball rules in this league specified that no "fast-breaks" were allowed (i.e., the offensive team could not bring the ball down until the defensive team had a chance to set themselves up at their end of the court). Pete Rose, the professional baseball player, has been characterized as the "ageless wonder" by an Associated Press writer as he approaches the National League hitting record at the ripe old age (in baseball) of 41. During the 1970s, George Allen, coach of the Washington Redskins professional football team, was known to recruit experienced and vintage defensive lineman and linebackers in their 30s–they were known as the "Over the Hill" gang. The United States Handball Association (as do other sport associations) stratify individuals by age when setting up tournaments; the Masters Handball tournaments are for individuals over 40, and the "Golden" Masters tournaments are for individuals over 50 years of age. The observance of an elderly female jogging in a rural West Virginia community is probably as frequent as the observance of sheep grazing in Brooklyn.

These examples serve to illustrate that age, like race or sex, is an attribute that clearly regulates many of the normative expectations affecting participation in sport and physical activity. Age-related norms tell us that kids go to school; adults get married; and the elderly should not be interested in sex or singles in tennis. Neugarten and Datan (1973) suggest that different sets of age expectations and age statuses operate across and within societies: "Every society has a system of social expectations regarding age-appropriate behavior, and these expectations are internalized as the individual grows up and grows old, and as he moves from one age stratum to the next [p. 59]." Through socialization, individual members of each cohort learn specific roles based on age, and the concomitant behaviors associated with each of these roles (Neugarten & Hagestad, 1976).

Conceptually, this system of age grading produces two forms of age-appropriate behavior—*ascriptive* age norms and *consensual* age norms (Neugarten & Datan, 1973). Ascriptive age norms are based on clearly specified societal age-regulated rules and constraints. For example, in many states it is legal to drive a car at 16 and drink at 18 years of age; mandatory retirement laws dictate retirement at age 70. In sport, entries into tournaments are stratified based on chronological age.

Consensual age norms specify the assumed age range in which people are expected to acquire or relinquish certain roles. In sport and physical activity, it is often assumed that one will retreat to doubles (rather than singles) in handball or tennis with advancing age. The playing of touch football would probably be viewed as childish for middle-aged men (and as abhorrent for middle-aged women). In fact, the promotion of "life-time" sports suggests the differential acceptability of participating in various sports at specific points in the life cycle.

In short, consensual age norms suggest that each of us have built-in time clocks that carefully regulate the roles we assume when we are on time, and relinquish when we are off time. Our sensitivity to this time clock influences our pride and estimates of self-worth (Neugarten & Datan, 1973). How many of us have enhanced (or protected) our self-esteem in sport by proclaiming, "Take it easy on the old man?" This self-debasing attitude toward participation in physical activity is particularly apparent among the elderly, who generally feel that their need for physical activity diminishes with increasing age and who tend to vastly exaggerate the risks involved in vigorous exercise (Ostrow, 1980).

Ageism

Age-role *stereotypes* refer to a set of commonly held beliefs about the way people are supposed to behave based on age. For example, old age is typically characterized as synonymous with isolation, poverty, and sickness. The older person is traditionally viewed as someone who moves and thinks slowly, who lacks creativity and ambition, and who is irritable, cantankerous, shallow, rigid, conservative, and enfeebled—in short, the picture of physical and mental decline (Butler, 1975). When our views about aging are discriminatory and prejudicial in nature, we are guilty of practicing *ageism* (Butler, 1969). Trippatt (1980), in an essay on ageism in *Time* magazine, warned that the foreclosure of the elderly from society's respect and admiration will mean serious generational conflict in the future. Robert Butler (1969) prophesied that ageism would parallel racism as the great issue of the remaining decades of this century.

The practice of ageism is rampant in our society. Perhaps the most visible example is the picture of older adults portrayed as consumers. Usually, they are seen as decrepit and toothless consumers of laxatives, denture adhesives, or sleeping pills. Most television commercials lead us to believe that fun and vigorous leisure activity belong solely to the young. How often have we seen a physically active older adult portrayed on television? Advertisers are beginning to recognize, however, that the older segment of our population is more diverse than homogeneous and that it is growing in importance. As the *Wall Street Journal* pointed out, older adults drink Pepsi too (Abrams, 1981).

In sport and physical activity, the practice of ageism is often less visible and apparent. There is an underlying assumption of decline, of declining reaction time, movement speed, and an overall reduction in physical function with increasing age. Opportunities and incentives for continued practice of proficiently executed motor skills diminish. The individual develops reduced expectancies for cardiovascular and psychomotor function. These diminished self-expectancies, coupled with social expectations that one should act his age and that one should be less competitive and expect less from a competitive outcome, lead many individuals to gradually disengage from sport and physical activity as they grow older.

Ageism is also evident in the blatant misuse of chronological age as the sole criterion for determining entry levels in competitive sport tournaments. Why have we not considered developmental function, as well as age, in assigning people to competitive slots? Ageism may also exist in professional sports, where athletes are encouraged to retire "early." An athlete who fails to recognize that age often dictates his or her potential usefulness is subtly (and sometimes mercilessly) eliminated from a squad.

Unfortunately, the empirical evidence shedding light on the phenomenon of ageism and age-role stereotyping in sport and physical activity is nonexistent. This is particularly surprising in view of the enormous attention devoted to racism and sexism in sport that has paralleled, in general, society's increasing concerns with these social issues. Although several authors (e.g., McPherson, Note 1; McPherson & Kozlik, 1979; Snyder, Note 2) have discussed the potential impact of ageism, age norms, and age stratification systems on participation in physical activity, carefully designed empirical investigations of these phenomena would appear warranted.

AGE-ROLE STEREOTYPING AND PHYSICAL ACTIVITY
PARTICIPATION: A PRELIMINARY REPORT

My colleagues and I (Ostrow, Jones, & Spiker, 1981; Ostrow & Spiker, Note 3) have intitiated a preliminary set of investigations designed to determine and contrast the stereotyping of sport participation based on age-role and/or sex-role appropriateness. Samples of 93 undergraduate female nursing students (Ostrow, Jones, & Spiker, 1981) and 444 students (Ostrow & Spiker, Note 3) enrolled in the physical education basic instructional program at West Virginia University were administered an Activity Appropriateness Scale (AAS) developed by the investigators and Bem's (1974) Sex-Role Inventory (BSRI). Subjects were asked to rate on the AAS how appropriate they felt it was for eight referent persons, who varied in assigned chronological age (20, 40, 60, or 80 years old) and assigned gender, to participate in 12 designated physical activities, including bowling, tennis, marathon racing, basketball, swimming, bicycling, and so on. For example, subjects were asked to rate how appropriate they felt it was for an 80-year-old healthy female, a 60-year-old healthy male, and so on, to participate in swimming (and 11 other physical activities). These 12 physical activities were selected based on (a) a literature review (Del Rey, 1976; Fisher, Genovese, Morris, & Morris, 1978) that identified certain physical activities as being stereotyped as more masculine or feminine; and (b) the intuitive judgment of the investigators that certain physical activities may be stereotyped as differentially appropriate at specific points in the life cycle.

Test–retest (10-day interval) reliability coefficients on independent samples of male subjects ($N = 54$) and female subjects ($N = 46$), averaged across sport, were low to moderate (.73 males; .64 females); similarly, test–retest reliability coefficients, averaged across referent person, were low to moderate (.76 males; .68 females). The order of presentation of the eight referent persons and 12 physical activities was randomly assigned on the AAS.

Bem's (1974) Sex-Role Inventory was administered to subjects in these two investigations to determine the relationship of their sex-role orientation to their typing of physical activity participation based on sex-role and/or age-role appropriateness. Subjects were classified into one of four possible sex-role orientation categories—masculine, feminine, androgynous, or undifferentiated. This was based on their responses to a set of positive, socially valued, but culturally sex-typed characteristics contained in the inventory that depicted either masculine or feminine role preferences. Subjects were sex typed as masculine or feminine based on the degree to which they endorsed masculine items to the exclusion of feminine items or vice versa. Subjects who endorsed equal proportions of masculine- and feminine-typed items were classified as androgynous, whereas subjects who failed to endorse either masculine- or feminine-typed items were classified as undifferentiated. Conceptually, the BSRI rejects the traditional notion that masculinity and femininity are bipolar dimensions on a unidimensional continuum; rather, an orthogonal two-dimensional model of sex roles forms the conceptual basis for Bem's construction of independent feminine and masculine scales (Kelly & Worell, 1977).

The data from both investigations were analyzed using a series of univariate ANOVA across physical activity. The results of both studies were remarkably consistent. Table 10.2 presents a summary of computed F-ratios depicting differences in these subjects' responses to the appropriateness of participating in various physical activities as a function of the age and gender of the referent person.

The main effect of age of the referent person accounted for an average of 27.99% and 28.28% of the variance of subjects' responses to the AAS in Study 1 (Ostrow, Jones, & Spiker, 1981) and Study 2 (Ostrow & Spiker, Note 3), respectively. The variance estimates accounted for by age for each physical activity were remarkably consistent across both investigations. Age-related social prescriptions appeared to be more evident for basketball, tennis, and racquetball than for bowling or achery. Subsequent comparisons revealed that participation was viewed as less appropriate with increasing age (i.e., from 20 to 40 to 60 to 80 years old) for *each* physical activity investigated.

The main effect of gender of the referent person accounted for an average of 1.45% and 2.97% of the variance of subjects' responses to the

TABLE 10.2. F-ratios Depicting Responses to Physical Activity Participation Appropriateness as a Function of the Age and Gender of the Referent Person[a]

Physical activity	Study 1 ($N = 93$)		Study 2 ($N = 444$)	
	Age	Gender	Age	Gender
Archery	143.49°	114.00°	490.99°	505.84°
	(17.44)	(4.62)	(14.19)	(4.87)
Ballet	182.35°	92.39°	771.45°	341.14°
	(21.69)	(3.66)	(21.12)	(3.11)
Basketball	281.56°	138.58°	1786.33°	1004.76°
	(36.61)	(6.00)	(41.89)	(7.85)
Bicycling	129.54°	3.25	713.41°	50.80°
	(24.62)		(24.79)	(0.01)
Bowling	74.82°	1.27	360.65°	89.30°
	(16.22)		(13.63)	(1.13)
Figure skating	263.09°	7.63°	1014.31°	54.58°
	(30.33)	(0.00)	(27.51)	(0.00)
Jogging	189.90°	7.53°	963.95°	129.06°
	(28.24)	(0.00)	(29.27)	(1.31)
Marathon race	295.89°	65.89°	1697.63°	509.09°
	(35.54)	(2.75)	(38.10)	(3.81)
Raquetball	374.42°	38.92°	1668.04°	426.75°
	(40.46)	(0.00)	(41.74)	(3.56)
Shot put	211.80°	177.43°	1143.06°	1182.36°
	(22.24)	(6.21)	(25.40)	(8.76)
Swimming	114.41°	1.09	593.41°	81.28°
	(21.43)		(19.92)	(0.01)
Tennis	290.58°	5.14°°	1496.86°	124.08°
	(41.04)	(0.00)	(41.81)	(1.16)

[a]Numbers in parentheses represent percentages of accountable variance in ANOVA model.
°$p < .01$.
°°$p < .05$.

AAS. Generally, subjects in both investigations viewed participation in physical activity across the life cycle as more appropriate for men than women. However, participation in ballet and figure skating was seen as more appropriate for women than men. Table 10.2 presents an overview of subjects' typing of physical activity based on gender appropriateness.

Neugarten and Hagestad (1976) suggested that it is fruitless to study age-regulated systems in isolation, since they always operate in conjunction with gender status. To test this premise, age of the referent person × gender of the referent person interactions were examined. Although few interactions (except for figure skating and shot put) were statistically significant in Study 1, these interactions (except for racquetball) were statistically significant in Study 2. Figure 10.1 illustrates and contrasts the nature of these interactions for basketball (an age-dictated activity) and ballet (a female-appropriate activity). For ballet and basketball, differences in perceived gender appropriateness generally decreased as the

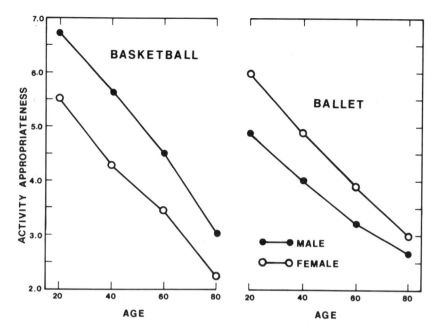

FIGURE 10.1. Subjects' (*N* = 444) ratings of physical activity appropriateness as a function of the age and sex of the referent person. (Data are from Ostrow & Spiker, Note 3.)

age of the referent person increased. Thus, age-regulated social prescriptions for physical activity appear to be different for men and women.

Surprisingly, in both investigations, subjects' sex-role orientation did not appear to interact with their typing of physical activity participation based on gender appropriateness. However, even more surprisingly were the numerous sex roles of the subject × age of the referent person interactions that were statistically significant. At this point, it is conceptually unclear to me why a subject's sex-role orientation should influence his or her age-role assignments for physical activity. Replicative and confirmatory investigations on this issue would appear to be warranted.

The results of both investigations provide evidence that age is a far more potent attribute than gender in dictating these subjects' perceptions of the appropriateness of participating in physical activity across the life cycle. Recently, Neugarten (1980) optimistically predicted that we were on the verge of becoming an age-irrelevant society—that the internal age-regulated time clock she used to write about was no longer as powerful or as compelling. It appears that her message has not yet reached these college students. They have clear, age-regulated social prescriptions regarding the extent to which we should be involved in physical activity as we grow older.

A CONCEPTUAL MODEL CHARACTERIZING
THE AGE-ROLE STEREOTYPING
OF PHYSICAL ACTIVITY

The data presented in the previous section, although restricted to college students, indicate that these individuals maintain age-regulated normative expectations which may regulate, to some extent, their involvement in physical activity across the life cycle. What is not clear is *why* these individuals perceive physical activity as differentially appropriate at specific points in the life cycle.

The Model

My colleague and I (Ostrow & Spiker, Note 4) propose a four-factor conceptual model that may depict, in part, why physical activity participation is perceived as differentially appropriate across the life cycle. We have labeled these four factors as (*a*) *somatic*; (*b*) *neurophysiological*; (*c*) *skill acquisition*; and (*d*) *emotional*. These proposed factors are based on a limited body of empirical evidence which sheds light on physical activity and aging.

Briefly, we suggest that these subjects' perceptions that physical activity participation is less appropriate with advancing age can be attributed to the traditionally accepted notion of aging as a process of decline and withdrawal. For example, there is ample evidence (e.g., Clarke, 1977; Shephard, 1978) to suggest that a gradual deterioration in the physiological functioning of the body takes place during the middle and later adult years. Of course, what is not clear is the extent to which exercise, proper diet, reductions in stress, and so on, can defer or retard the body's decline. We believe, however, that college students typically see advancing age as a period of physiological decline with concomitant reductions in cardiovascular fitness and muscular endurance and strength. Older people are often stereotyped as ill, weak, and tired (McTavish, 1971; Tibbitts, 1979). Therefore, we propose a *somatic* factor that we believe articulates physiological decline with advancing age.

Similarly, there is evidence (e.g., Shephard, 1978; Welford, 1977) to suggest psychomotor decline as we grow older. Welford (1977), in an extensive review of industrial and human factors research, concluded that reaction time and movement time increase with advancing age. This is particularly true if movements involving manipulation cannot be prepared in advance. Older adults sometimes develop alternative strategies, such as increased cautiousness, meticulousness, and precision, in attempting to minimize movement decrements. It is not clear, however, to what extent these decrements can be slowed or reversed by continued practice of psychomotor skills. As Welford (1977) has postulated, exercise may reverse the commonly reported declines in movement by reducing the potential for cardiovascular impairment and by facilitating stimulation of the central nervous system. Traditionally, however, the middle and later adult years are associated with rapid declines in psychomotor capacity and efficiency. Older people are stereotyped as slow, forgetful, restricted in movement, and unable to learn new skills (McTavish, 1971; Tibbetts, 1979).

To account for perceptions of psychomotor decline, we propose two factors that we have labeled as *neurophysiological* and *skill acquisition*. The neurophysiological component focuses directly on perceptions of deterioration in reaction time and movement speed with advancing age. The skill acquisition factor relates to one's gradual inability to execute with proficiency and accuracy complex skills that are inherent in various sport activities (e.g., shooting foul shots in basketball with accuracy). We believe that this skill acquisition factor will explain the stereotype that older people cannot benefit from practice in their attempt to master complex motor skills.

Finally, we propose an *emotional* factor that is intricately tied to success in competitive sport activities. Older persons are often stereotyped as withdrawn and anxious (McTavish, 1971; Tibbitts, 1979). Welford (1958) has observed that the elderly evidence few risk-taking behaviors when performing motor skills, whereas Conrad (1976) has suggested that older adults vastly exaggerate the risks involved in exercise. We suggest that younger people will associate advancing age with decreased self-confidence and increased anxiety and avoidance behaviors during competive motor skill performance—behaviors that we feel will account, in part, for the age-role stereotyping of physical activity.

Validation of the Model

To establish the construct validity of this four-factor conceptual model, we have developed a 20-item Likert-format questionnaire (5 items/factor) for the physical activities of basketball and tennis. Basketball and tennis were the targeted activities based on the large variance estimates derived for the main effect of age in the two studies (Ostrow, Jones, & Spiker, 1981; Ostrow & Spiker, Note 3) described in the previous section.

Originally, a pool of 40 items (10 items/factor) was established for each activity. These items were carefully evaluated by a panel of six graduate students in physical education at West Virginia University to assess their clarity and content validity. Based on their review, and after several item revisions, 20 items per physical activity were retained for further analyses. Figure 10.2 illustrates items that were generated for each hypothesized factor in tennis.

Students ($N = 116$ males; $N = 112$ females) enrolled in the physical education basic instructional program at West Virginia University were administered both questionnaires (in random order). These subjects were asked to respond on a 7-point ordinal scale the extent to which they felt each item characterized the basketball or tennis performances of eight referent persons of varying assigned chronological ages (20, 40, 60, or 80 years old) and gender. For example, they were asked whether they agreed, disagreed, strongly disagreed, and so on, that a 60-year-old female could hit a tennis serve with accuracy. Several of the items per factor on each questionnaire were counterbalanced to minimize the potential response set of acquiescence. The order of presentation of each item and each referent person was randomly established within each questionnaire.

Exploratory factor analyses were performed on subjects' responses to each physical activity. Principal component analyses followed by both orthogonal (varimax) and oblique (promax) rotations were conducted. Although the data for basketball are currently being analyzed, preliminary analyses of the tennis data suggest partial conformation of the model. The skill acquisition and somatic factors appear to be most viable at this point, whereas there appears to be little support for the proposed emotional and neurophysiological factors as explanations for the age grading of tennis.

Most interestingly, skill acquisition appears to become the most prominent explanatory factor with the advancing age of the referent person. In other words, there seems to be a subtle suggestion that these college students feel that older persons should reduce their involvement in tennis because they cannot continue to perform the complex motor skills required in tennis with accuracy and authority.

It is apparent that this research needs to be extended across a variety of

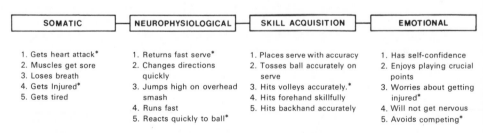

FIGURE 10.2. A conceptual model characterizing age-role stereotyping in tennis. *Reverse scored item. High score equals positive attitude toward aging.

physical activities that have been shown to be age-dictated. Furthermore, the age grading of physical activity must be verified among a number of cohorts (besides college students). In addition, continued item sampling and revision must occur if we are to understand why participation in physical activity is perceived as differentially appropriate across the life cycle. It is suggested, however, that theoretical and empirical models must be carefully linked if we are to understand why age-regulated social prescriptions exist for participation in physical activity.

SUMMARY AND RECOMMENDATIONS

This chapter has proposed the thesis that a decline in involvement in physical activity with advancing age may be attributable, in part, to the age grading of physical activity participation. A conceptual framework for understanding the age grading of human behavior was first presented. Data from two recent investigations were then reviewed in an attempt to document the finding that college students have clear, age-regulated social prescriptions regarding the extent to which we should be involved in physical activity as we grow older. Finally, the construct validity of a proposed conceptual model was examined which may help us understand why participation in physical activity is perceived as differentially appropriate across the life cycle.

Clearly, a number of cohorts need to be asked to what extent continued participation in physical activity is appropriate as we grow older. Of particular interest to this author is the important developmental question of when and how age-role expectancies for physical activity participation first evolve. Young children seem to already have clear social prescriptions for what older persons can and cannot do (McTavish, 1971). How important are physically active parents and grandparents as role models for our children? What impact has television had in portraying the older adult as listless and decrepit, rather than as active and alive?

It would be fallacious to assume that the age grading of human behavior can account for the myriad of variables that preclude our involvement in physical activity with advancing age. Similarly, it would be fallacious to promote vigorous physical activity participation for all adults without first adapting and prescribing physical activities based on individual tolerance levels. What is clear, however, is that participation in physical activity must be based on developmental appropriateness rather than age appropriateness and that age stereotypes and other social barriers must be eliminated if participation in physical activity is to occur across the life span of each individual.

REFERENCE NOTES

1. McPherson, B. D. *Aging and involvement in physical activity: A sociological perspective.* Paper presented at the International Congress of Physical Activity Sciences, Quebec City, 1976.
2. Snyder, E. E. *A reflection on commitment and patterns of disengagement from recreational physical activity.* Paper presented to the North American Society for the Sociology of Sport convention, Denver, 1980.
3. Ostrow, A. C., & Spiker, D. D. *The stereotyping of sport participation based on age role and sex role appropriateness.* Paper presented at the North American Society for the Psychology of Sport and Physical Activity annual convention. Monterey, California, 1981.
4. Ostrow, A. C., & Spiker, D. D. *Validation of a conceptual model characterizing the age role stereotyping of physical activity.* Research in progress, 1981.

REFERENCES

Abrams, B. Advertisers start recognizing cost of insulting elderly. *Wall Street Journal,* March 5, 1981, p. 27.

Adams, G. M., & deVries, H. A. Physiological effects of an exercise training regimen upon women aged 52 to 79. *Journal of Gerontology,* 1973, *28,* 50–55.

Atchley, R. Retirement and leisure participation: Continuity or crisis? *The Gerontologist,* 1971, *11,* 13–17.

Atchley, R. C., & Seltzer, M. M. *The sociology of aging: Selected readings.* Belmont, California: Wadsworth, 1976.

Belloc, N. B. Relationship of health practices and mortality. *Preventive Medicine,* 1973, *2,* 67.

Bem, S. L. The measurement of psychological androgyny. *Journal of Consulting and Clinical Psychology,* 1974, *42,* 155–162.

Bengtson, V. L. *The social psychology of aging.* New York: Bobbs–Merrill, 1973.

Butler, R. N. Age-ism: Another form of bigotry. *The Gerontologist,* 1969, *9,* 243–246.

Butler, R. N. *Why survive? Being old in America.* New York: Harper & Row, 1975.

Clarke, H. H. (Ed.). National Adult Physical Fitness Survey. *President's Council on Physical Fitness and Sports Newsletter,* 1973, 1–27.

Clarke, H. H. (Ed.). Exercise and aging. *Physical Fitness Research Digest,* 1977, *7,* 1–27.

Conrad, C. C. When you're young at heart. *Aging,* 1976, *258,* 11–13.

Cumming, E., & Henry, W. E. *Growing old: The process of disengagement.* New York: Basic Books, 1961.

Cureton, T. H. Improvement of psychological states by means of exercise fitness programs. *Journal of Association of Physical and Mental Rehabilitation,* 1963, *17,* 14–17.

Del Rey, P. In support of apologetics for women in sport. In. R. W. Christina & D. M. Landers (Eds.). *Psychology of motor behavior and sport–1976.* Champaign, Ill.: Human Kinetics, 1976.

deVries, H. A., & Adams, G. M.|Electromyographic comparison of single doses of exercise and meprobamate as to effects on muscular relaxation. *American Journal of Physical Medicine,* 1972, *3,* 130–141.

Fisher, A. C., Genovese, P. O., Morris, K. J., & Morris, H. H. Perceptions of women in sport. In D. M. Landers and R. L. Christina (Eds.), *Psychology of motor behavior and sport–1977.* Champaign, Ill.: Human Kinetics, 1978.

Gordon, C., Gaitz, C., & Scott, J. Leisure and lives: Personal expressivity across the life span. In R. H. Binstock & E. Shanas (Eds.), *Handbook of aging and the social sciences*. New York: Van Nostrand Reinhold, 1976.

Harris, D. V. *Involvement in sport: A somatopsychic rationale for physical activity*. Philadelphia: Lea & Febiger, 1973.

Johnson, W. R., & Buskirk, E. R. (Eds.). *Science and medicine of exercise and sport*. New York: Harper & Row, 1974.

Kelly, J. A., & Worell, J. New formulations of sex roles and androgyny: A critical review. *Journal of Consulting and Clinical Psychology*, 1977, *45*, 1101–1115.

Kleiber, D. A., & Kelly, J. R. Leisure, socialization and the life cycle. In S. E. Iso-Ahola (Ed.), *Social psychological perspectives in leisure and recreation*. Springfield, Ill.: Charles C Thomas, 1980.

Levin, J., & Levin, W. C. *Ageism: Prejudice and discrimination against the elderly*. Belmont, California: Wadsworth, 1980.

Maddox, G. L., & Wiley, J. Scope, concepts, and methods in the study of aging. In R. H. Binstock & E. Shanas (Eds.),*Handbook of aging and the social sciences*. New York: Van Nostrand Reinhold, 1976.

McPherson, B. D., & Kozlik, C. A. Canadian leisure patterns by age: Disengagement, continuity, or ageism? In V. W. Marshall (Ed.), *Aging in Canada: Social perspectives*. Pickering, Ontario: Fitzhenry & Whiteside, 1979.

McTavish, D. G. Perceptions of old people. A review of research methodologies and findings. *The Gerontologist*, 1971, *11*, 90–108.

Neugarten, B. L. Acting one's age: New rules for old. *Psychology Today*, 1980, *14*, 66–80.

Neugarten, B. L., & Datan, N. Sociological perspectives on the life cycle. In P. B. Baltes & K. W. Schaie (Eds.), *Life-span developmental psychology: Personality and socialization*. New York: Academic Press, 1973.

Neugarten, B. L., & Hagestad, G. O. Age and the life course. In R. H. Binstock & E. Shanas (Eds.), *Handbook of aging and the social sciences*. New York: Van Nostrand Reinhold, 1976.

Olson, M. I. *The effects of physical activity on the body image of nursing home residents*. Unpublished Master's thesis. Springfield, Mass.: Springfield College, 1975.

Ostrow, A. C. Physical activity as it relates to the health of the aged. In N. Datan & N. Lohmann (Eds.), *Transitions of aging*. New York: Academic Press, 1980.

Ostrow, A. C., Jones, D. C., & Spiker, D. D. Age role expectations and sex role expectations for selected sport activities. *Research Quarterly for Exercise and Sport*, 1981, *52*, 216–227.

Palmore, E. Predictors of successful aging. *The Gerontologist*, 1979, *19*, 427–431.

Riley, M. W. Social gerontology and the age stratification of society. *The Gerontologist*, 1971, *11*, 79–87.

Riley, M. W. Age strata in social systems. In R. H. Binstock & E. Shanas (Eds.), *Handbook of aging and the social sciences*. New York: Van Nostrand Reinhold, 1976.

Robinson, J. Time expenditure on sports across ten countries. *International Review of Sport Sociology 1967*, *2*, 67–87.

Shephard, R. J. *Physical activity and aging*. Chicago: Year Book Medical Publishers, 1978.

Shivers, J. S., & Fait, H. F. *Recreational service for the aging*. Philadelphia: Lea & Febiger, 1980.

Sidney, K. H., & Shephard, R. J. Attitudes toward health and physical activity in the elderly: Effects of a physical training program. *Medicine and Science in Sports*, 1976, *8*, 246–252.

Sidney, K. H., & Shephard, R. J. Maximum and submaximum exercise tests in men and women in the seventh, eighth, and ninth decades of life. *Journal of Applied Physiology*, 1977, *43*, 280–287.

Spirduso, W. W. Physical fitness, aging, and psychomotor speed: A review. *Journal of Gerontology*, 1980, *35*, 850–865.

Teague, M. L. Aging and leisure: A social psychological perspective. In S. E. Iso-Ahola (Ed.), *Social psychological perspectives on leisure and recreation*. Springfield, Ill.: Charles C Thomas, 1980.

Tibbitts, C. Can we invalidate negative stereotypes of aging? *The Gerontologist*, 1979, *19*, 10–20.

Trippatt, F. Looking askance at ageism. *Time*, March 24, 1980, p. 88.

Welford, A. T. *Aging and human skill*. London: Oxford University Press, 1958.

Welford, A. T. Motor performance. In J. E. Birren & K. W. Schaie (Eds.), *Handbook of the psychology of aging*. New York: Van Nostrand Reinhold, 1977.

11

Working with Older People: The Patient–Physician Milieu[1]

LUCILLE NAHEMOW

The patient–physician milieu is a series of environments, each of which contains a unique collection of behavior settings.[2] For example, hospitals have many behavior settings, such as admitting offices and operating rooms, each of which requires different kinds of behavior. People play different roles inside the hospital than they do outside the hospital: such as doctor, nurse, administrator, or patient, rather than father, parishioner, or salesman. Parsons (1975) was the first to call attention to the fact that the sick person plays a socially defined role which cannot be explained in terms of illness alone. Most of us can remember a time when we were working, despite a headache and scratchy throat, and suddenly thought, "I'm really sick!" Our behavior changed markedly. We went home to bed. The illness had not increased during the 5-minute interval; the difference involved assumption of the sick role. A characteristic of the sick role is dependency. It represents a way in which one can avoid the demands of everyday living. In exchange for not having to make the usual life decisions, one delegates the right and obligation to do so to another.

---

[1]Funded in part by Grants #90-A1825 and #2A-51A from Model Projects in Aging Program, Administration on Aging, Office of Human Development Services; Department of Health and Human Services, Washington, D.C. 20201.

[2]A behavior setting is a place in which specific activities take place; the same people and objects are transformed into different patterns as they pass from one behavior setting to another, and conversely, different sets of people and objects exhibit the same pattern within a particular behavior setting (Barker, 1976).

AGING AND MILIEU:
ENVIRONMENTAL PERSPECTIVES
ON GROWING OLD

The environments comprising the patient–physician milieu can be seen as falling along a continuum in terms of size and complexity:

Hospital	Long-term-care institution	Clinic	Doctor's office	Home care

The hospital milieu is so complex that it has been likened to a city. At the other end, one's own home becomes a temporary patient–physician behavior setting.

These environments could be delineated in an almost infinite variety of ways. Moos (1980) provides a multidimensional conceptual framework which considers the provision of opportunities for choice and control by the older individual in the environmental setting. French, Rodgers, and Cobb (1974), Kahana (1975), and Lawton and Nahemow (1973) all developed theories of person–environment fit. Labouvie-Vief and Chandler (1978) developed a theory which takes into account the total context of the individual. All of the medical environments could be studied from each theoretical vantage point, exploring the physical environment, and each would provide some insights. However, the most critical factors operating within the patient–physician milieu tend to be the unseen.

Calhoun (1968), in *Space as a Strategy of Life* talks about the human capability to substitute conceptual space for physical space. The more advanced the civilization, the more the conceptual or the metaphorical substitute for the concrete. The medical environment, it seems to me, can only be understood in terms of this conceptual space. In *Illness as Metaphor*, Sontag (1978) discusses the imbedded environmental meaning in beliefs regarding tuberculosis and cancer. To a being from Mars, a house and street would be comprehensible places, whereas a hospital would not. Similarly, the emotions elicited by a thunderstorm or a tidal wave would be obvious, but the emotions in a doctor's office are tied to beliefs rather than to physical reality. Hypertension, diabetes, and the other chronic illnesses to which old people are prone may not be visible, but they are very real, and they dominate the transactions which occur. The fear of death created by the word *cancer* can be palpable. If we look at the continuum of environments comprising the patient–physician milieu, they seem to vary in the dominance of the conceptual, or "hidden," dimension. Perhaps because of its novelty and complexity, and perhaps because it elicits strong emotions, in the hospital environment the conceptual dimension is paramount.

Most doctors have their initial contact with patients in hospitals. During 3 years of residency, physicians spend almost all their time in the hospital.

They see many geriatric patients and deal with issues of life and death; they also eat there and make friends there. Eventually, the hospital becomes a place in which doctors feel comfortable, in which they are "at home." In contrast, patients are singularly uncomfortable. They usually associate hospitals with unhappy memories and find the hospital a disorienting, painful, and frightening place. Patients are in a position of dependency and powerlessness. Usually they are aware of their lack of control over the environment. This knowledge adds to the fear produced by the knowledge of the illness itself.

Power and helplessness will be the theme of this chapter. It is a theme that I believe to be a dominant one in patient–physician transactions. Power imbalance is ubiquitous to the patient–physician milieu. Rodin and Janis (1979) examined the sources of social power and influence that affect the degree to which patients adhere to recommended regimens for prevention or treatment and their rate of recovery. Using the following classification of ways in which authority figures exert social influence (coercive power, reward power, legitimate power, and referent power), they postulate that "referent power" would be most likely to promote patient compliance. They state

> Persons have referent power for those who perceive them as likeable, benevolent, admirable, and accepting, and their motivating power derives from this source. We further expect that the same circumstances that promote internalization also serve to increase patients' feelings of choice and control because they perceive themselves to be acting on the basis of internal, self-motivated norms and goals. Research has shown that greater feelings of control increase behavioral commitment and play an important role in facilitating adherence [p. 62].

The article discusses ways in which the health care professional can establish, use, and maintain "referent power."

Bain (1976) studied doctor–patient communication in general practice consultation and found that the doctor typically initiated more verbal interactions than the patients, who frequently accepted a subordinate role in which the main verbal contribution involved symptom presentation. In a review of the literature on compliance with medical regimens, Marston (1970) concluded that patient report is the easiest method for measuring patient compliance, but discrepancies between patient reports and more objective measures such as pill count and excretion tests made the former suspect. Davis (1966) reviewed the literature finding that doctors attributed most noncompliance to either the patient's inability to understand or to an "uncooperative personality," and Roter (1977) discovered "the preponderance of sociological and psychological models characterizing

the patient role in medically related interactions [to be] passive [p. 304]."
When belief and knowledge are involved, discussions of the patient–
physician milieu have typically been from the point of view of the health
care provider. The patient's beliefs about health and illness have usually
been reduced to studies of compliance or "adherence" to medical recom-
mendation (see DeMatteo & Friedman, 1979).

PATIENT BELIEF SYSTEMS

Becker (1974) developed a health belief model, which stated that for
individuals to seek out a doctor they must first believe themselves to be
susceptible to illness, then perceive the health problem as serious and
possible action as beneficial. Such beliefs are strongly influenced by
culture and socioeconomic level.

A pilot study is now underway at New York University Medical Center
in which Meryl Domenitz, Pam Davis, and I have been interviewing
patients waiting at the new medical Geriatric Clinic in Bellevue Hospital
in order to investigate the beliefs that patients have about their illnesses,
their bodies, and their treatments. This clinic is unusual in that it is
attended by physicians with high academic rank and subspecialty board
certification (Freedman, in press). The clinic began 3½ years ago, at which
time there was one physician, a nurse, and a social worker who met two
afternoons each week and served 100 frail, elderly people. Today there
are 14 physicians, nurse practitioners, social workers, and a host of support
staff and students in medicine and social work. The clinic also has
considerable research and a strong teaching component. Third- and
fourth-year students do clinical rotations there, and the clinic staff
developed 9 hours of instruction in geriatrics, which is required for
second-year students. The clinic is currently caring for approximately
1500 people. It is a good place to do research on patient beliefs for many
reasons, not the least of which is that the physicians are cooperative,
interested, and secure enough in their clinical manner that they are
prepared to collaborate and openly discuss their views.

Thus far, 50 patients have been interviewed. Considerably more women
than men attend the clinic, and more women were interviewed for this
investigation. The median age was 78 years (those interviewed ranged
from 55 to 91). In answer to the first question, "Why are you here today?",
one–half responded that they had appointments with the doctor or nurse-
practitioner and had come for either a checkup or a specific procedure.
Most needed additional medication. The remaining people mentioned
particular illnesses, functional problems, or the need for pain control. One

woman came to accompany her husband. When the data was tallied for specific ailments mentioned, a potpourri of medical problems emerged— 27 in all. The most frequently mentioned were arthritis (15), hypertension (8), and heart trouble (5). Five patients complained that they had difficulty walking.

Some of those who attend are picked up in the morning by a minibus. Consequently, they may have considerable waiting time in the clinic. Although they may wait for an hour or two, when asked if they would talk to us for a few minutes, most patients said uneasily,"I don't know; my doctor may call me any minute."

Patients were asked about their illnesses (most had several). For each condition, they were asked about the symptoms, the medications they took, and how those medications worked. In order to elicit as much detail as possible, we asked such questions as "what would happen if you did not take your medications?" "If you went away and forgot [each medication], what would you do?" and "If you had a question and your doctor was not available to answer it, what would you do?" There was also a series of questions about life-style issues including diet, which was explored in great detail.

All of the patients had enough of an idea about what their medications were so that they could obtain them at the pharmacy. However, many referred to the medications by appearance rather than by name. Whether that was because they did not know the name or thought that we did not is unclear. Unfortunately, because Bellevue is a public facility, the pharmacy must obtain the lowest bidder's drug supplies, and consequently, suppliers change and the appearance of standard medications changes. The pink, round one this month could conceivably become the yellow, oval one next month. About one-half of the patients could give a simple functional explanation for how the major medications worked, for example, "it thins the blood so the heart can pump it," or "it helps my heart beat stronger." However, virtually no one provided an explanation of how it helped the heart beat stronger (each person was asked the question: "What is the way that it works?").

The most interesting answers came in response to questions regarding what they would do if the expected supports were not available, that is, if the doctor were unavailable or if they ran out of medication. A few patients referred to God as a support. For example, one patient said that if the doctor were not available to answer her question, she would ask God what she should do. I think that this kind of response is an outgrowth of the extraordinary status and power with which the doctor is invested.

There appears to be a high proportion of psychogenic explanations of illness offered by older people. Years ago, when I taught a class in the social psychology of health, students asked the following question of an older person and a peer: "Remember the last time you were sick; tell me what was the matter and what caused it." The younger peers were more likely to give mechanistic responses, for example, "I caught a virus from a friend who was ill," and the older people were more likely to give psychogenic responses, for example, "I got sick from aggravation." Despite the fact that older people are commonly thought of as not being "psychologically minded," they were highly likely to recognize the interdependence of mind and body at the functional level.[3]

In the geriatric clinic, many patients referred to "stress" as one of their problems and tended to emphasize its importance. Health care professionals often refer to the complex interactions between mind and body. Inquiry into patient belief systems reveals that patients often have a functional understanding of these interactions. With that comes the capability of monitoring themselves. With the doctors' support, there is potential for control of the illness in this process. However, when hidden from the doctor, this healing capability may be seen as noncompliance and become destructive of good health.

THE CASE OF MRS. DeANGELO

Since it seems easier to understand the findings and implications of this research through the use of the individual case, I will describe an interview I conducted with a patient. The patient, whom we will call Mrs. DeAngelo, was a somewhat obese woman who said she was 73 years old (her doctor said she was 75). She walked with a cane and occupied two chairs in the waiting room, one with an assortment of shopping bags. She lives in a housing development within 2 blocks of the hospital and has attended the clinic ever since she moved in 2 years ago. She lives alone in a small apartment. She was neatly dressed and seemed to be looking forward to seeing the doctor.

When asked why she had come to the clinic, she explained that she was there for a checkup, adding, "after 65, everything seems to go wrong." Normally, she said, she came to the clinic every 3 months. This time she came early, however, because she had been mugged last week. She was pushed to two young boys and knocked down, skinning her knee. She felt that the incident had exacerbated her edema. With some pride, she showed me her knee encased in its nylon stocking.

Mrs. DeAngelo began the interview by telling me that 16 years ago she had actinomycosis, "which is fatal." She was in New York Hospital at the

---

[3]A variable used in research on the outcome of psychotherapy, which refers to sophisticated awareness of psychological factors underlying appropriate functioning.

time, and she prayed to God. An evangelist in Ohio saved her life, and she is now okay except that she "is 73 years old." She is convinced that the faith healing is what cured her "fatal" condition. She repeated this story with embellishments several times during the course of the interview, emphasizing the word *fatal* each time. She would go out to Ohio now if she could afford the trip. She is saving up to go.

She described her health problems as follows:

1. *Congestive heart failure*: Her heart trouble began when she was 60, although she had had a murmur preceding the symptoms of heart failure. She takes digoxin and Lasix® once a day (she stated that she should take the Lasix® twice a day but does not; instead she takes two pills at once). She also takes potassium. When questioned, she explained that the water pill draws potassium out of her body and she must replace it.

2. *Water in her lungs*: She gets waterlogged, blows up all over; water is invading her body (and, presumably, all of the internal organs are waterlogged). The doctor cannot explain why this happens, so she says that she cannot tell me. That is what the Lasix® is for. Recently, the doctor prescribed two pills, which is a double dosage. It is very powerful medication. If she took three pills, she would most likely die. Nevertheless, the two pills do not quite work. She is always waterlogged. Once or twice she became dehydrated, however. It felt awful—her tongue was like wood, and she drank and drank. Several questions revealed that she has little sense of managing her medication. She kept repeating like a litany that she follows doctor's orders and does not vary.

3. *Hiatal hernia*: This is a condition of long standing. The doctor prescribed Maalox® but she stopped taking it. She does not know why, except that she did not want to keep taking "stuff." She assumed that it helped, but she just did not want to take it, so she stopped drinking coffee (that was evidently her idea rather than the doctor's).

4. *Buzzing in her right ear*: She is hearing it right now, all during the interview. Nothing can be done about it. She tried a noisemaker placed over her ear, but it was as annoying as the problem, so she stopped using it. She gets recurrent infections in her left ear which she sees as a related condition.

5. *Fatigue*: She has suffered from this for many years. It is important; she knows it is, although no one has found out what causes it. She explained with feeling that her doctor was the first one who took it seriously and was checking it out in a way that made sense

(although repeated questioning revealed that she did not know what the doctor was doing or why it made sense).

6. *Overweight*: Interestingly, she sees this as a problem which continues even though she has lost 35 lb (she now weighs 148 lb). Prior to coming to the clinic, she had been prescribed thyroid pills to help with the weight loss.

The patient interview was followed by one with Mrs. DeAngelo's physician. He sees her as a difficult patient because she has several very serious diseases. At the same time, she complains of various maladies which make little sense. Because she is so ill, all of her complaints must be taken very seriously. She has valvular heart disease, recurrent urinary tract infections, and may have adrenal disease. She has an abnormal chest X ray (her chart showed a series of repeated X rays showing a small density infiltrate) and a variety of other problems. She reports her problems in a manner that the physician sees as halfway between hypochondriasis and "La Belle Indifference." She describes everything in detail but seems to have blocked off her emotional response to the conditions. He noted that she apparently enjoys taking off her clothes for examination, unlike many other older female patients who seem embarrassed; he feels that she has sexualized the patient–doctor relationship.

Let us look at Mrs. DeAngelo's understanding of her problems and her medications. She seems to have a good working understanding of her congestive heart failure. She takes her medications when she should and understands the need for potassium replacement. Contrary to her belief, it makes no difference that she takes two Lasix® tablets once a day instead of spacing them. Consequently, regarding the problem that demands management, Mrs. DeAngelo is compliant. She has very strange beliefs, however, regarding her tendency to hold water. As she talks, one gets the image of a body without dividing membranes in which water sloshes around indiscriminately.

She presents her reactions to the hiatal hernia as though she is noncompliant and determinedly so. Actually, the Maalox® would be discretionary under any circumstances. Although another patient might have presented the same information in such a manner as to seem knowledgeable and sensible, Mrs. DeAngelo presented herself as though she were a child disobeying her father. Her analysis regarding the buzzing noise in her ear is accurate and presented straightforwardly. However, her linking the ear infections with the buzzing is wrong. In terms of treatment, however, it does not matter.

She is absolutely accurate about her fatigue. The only difference between her slightly bizarre account and that which might be expected from a good student summation at rounds is simply in the style of presentation. Her doctor is taking the symptom seriously and certainly should do so. A differential on fatigue is probably one of the most difficult diagnostic tasks. Moreover, practically everything wrong with her, plus the variety of things that could be wrong, would all produce fatigue.

This patient presents with almost classical hysterical symptoms. Interestingly, in my practice as a psychotherapist, I have not seen this type of symptom complex. The literature in the domain of psychotherapy indicates that such presentation is rare today.[4] Historically, the hysterical symptomatology is very important. Freud's original work developed from his interactions with hysterical patients. Were it not for some of those cases, Freudian theory would not have assumed the form that it did. Consequently, the fact that conversion hysteria is uncommon in the office practice of most psychotherapists is worth noting and has been noted repeatedly. The fact that Mrs. DeAngelo shows up in the geriatric clinic is important and has at least two implications. First, there are patterns in illness and in health that change from generation to generation. Mrs. DeAngelo is from a generation in which women repressed their sexuality, which then found pathological expression in conversion symptoms. We might expect the interaction between the physical and the psychological to differ by generations. Second, Mrs. DeAngelo's case underlines the fact that beliefs affect the diagnosis, course, and treatment of illness, and that patient compliance is much more idiosyncratic than the literature on the subject would have us believe.

Patients do not simply comply or not comply. There are almost infinite variations on the theme. To what do they comply? When do they veer from their intentions? Most importantly, how does a patient interpret a change of state? In general, we would expect that a patient's behavior in an emergency will be dependent upon his or her system of beliefs. How does a patient define an emergency? Noncompliance can be life-threatening, but what about blind compliance? Particularly for the old, who have several chronic conditions for which they are usually involved in a variety of treatments, management may demand that the individual be in tune with his or her body. Frequently, it is the patient who is the first to sense that "something is wrong." Any good clinician knows that this is very important information. Patients may be right to use their own judgment to monitor their bodies' responses. It is not clear why Mrs. DeAngelo stopped taking the Maalox® and simultaneously stopped drinking coffee in

---

[4]An exception is the Hispanic community, in which *attaques* are not uncommon (Garrison, 1977).

the treatment of her hiatal hernia, but I think most would agree that it was a good idea.

With an hysterical patient, the problem of compliance is both exaggerated and confounded. It is a tribute to a superb physician that Mrs. DeAngelo is functioning as well as she is and that she evidently is using her resources to maintain her healthy status. A very subtle change in emphasis could have this patient working against herself. Not very many doctors untrained in clinical psychology could manage to circumvent the pitfalls that this case presents. Even here, it would be a help to have a trained therapist available to work with this patient. Hysterics respond so well and so dramatically to treatment that it could be potentially very helpful. However, she is doing well. The physician focused determinedly on one fact: Mrs. DeAngelo is functioning very well in her own apartment in the community. It was clearly his major goal to keep her there, and because both physician and patient had their eye on the same ball, they were working very well together.

Mrs. DeAngelo is fortunate to have a physician with whom she can work to maintain her health. Older people are painfully aware that once they become patients, the power discrepancy between their doctor and themselves is very great. The avoidance of needed medical care might be more typical of men than of women. Men of the older generation seem particularly sensitive to any implications that they are seen as inferior. Most have lost some of the status positions that they occupied during the bulk of their lives, and any challenge to their self-esteem, real or imagined, is intolerable. They may be more protective of their self-esteem than of their physical health, and, if they see the physician–patient milieu as a threat, they will avoid it. Women of this generation developed strategies to cope with their relative lack of power and status.

THE PEOPLE-CARE-FOR-PEOPLE PROJECT

The Division of Gerontology, at NYU Medical Center, conducted a model project called "People-Care-For-People," which involved the informal support network of older people. The idea underlying the project was that there were times when people needed reassurance as well as information and assistance to permit them to continue to live in the community. Older people are likely to have multiple medical problems, many of which are chronic in nature—which means that they require management since cure is impossible. Management can be arranged outside of a hospital or a nursing home, but, wherever the locus of care, successful treatment requires two things: knowledge and assistance, when necessary. The patient must know whether each new development needs to be taken seriously enough to get outside help and exactly when outside help must be obtained. If the support system is working well, assistance will not be necessary until later. In general, if a person knows what to do in an emergency and is not anxious about it, he or she will be able to hold out longer.

Because it was felt that some older people might be so awed by professionals that they would be able to work more easily with a student, we enlisted students to act as go-betweens, linking the informal caregiver to the formal system. Thus in the heart of midtown Manhattan, outreach efforts were conducted to form groups of caregivers for the frail elderly people who reside in the area. Groups were to introduce people to others with similar responsibilities and problems related to the care of the elderly. The intent was to provide the group members with information about illness and about available services in the area. Both were to be tailored to their needs. In other words, we would not offer them a lecture on diabetes unless it was specifically requested, and even then the main thrust would be on eliciting questions and finding the answers.

The outreach efforts revealed that the day-to-day social support network of the urban elderly was often composed of friends who were age peers, rather than kin. Families were very supportive, but they often lived an hour or more away. In addition, a significant proportion of inner-city elderly are without families. (I became aware of this fact when I worked in a nursing home with a high proportion of German Jews who had escaped their native land during World War II without their families.) In an earlier study of the transportation and visiting patterns of the elderly people in New York City, we found that most people saw their families about once a month, whereas close friends and neighbors were usually visited daily. Consequently the groups of caregivers who were the community linkage for the model project tended to be the older people themselves (Nahemow & Kagan, 1971).

Let us digress for a moment to describe the nature of the Model Project. Once a week, students of nursing, social work, and medicine convened to learn gerontology and geriatrics, to develop tools to assess client–patient–caregiver needs, to then collect their questions and to develop a syllabus for the community groups. Since learning to teach is very different from learning for its own sake, there was an intensity to the classes that is not typical of students—they really needed to know things lest they be asked a question about it. It was in this atmosphere that the faculty members of the different schools came together, and Friday afternoon became a high point of our week.

A series of talks were arranged for the groups of caregivers. The physicians who served in the geriatric clinic were eager to talk to the groups about their areas of specialization and about general health issues. There was both interest and goodwill; certainly there was information to transmit, and the most knowledgeable people to transmit it were academic physicians. The questions that individuals have regarding their own medical conditions are often very complex. Like the penetrating questions that children sometimes ask, they may be hard to answer and require in-depth knowledge of a field to answer well. The physicians were excellent; they were among the best that a major medical center could produce. Their talks were not only clear and well prepared, but they were also intended to invite response. Yet there was a problem. The group members were particularly critical of doctors. They felt that the talks were too technical, that they could not ask questions. Although the groups had been animated when addressed by the students, they were unresponsive to the physicians.

We discovered that our initial "gut" feeling that students would be good supporting links for the caregivers was correct. Even though they had to tell the group member that they did not know an answer and would have to look it up, or talk to their teacher, many more questions were asked. Group members seemed quite willing to wait for the answers to their questions. Although we had predicted that this would happen, the reason for it was not clear. The physicians seemed to me to be warm and responsive. Why were the group members so cold? Exactly what was going on here?

The answer came from an unexpected source. As a spin-off of the model project, Stephanie Glickman and Sheila Ryan conducted a series of videotaped sessions with elderly people in the lounge of a local housing development. In order to help the older people become more comfortable in front of the camera, a series of theater games were played. On camera, the old people played themselves trying to get up the courage to ask the doctor a question. They reviewed how they would do it and what would be likely to happen. Watching the tape, one found oneself drawn into the drama, as older people responded with rage to an imaginary doctor accusing them of being "senile." The results of the exercise far exceeded our expectation as a vehicle for airing the patient's view of the patient–physician milieu to both themselves and others. It is our hope that the film (for we are currently in the process of developing it into a 30-minute patient-advocacy tape) will be useful to both old people and their doctors as a way of showing a clear picture of the patient–physician milieu as it exists in the older patient's mind. During the process of development, the film was shown to academic physicians, community people, and medical students. Most found it compelling.

It is clear to the viewer that underneath the selfeffacing demeanor of some older people, there was considerable anger. Older people felt that they had been demeaned at some point when they had assumed the patient role. They resented their powerlessness and resented the doctor for being powerful. They felt rejected and hurt. This feeling was not expressed openly, often not even to themselves. Consequently it interfered with their ability to seek help. Patients sometimes talked of "doctors" as though they were all alike. The videotape shows that when people can express some of the anger and hurt they feel, they can once again deal with the question of how to get their needs met and how to work *with*, rather than *against*, their doctor.

ATTRIBUTION THEORY

Attribution theory states that in a social environment we behave toward other people in ways that are determined by the motivations that we attribute to them. If someone steps on your foot and you feel that it was an accident, you will behave differently than you would if you assumed that it was a purposeful act. We are all likely to attribute more differentiated motivations to ourselves than to others. The result of several years of research in attribution theory shows that our own motivations are seen as situational and others' are inherent in their nature, that is, *I* was inconsiderate to you because I was unbearably hassled; there were a long series of contributory events making me late and your interruption was badly timed. *You* were inconsiderate toward me because you are a rude person.

We attribute complex, changing motivation to ourselves. The better we know someone, the more likely we are to see alterations from day to day. Our best friend is behaving strangely today. He is being unlike himself, in the same way that my own inconsiderate behavior was unlike me. The more remote the other person is from my personal world, the more I chunk and categorize. Carol Burnett once said that she disliked men who categorized women—and the fewer the categories, the less she liked the men. Any man who began sentences with, "women like" was, by this criterion, to be avoided. With only one category to cover all of womankind, it was unlikely that she could achieve the individual person status she desired.

I submit that because of the enormous differential in status and power between physician and patient, patients are likely to generalize broadly about doctors. After a bad experience, we will hear that "Doctors are inconsiderate, arrogant. . . ." The implication is that this is true of all doctors. Interestingly, because most older people's contact with doctors has been rather extensive, there is also the opposing tendency to make exceptions. "My doctor is wonderful. . . ." When we visited the home-bound elderly in the community, there were sometimes pictures of the family doctor on the mantle, which were proudly shown to visitors. Thus we have two contradictory psychic forces or beliefs operating: One image can do nothing wrong, and the other can do nothing right.

The patient, perceiving the exalted status and very real power of the physician, can deal with his or her relative powerlessness in several ways:

1. By avoiding those environments in which the power differential is greatest. The high priest may be less awesome outside of the temple. Thus one stays far away from the hospital and when possible tries to "collar" the doctor away from his working environment, that is, all physicians are familiar with the cocktail party pest who attempts to get a diagnosis from anyone who mistakenly admits to being an M.D.

2. By establishing distance, not physically, but psychologically, by using such defense mechanisms such as denial, rationalization, and so on. This route will result in noncompliant behavior on the part of the patient. The patient will use whatever justification he or she can find in the interest of this self-destructive behavior. Noncompliance is one of the most troublesome facts of modern medicine. It is the medical equivalent of the surgical, "the operation was a success, but the patient died," and it is enormously widespread (see Stone, 1979, for a comprehensive review of the literature). It is reasonable to question why a patient would go to the trouble and expense to obtain a diagnosis and purchase drugs, and then not use them. From the point of view of the patient who has been unable to come to terms with the power of the physician, it makes sense (psychological sense, that is, it is *not* logical or rational behavior).

3. By establishing a *personal* connection with the physician. Then, the contact that is made involves interaction on two levels: One is expert–client, but the other is that of ordinary friendship in which the status discrepancy is reduced. If the patient can get the physician to be a friend, then the patient will have enough sense of power to take a dependent stance trusting that he or she will be taken care of adequately.

Thus, many patients are highly motivated to develop a relationship which would create considerable "referent power" for the doctor. More than anything, most patients want the doctor to like them and be their friend. Rodin and Janis' (1979) concern about ways in which the health care professional can develop referent power almost seems unnecessary. Given half a chance, patients will go to great length to establish a personal connection with the doctor. The physician needs to be relaxed enough to let it happen. It is my impression that this requires no additional time, but research is needed to find out.

Roter (1977) finds that the patient–provider relationship appears to be the variable most consistently related to patient compliance." Bertakis (1977) found that simply asking patients to restate information in their own words and giving them feedback improved not only retention of information about their illness, but also improved patient satisfaction. Over and over the literature on patient compliance or adherence states that the doctor must rely upon his ability to establish good rapport in order to inculcate in patients a positive orientation and commitment to the relationship so that ultimately the patient will follow the doctor's advice (Blackwell, 1976).

We noted at the beginning of this chapter that most of the compliance literature was one-sided in that it asked the question: "How can we obtain compliance from patients?" Thus the vantage point is that of the health-care provider. However, when it comes to discussing feelings, it is the patient who is considered. The doctor's feelings are not mentioned. Given the strong nonrational component in the interaction, we might well ask the question, How is the physician to deal with a patient's perception of him or her as a godlike person who either can do nothing right or can simply do nothing wrong. A repeated theme I hear from physicians who seem to be successful in getting difficult patients to work with them is "I don't feel personally attacked or psychologically threatened by patients who don't do what I say; I try to find out why not, what the problem is." It seems to me that in the wake of all the lay literature concerning the impersonal physician who is unable to meet patients' needs, we sometimes forget that physicians *can* be psychologically minded and sensible as well as technically competent.

There has been a polarization of feelings regarding the medical profession in which physicians are depicted as either wonderful or dreadful. That most fall somewhere in between should not come as news to anyone. However, the polarization of attributions and expectations makes it difficult for the physician to respond with simple humanity, which is, after all, what we all want.

REFERENCES

Bain, D. J. G. Doctor–patient communication in general practice consultations. *Medical Education*, 1976, *10*, 125–131.

Barker, R. On the nature of the environment. In H. Proshansky, W. Ittelson, & L. Rivlin (Eds.), *Environmental Psychology*. New York: Holt, Rinehart, & Winston, 1976.

Becker, M. H. The health belief mode of personal health behavior. *Health Education Monographs*, 1974, *2*, 324–511.

Bertakis, K. D. The communication of information from physician to patient: A method for increasing patient retention and satisfaction. *Journal of Family Practice*, 1977, *5*, 217–222.

Blackwell, B. Treatment adherence. *British Journal of Psychiatry*, 1976, *129*, 513–531.

Calhoun, J. B. *Space and the strategy of life.* Paper presented at the American Association for the Advancement of Science 135th annual meeting, Dallas, Texas, 1968.

Davis, M. S. Variations in patients' compliance with doctors' orders: Analyses of congruence between survey responses and results of empirical investigations. *Journal of Medical Education*, 1966, *41*, 1037–1048.

DiMatteo, M. R., & Friedman, H. S. (Eds.), Interpersonal relations in health care. *Journal of Social Issues*, 1979, *35*, pp. 1–206.

Freedman, M. L. Establishment of an academic division of geriatrics in the department of medicine at NYU–Bellevue medical centers. In L. Nahemow, A. Miles, M. Stern, & J. Mintz (Eds.), *Establishing Geriatric Programs in Medical Schools.* New York: Springer Publishing, in press.

French, J. P. R., Rodgers, W., & Cobb, S. Adjustment as a person–environment fit. In G. V. Coelho, D. A. Hamburg, & J. E. Adams (Eds.), *Coping and adaptation.* New York: Basic Books, 1974.

Garrison, V. Doctor, espirista, or psychiatrist? Health seeking behavior in a Puerto Rican neighborhood in New York City. *Medical Anthropology*, 1977, *1*, 65–180.

Kahana, E. A congruence model of person–environment interaction. In P. G. Windley, T. O. Byerts, & F. G. Ernst (Eds.), *Theory development in environment and aging.* Washington, D.C.: The Gerontological Society, 1975.

Labouvie-Vief, G., & Chandler, M. J. Cognitive development and life-span developmental theory: Idealistic versus contextual perspectives. In P. B. Baltes (Ed.), *Life-span development behavior* (Vol. 1). New York: Academic Press, 1978.

Lawton, M. P., & Nahemow, L. Ecology and the aging process. In C. Eisdorfer & M. P. Lawton (Eds.), *The psychology of adult development and aging.* Washington, D.C.: American Psychological Association, 1973.

Marston, M. V. Compliance with medical regiments: A review of the literature. *Nursing Research*, 1970, *19*, 312–323.

Moos, R. H. The environmental quality of residential care settings. In R. R. Stough (Ed.), *Optimizing environment: Research practice and policy.* Washington, D.C.: Environmental Design Research Association (II), 1980.

Nahemow, L., & Kogan, L. S. *Reduced fare for the elderly: Final report.* New York: New York City Office for the Aging, 1971.

Parsons, T. The sick role and the role of the physician reconsidered. *Milbank Memorial Fund Quarterly*, 1975, *53*, 257–275.

Rodin, J., & Janis, I. L. The social power of health-care practitioners as agents of change. *Journal of Social Issues*, 1979, *35*, 60–81.

Roter, D. L. Patient participation in the patient–provider interaction: The effects of patient question asking on the quality of interaction, satisfaction, and compliance. *Health Education Monograph*, 1977, *5*, 282–314.

Sontag, S. *Illness as a metaphor.* New York: Farrar Straus & Giroux, 1978.

Stone, G. C. Patient compliance and the role of the expert. *Journal of Social Issues*, 1979, *35*, 34–59.

IV

CHANGING MILIEU:
PERSPECTIVES ON RELOCATION

12

Environmental Displacement:
A Literature Reflecting
Old-Person–Environment Transactions

LEON A. PASTALAN

Beginning in 1938, Camargo and Preston (1945) undertook a 3-year survey of first admissions of patients over 65 years of age to the Maryland state mental hospitals. A total of 683 cases were examined. In the first year following admission 47% of the patients died, with approximately 16% dying during the first month. After the second year another 11% died. Whittier and Williams (1956) conducted a similar investigation and found a 20% mortality rate within 30 days from the date of admission. After 1 year, one-half of the study population had died.

Both studies were designed to be descriptive and not intended to prove any causal relationships. Yet, the numbers were too striking to ignore and suggested that further study was needed regarding the consequences of moving an older adult from one environment to another. Since that time much discussion has evolved on the notion of "transplantation shock" or the "relocation effect" experienced by elderly individuals upon changing living environments. Two major questions arise. Do all older people under all conditions experience negative consequences following a move, or are certain types of individuals more susceptible to a move under certain conditions? What, if anything, can be done to facilitate adjustment to a new setting and reduce the potential "transplantation shock"?

A careful review of the literature reveals apparently contradictory results. Aldrich and Mendkoff (1963), Killian (1970), Markus, Blenkner, Bloom, and Downs (1972), and Pablo (1977) have found that relocation has negative consequences such as increased mortality, depression, stress, and decreased life satisfaction. In contrast, Carp (1967–1977), Lawton

189

AGING AND MILIEU:
ENVIRONMENTAL PERSPECTIVES
ON GROWING OLD

and Yaffe (1970), and Lieberman, Tobin, and Slover (1971) have failed to find negative consequences in terms of survival, longevity, and general well-being of the elderly. In fact, in some instances significant positive results have been noted following a move to a new environment.

A major reason for the apparently contradictory findings is that underlying all the conclusions are qualifying factors such as the characteristics of the people being moved, the reasons for the move, and its meaning to the mover; and the helping techniques used to facilitate the moves. The results can be said to revolve around five major factors: (a) the degree of choice in making the move; (b) the degree of environmental change; (c) the degree of health; (d) the degree of preparation; and (e) the methodology utilized in the study.

It is the purpose of this chapter to compile a relocation "state of the art" revolving around these five major qualifying factors for a variety of settings, diagnostic categories, demographic characteristics, and social factors. In addition, specific studies that will identify individuals who are least and most vulnerable to relocation will be cited. Finally, longitudinal studies that provide methodology, techniques, and data on the preparation of patients and families for relocation, as well as the effects of these processes on facilitating adjustment to new settings, will be highlighted.

AN OVERVIEW

Schulz and Brenner (1977) postulate that negative response to a stressful event will be lessened to the extent that the individual feels it is predictable and/or controllable. Given this assumption, the greater choice an individual has, the less negative will be the effects of displacement. The *degree of choice*, in terms of whether the move is *voluntary* or *involuntary*, thus becomes an important qualifying factor that must be examined separately. Furthermore, an individual's response to a new environment will be a function of that individual's past experiences and environmental cues. It therefore becomes necessary to note the nature of the pre-relocation environment. These *degrees of environmental change* can be summarized into three general categories: (a) a move from one private residential setting to another (home-to-home); (b) a move from a home to an institution (home-to-institution); and (c) a move from one institution to another (institution-to-institution). In sum, the nature of the many qualifying factors should be considered within the overall framework of whether the move was voluntary or involuntary, and whether the move was from home-to-home, home-to-institution, or institution-to-institution.

Voluntary Move

HOME-TO-HOME

Numerous studies have examined the effects of moving aged individuals voluntarily from one home to another. Carp (1967) was one of the first investigators to consider this situation. She did a follow-up examination of these same individuals 8 years later (Carp, 1977), providing one of the few longitudinal studies regarding the relocation experience. The research was conducted at Victoria Plaza, San Antonio, an apartment complex for the elderly, and consisted of comparing applicants who were accepted into the home with a matched set of applicants who did not become residents. Most of the relocated subjects were coming to an environment that was substantially "better" than the one they were leaving. Carp found that residents were more satisfied with their housing than nonresidents, had less need for special services, had more memberships in clubs, and had more friends. No differences were found between the relocation experience of men and women. Consistently, attitudinal scores of residents improved, whereas those of the nonresidents showed slight decrements or no change. In addition, pre- and postmeasures taken 12–15 months apart revealed that residents spent less time in bed on account of illness and less time in health care activities following relocation. Thus, the author concluded that more time should be spent on examining the role of the setting in determining the experience of the people living within it.

Citing the fact that most studies tend to report on the first year of tenancy following relocation, Carp again examined the Victoria Plaza residents 8 years later (Carp, 1977). At that time, 26% of the 204 original subjects moved into Victoria Plaza and 37% of the 148 comparison group were dead. These findings suggest that there can be a health benefit of a good living environment over the long range as well as the short. Carp suggests that the new living environment facilitated satisfaction and reduced stress, which brought about, among other direct consequences, improved health status and a declining death rate.

Lawton and Yaffe (1970) also examined a move from one housing environment to new housing which was substantially better. Three groups of older people were matched for sex, age, and health at the beginning of the study: (a) a congregate housing relocated group; (b) a congregate housing nonrelocated group; and (c) a community nonrelocated group. The postmove mortality rate was found to be low in all three groups (a 12-month rate of 7.4%), with no significant differences between the voluntarily relocated group and the two matched control groups. However, Schulz (1976) warns that care should be taken in extrapolating these findings to other relocation questions, since, in the absence of random assignment, it might be questioned what consequences might arise from comparing a group that had a desire to move with control groups that did not.

Like Lawton and Yaffe, Wittels and Botwinick (1974) found no differences in mortality rates between voluntary relocation groups and control groups. The subjects had to be healthy to be included in the study and were moved to a setting that stressed activities and group participation. Within 1 year of the move it was found that on the average the deceased tended to be older by nearly 3 years, were in less good initial health, and included a larger percentage of men. No significant differences were observed between those surviving after 1 year in terms of occupation, education levels, or marital status. These findings are compatible with those of Storandt and Wittels (1975) in which decisional control was exercised by the relocated subjects, and a maximum of predictability was maintained. No decrements in voluntarily relocated persons from pretest to posttest were recorded.

Lawton and Cohen (1974) utilized a longitudinal comparison group design by examining the change over time among relocated subjects to that among the comparison subjects by means of multiple regression analysis which controlled for the original state of well-being, demographic characteristics, and initial state of health. Five housing sites limited to people 62 years of age and over were studied. All subjects were interviewed prior to occupancy, and 83% were reinterviewed 12 months after relocation. Results showed that relocated subjects were significantly poorer in functional health than were community comparison subjects. Yet, relocated subjects were significantly higher in morale, more satisfied with their housing, more involved in external activities, and more satisfied with the status quo than were the community residents. Although the authors are not sure why morale was higher while health was poorer, they suggest that a positive advantage can result from rehousing the elderly based on the judgment made by the older person evaluating his or her current condition.

In sum, the results reveal that the vast majority of subjects who moved voluntarily from one house to another maintained or improved their quality of life based on various attitudinal indicators. In addition, although most of the existing studies dealt only with healthy subjects, there are indications that those who are older and in worse physical health initially will not fare as well after the move. Conflicting evidence was reported regarding postrelocation adaptation differences between men and women.

HOME-TO-INSTITUTION

In most instances when an older person moves from one home environment to another it usually means an improvement in living conditions. However, when an older individual moves from a home or residential environment to an institution voluntarily, it is not always the desire for a better living environment which precipitates the move. Often the older adult is faced with a life crisis that makes a move to an institution necessary. Consequently, the fact that a person entering an institution for the first time may also be experiencing another life crisis at the same time makes this type of move slightly different from the home-to-home move.

In 1963, Farrari compared two groups moving from a home environment to an institution—one entering voluntarily and the other without an alternative. Examination of the mortality rates 10 weeks after relocation revealed that 94% (16 of 17) of those relocated involuntarily died, whereas 2.8% (1 of 38) in the voluntary group died within the same period. Therefore, even though health was a confounding variable in this situation, the study provides some evidence that a voluntary move from a home to an institution does not necessarily mean a high mortality rate shortly after relocation.

Schulz and Aderman (1973) and Sherwood, Glassman, Sherwood, and Morris (1974) examined in-depth the prerelocation environment and attitudes of voluntarily relocated subjects. Schulz and Aderman conclude that those people who are used to exercising control over their home environment suffer more from feelings of helplessness upon entering an institution than do people who move from one institution to another. As a result, those who move to an institution from a home have more difficulty adapting to a new environment than do those who move from another institution. Sherwood, Glassman, Sherwood, and Morris (1974) divided a group of voluntarily relocated subjects into two subgroups. Those who had previously exercised a good deal of control were classified as less suitable for institutionalization, and vice versa. Pretest attitudinal measures revealed that the more suitable group was more dissatisfied with life than the group classified as less suitable for institutionalization. The posttest results showed that the life satisfaction scores of the suitable group went up. Consequently, this study provides further evidence that the postrelocation experience is a function of prerelocation environments and attitudes.

Turner, Tobin, and Lieberman (1972) examined subjects who were voluntarily relocated to institutions but focused more attention on the nature of the post-relocation environment. In an environment that stresses high levels of interaction, activity, and aggressiveness, the authors conclude that a vigorous, if not combative, style facilitates adaptation. In examining a group of healthy, older adults they found that those who interacted with the environment adapted better than those who tended to disengage.

In a similar type of study, Havens (1968) examined a group of voluntarily relocated subjects who possessed some handicaps, but who were nevertheless capable of self-maintenance. These subjects' moves were involuntary in the sense that they had no alternative but to leave their former residences, but they did choose to live in that particular environment. Examination of pre- and postrelocation attitudinal tests revealed that a low level of adjustment tended to be associated with discontinuity between environmental conditions and that a high level of adjustment was associated with a continuity of environments. Age, sex, and marital status did not prove to be good predictors of postrelocation adjustment.

Blenkner (1967) utilized a random assignment procedure to assign those living in the community to prerelocation service programs providing minimal, moderate, or maximal care and information. Those who received a more intensive level of professional services were more likely to be placed in an institution. In addition, for those who were relocated, there was evidence that if the older person's intellectual capacity, memory, and orientation to time, place, and person were seriously impaired, his or her chances of survival following relocation was considerably lower than that of a person displaying no or only minimal signs of impairment, regardless of the level of emotional or social disturbance or maladjustment of the individual.

In sum, home-to-home institution studies tended to focus on examining the effects of the previous life-style and environments on relocation adjustment. Most indicated that the response to institutionalization is a function of the nature of the prerelocation environment. In addition, the sudden change from an environment where control was prevalent to an institution where there is less control available was shown to lead to stress and greater life dissatisfaction in the new environment. Finally, there was some evidence that those who sought interaction following the move adjusted better than did those who withdrew from activities.

INSTITUTION-TO-INSTITUTION

Most of the literature regarding relocation of the elderly has been concerned with the change from one institution to another. However, the vast majority of these studies have examined older people who were forced to relocate. Jasnau (1967) and Zweig and Csank (1975) represent the studies which have utilized a voluntary population sample. Both investigations involved the use of a carefully planned prerelocation preparation program. Jasnau compared a group who were mass-moved to another group in which each person was given extensive individual preparation. All patients were prepared for the move, and no patient was moved against his or her will. Those given individual attention were given extensive psychological and emotional preparation by trained social casework services. Those who were undecided about moving were given a second chance to change their minds later and were also given further personal attention. The mass-moved group had a mortality rate 35% greater than the death rate for the same institution 1 year before relocation. The group given individual attention had lower than expected mortality rates. Although Jasnau did not examine other possible reasons for the change in the death rate, the results indicate that adequate preparation can reduce the trauma associated with change for older adults transferred from one institution to another.

Zweig and Csank (1975) investigated the voluntary transfer of about 350 male war veterans who were over 64 and suffering from some chronic incapacity requiring more or less constant attention. The move was not sudden. A preparation program was implemented in order to "relieve pressure, allay anxiety, and build up realistic expectations of what the future held in store [p. 135]." From the year before relocation to one year after, there was a 6.82% decrease in mortality. Like Jasnau, Zweig and Csank point to the relocation preparation program as the probable reason for the success.

In sum, very few studies exist regarding the voluntary move from one institution to another. No results compared individuals relocated specifically in terms of diagnostic categories, age, sex, race, education, or income. Some indication was obtained that the existence of a preparation program can reduce the trauma of relocation.

Involuntary Move

HOME-TO-HOME

The results in this category are contradictory in some instances, while being consistent in others. Kasteler, Gray, and Carruth (1968) compared a group of people forced to move because of highway construction with a matched sample of nonrelocated elderly subjects. The nonrelocated group had significantly more persons with a good or average rating regarding health, friends, work, economic security, religion, feelings of usefulness, and happiness. Thus, the nonrelocated subjects seemed to score higher on measures of personal adjustment and amount of activity.

Brand and Smith (1974) initiated a similar study and found that the nonrelocated group also scored significantly higher than the relocated group on a life satisfaction index. In addition, it was discovered that those who were the most unhealthy were more susceptible to the stress of relocation than were those who were healthy. Relocation had a more adverse effect on females than on males, and blacks seemed to adjust better than whites. No difference was observed between the relocated and nonrelocated groups with regard to health status.

In contrast to the findings of Brand and Smith, Kral, Grad, and Berenson (1968) found that normal aged men appeared to suffer more from relocation than normal aged women. Within 23 months, the mortality rates were 42% for men and 20% for women. Yet, they also discovered that those who were unhealthy and those who were psychotic did not adjust as well to the move as did those who were healthy.

Shahinian, Goldfarb, and Turner (1968) compared death rates for involuntarily relocated subjects to a control group that was not relocated. Support was revealed for the previous findings that those having moderate physical impairment, severe brain syndrome, and severe motor impairment are likely to experience negative consequences and higher mortality rates.

In sum, the literature regarding forced relocation from one home to another was not as favorable as it was for the subjects who voluntarily moved from one home to another. Most studies found some negative consequences associated with the move. In particular, those people with physical and mental health disabilities consistently showed up as being more vulnerable to a move. Those who were forced to relocate did not tend to score as well on attitude tests following relocation as did their nonrelocated control groups. Conflicting evidence was reported regarding the differences of forced relocation on males and females.

HOME-TO-INSTITUTION

The majority of the studies involving home-to-institution moves have been voluntary in nature, with a couple of exceptions. As mentioned earlier, Farrari (1963) compared a voluntary group to an involuntary group and found that within the first 10 weeks of residence, the involuntary group had a mortality rate of 94%.

Schulz and Aderman (1973) found that those patients who came to the institution from a similar environment survived on the average nearly 1 month longer than those patients who came from dissimilar home environments.

In sum, very little research has been done in this category, but what has been done provides further evidence that those who are forced to move and those who come from dissimilar backgrounds are more often among those who die following relocation than are those people who move voluntarily and who move to a receiving environment which is similar to the one they just left.

INSTITUTION-TO-INSTITUTION

Results of studies involving moves from one institution to another often suggest conflicting conclusions. For instance, Aleksandrowicz (1961) examined mortality rates following relocation and found a 20% death rate during the 3 months following the move, compared to 7.5% during the 3 months preceding relocation. Likewise, Killian (1970) found mortalilty rates to be from 4.98 to 8.99 times greater for relocated patients than for nontransferred patients. However, Miller and Lieberman (1965) reported a death rate of 4 out of 45 patients in 18 weeks, a figure that was not statistically significant. Further support of this finding comes from Markson and Cumming (1974) who recorded a mortality rate of less than 1 in 10 during an 11-month period following relocation.

One of the most frequently cited relocation studies is by Aldrich and Mendkoff (1963). Calculations of the annual survival rate for patients based on records for the institution during the decade prior to relocation were compared to the actual death rate. It was discovered that the actual death rate was substantially and significantly higher than the anticipated rate. Furthermore, an analysis of the breakdown of deaths during the first 3 months following relocation revealed that for patients over 70 years of age the actual rate was 3½ times greater than the expected death rate, and for all patients it was 3 times higher than expected. Higher death rates for the psychotic or near-psychotic were also found to be statistically significant. In terms of attitude, results revealed that those people with a philosophical or angry response to the news of relocation had a lower than average mortality rate, whereas those who denied the reality of the move tended to be more prevalent in the group that died.

Bourestom and Pastalan (1975) divided relocated subjects into two groups: One group had to adjust to a new staff, a new program, a new physical environment, and a new patient population (radical change group), whereas the other group only has to adjust to a physical environment change. A higher mortality rate was found for both relocated groups, with 43% of the radical change group dying in the 6 months preceding and one year following relocation. The authors concluded that the more severe the change in the type of environment, the greater the negative effects of relocation.

Lieberman, Tobin, and Slover (1971) also found the nature of the environment to be the most important factor in relocation, concluding that cold, dehumanizing environments tend to cause declines following a move, whereas autonomy-fostering environments are more likely to result in the patient staying the same or improving. In contrast, Marlowe (1974) concluded that it is not the nature of the physical environment which is of importance, but rather, the amount of control or perceived control which is of most importance.

In sum, although conflicting results have been reported regarding postrelocation rises in mortality rates, most of the studies indicate that the greatest danger appears to be among the helpless and psychotic. Furthermore, those patients who took an agry or philosophical attitude toward the move showed better adjustment than those who tried to deny the move. Some conflicting evidence exists as to whether it is the nature of the environment that is of major importance or whether control is a major factor. Studies involving other types of environments would indicate that both the nature of the environment and the amount of control exercised by the relocated individual are of major importance in terms of adjustment.

DISPLACEMENT PREPARATION PROGRAMS

Many of the relocation studies have indiciated that older individuals frequently do not readily adapt to a new environment. A common theme running throughout the relocation literature has been the role that stressful situations play in increased morbidity and mortality. Control, or perceived control, has been cited as an important factor in reducing the amount of stress associated with a change in living environments. Thus, the question arises: What, if anything, can be done to facilitate adjustment to a new setting and reduce the potential "transplantation shock"? Several relocation studies have implemented programs designed to prepare patients, families, and staff for the move. The findings of these studies are summarized, in the following section and potential techniques for facilitating adjustment are highlighted.

Preparation Program Research

Determining the benefits of a preparation program is made more difficult by the many qualifying factors involved. In addition, once a program is designed and implemented, it is difficult to assess what part each component of that program had in determining the overall results. The positive effects of the program discussed by Jasnau (1967) and Zweig and Csank (1975) have previously been summarized. Gutman and Herbert (1976) implemented a program for 81 extended-care male patients who were forced to move. The move was well planned to prevent confusion. Patients were assigned to rooms according to friendships and compatibilities. In addition, all personal possessions were transferred. A one year follow-up of mortality rates found no significant difference between the expected and anticipated rates. No relationship was found between mortality rates and age, length of hospitaliation, or mental status.

Pastalan (1976) implemented an extensive preparation program for involuntarily relocated patients in Pennsylvania. The impact of the program was measured by comparing mortality rates between the relocated population and the nursing home population at large. For 236 persons relocated between July 1975 and July 1976 the mortality rate was 11%, as compared to 26.6% for Pennsylvania and 27.5% for the United States. In addition, several factors were compared to postrelocation mortality. It was found that advanced age, poor prognosis, and confused mental status were strong predictors of mortality following the move. Distance moved and length of hospitalization by themselves did not present a clear picture of vulnerability. Mortality was 41% among those with a postmove rejecting attitude and 14% among those who accepted relocation.

Three major components of the preparation program (site visits, personal counseling, and group discussion) were correlated with mortality for individuals differing in mental and physical status and age. Site visits were found to reduce mortality in the 66–80-year-old age group, for persons with a fair prognosis and for patients who were confused at the time. Yet, site visits had little or no impact on the under-66 age group, those with an excellent prognosis and those who were alert most of the time. Group discussions tended to help the alert patients but in general had little to do with survival. Counseling sessions dramatically reduced mortality in the over-81 age group, those with a poor prognosis, and both the confused and alert patients.

In sum, most of the programs reviewed here found that, although there is a danger in relocating some types of elderly people in some situations, a carefully designed and implemented program can reduce the danger to some degree and facilitate postrelocation adjustment.

In terms of program content most of the more successful ones reflected the following elements: The person being relocated is involved in decision making to the greatest extent possible; multiple site visits are made to the new setting; continuous personal and group counseling is provided; staff at both the sending and receiving facilities are involved in the entire process; family or significant other(s) are involved in the move; and a means of having belongings accompany the person being relocated is provided.

Little mention was made in the preparation programs as to the length of time that group discussions and individual counseling should continue after relocation. It is unclear how each particular element of the program affected patient outcome or what the interactive affects were.

SUMMARY AND CONCLUSION

1. For those people who move voluntarily from one home setting to another, little evidence was found of postrelocation decrements, and the move was often found to be helpful in the case where the nature of the environment was an improvement.
2. The greater the choice and control the individual had in being relocated, the less negative the effects of relocation tended to be. The more predictable the new environment was, the less negative the results were, in general.
3. Those people of advanced age, poor prognosis, and confused mental status did not fare as well as those who were healthy.
4. There was some indication that those people who took an angry or philosophical attitude toward the move showed better adjustment than those who tried to deny the move or withdraw from activities.
5. Most of the studies did not find a relationship between length of hospitalization, educational level, occupation, or income and postrelocation adjustment.
6. The findings for adjustment differences between males and females were contradictory. There was some indication, however, that involuntary relocation is less traumatic for males than for females.
7. There were virtually no studies done relating race to postrelocation adjustment. The few studies that did mention it had a very small sample to base conclusions on.
8. Many of the studies found that the first 3 months immediately following the move are the most dangerous in terms of increased mortality rates.
9. There was some indication that the attitudes of the family and the staff toward patient relocation were not significantly related to mortality.
10. Site visits seemed to decrease mortality following relocation most emphatically for persons aged 66–80, for persons with a fair prognosis, and for those who were against the move.
11. Group discussions seemed to help the alert patients, but there was an indication that it was a negative factor for those with a poor prognosis.
12. Individual counseling was found to have a favorable impact on adjustment.

13. Counseling sessions were most dramatically associated with reduced mortality in the advanced age groups (over 81), those with a poor prognosis, and both the confused and alert patients.
14. Those who moved involuntarily from home-to-home showed greater decreases in life satisfaction than those who made the same type of move voluntarily.
15. Studies of the home-to-institution move showed a clear distinction between those who moved voluntarily and those who were forced to move. Consistently, those subjects who moved voluntarily showed more positive results than those who did not. The degree of control in the prerelocation environment was found to be an important predictor in the degree of adjustment following the move.
16. The institution-to-institution research tended to show that those who were forced to move had higher mortality rates than nonrelocated control groups.
17. In general, prerelocation preparation programs increased the predictability of the new environment and effectively reduced mortality rates.

This review makes it clear that, in assessing and predicting relocation risk, the conditions of the relocation experience and the characteristics of the preparations must be specified. The question is no longer whether relocation has negative or positive effects but under what conditions and with what kinds of populations are those negative or positive effects most likely to be observed. Finally there is evidence that relocation effects are modified by the degree and perhaps type of preparation for relocation programs that are implemented.

REFERENCES

Aldrich, C., & Mendkoff, E. Relocation of the aged and disabled: A mortality study. *Journal of American Geriatric Society*, 1963, *11*, 185–194.

Aleksandrowicz, D. Fire and its aftermath on a geriatric ward. *Bulletin Menninger Clinic*, 1961, *25*, 23–32.

Blenkner, M. Evnrionmental change and the aging individual. *The Gerontologist*, 1967, *7*, 101–105.

Bourestom, N., & Pastalan, L. *Forced relocation: Setting, staff, and patient effects.* Final Report, Institute of Gerontology, University of Michigan, Ann Arbor, April 1975.

Brand, F., & Smith, R. Life adjustment and relocation of the elderly. *Journal of Gerontology*, 1974, *29*, 336–340.

Camargo, O., & Preston, G. H. What happens to patients who are hospitalized for the first time when over 65 years of age. *American Journal of Psychiatry*, 1945, *102*, 168.

Carp, F. The impact of environment on old people. *The Gerontologist*, 1967, *7*, 106–108.

Carp. F. Impact of improved living environment on health and life expectancy. *The Gerontologist*, 1977, *17*, 242–249.

Farrari, N. Freedom of choice. *Social Work*, 1963, *8*, 105–106.

Gutman, G. M., & Herbert, C. P. Mortality rates among relocated extended care patients. *Journal of Gerontology*, 1976, *31*, 352–357.

Havens, B. J. An investigation of activity patterns and adjustment in an aging population. *The Gerontologist*, 1968, *8*, 201.

Jasnau, K. F. Individual or mass transfer of non-psychotic geriatric patients from mental hospitals to nursing homes, with special references to death rate. *Journal of American Gerontological Society*, 1967, *15*, 280–284.

Kasteler, J., Gray, R., & Carruth, M. Involuntary relocation of the elderly. *The Gerontologist*, 1968, *8*, 276–279.

Killian, E. Effects of geriatric transfers on mortality rates. *Social Work*, 1970, *15*, 19–26.

Kral, V., Grad, B., & Berenson, J. Stress reaction resulting from the relocation of an aged population. *Canadian Psychiatric Association Journal*, 1968, *13*, 201–209.

Lawton, M. P., & Cohen, J. The generality of housing impact on the well-being of older people. *Journal of Gerontology*, 1974, *29*, 194–204.

Lawton, M., & Yaffe, S. Mortality, morbidity and voluntary change of residence by older people. *Journal of American Geriatric Society*, 1970, *18*, 823–831.

Lieberman, M., Tobin, S., & Slover, D. *The effects of relocation on long-term geriatric patients.* Illinois Department of Health and Committee on Human Development, University of Chicago, Chicago, 1971.

Markson, E., & Cumming, J. A strategy of necessary mass transfer and its impact on patient mortality. *Journal of Gerontology*, 1974, *29*, 315–321.

Markus, E., Blenkner, M., Bloom, M., & Downs, T. Some factors and their association with post-relocation mortality among institutionalized aged persons. *Journal of Gerontology*, 1972, *27*, 376–382.

Marlowe, R. A. *When they closed the doors at Modesto.* Paper presented at NIMH Conference on Closure of State Hospitals, Scottsdale, Arizona, 1974.

Miller, D., & Lieberman, M. The relationships of affect state and adaptive capacity to reactions to stress. *Journal of Gerontology*, 1965, *20*, 492–497.

Pablo, R. Intra-institutional relocation: Its impact on long-term patients. *The Gerontologist*, 1977, *17*, 426–435.

Pastalan, L. *Report on Pennsylvania nursing home relocation program.* Interim Research Findings, Institute of Gerontology, University of Michigan, Ann Arbor, 1976.

Schulz, R. The effects of control and predictability on the physical and psychological well-being of the institutionalized aged. *Journal of Personality and Social Psychology*, 1976, *33*, 563–573.

Schulz, R., & Aderman, D. Effect of residential change on the temporal distance to death of terminal cancer. *Omaga: Journal of Death and Dying*, 1973, *4*, 157–162.

Schulz, R., & Brenner, G. Relocation of the aged: A review and theoretical analysis. *Journal of Gerontology*, 1977, *32*, 323–333.

Shahinian, S., Goldfarb, A., & Turner, H. *Death rate in relocated residents of nursing homes.* New York State Department of Mental Hygiene Office of the Consultant on Aging, Albany, New York, 1968.

Sherwood, S., Glassman, J., Sherwood, C., & Morris, J. N. Pre-institutional factors as predictors of adjustment to a long-term care facility. *International Journal of Aging and Human Development*, 1974, *5*, 95–105.

Storandt, M., & Wittels, I. Maintenance of function in relocation of community dwelling older adults. *Journal of Gerontology,* 1975, *30,* 608–612.

Turner, B., Tobin, S., & Lieberman, M. Personality traits as predictors of institutional adaptation among the aged. *Journal of Gerontology,* 1972, *27,* 61–68.

Whittier, J., & Williams, D. The coincidence of constancy of mortality figures for aged psychotic patients admitted to state hospital. *Journal of Nervous and Mental Diseases,* 1956, *124,* 618–620.

Wittels, I., & Botwinick, J. Survival in relocation. *Journal of Gerontology,* 1974, *29,* 440–443.

Zweig, J., & Csank, J. Z. Effects of relocation on chronically ill geriatric patients of a medical unit: Mortality rates. *Journal of American Geriatric Society,* 1975, *23,* 132–136.

13

Environmental Continuity, Futurity, and Adaptation of the Aged

EVA KAHANA   BOAZ KAHANA

Within the field of gerontology there has been a growing recognition in recent years of the great differences that exist in the ways people cope with aging. It is now established that age serves as an important variable which affects human behavior during the later years. Social influences on people are also known to differ based on age, as do environmental influences. Nevertheless, recently the focus has shifted from searching for generalization regarding characteristics of the aged or for optimal environments to serve them to a more differentiated and complex view that takes into account the many personal and situational influences which mediate the effects of aging.

The negative influences of the later years in terms of physiological changes, social losses, diminished roles and opportunities, and environmental vulnerability have been extensively documented. Understandably and appropriately, a social movement was set into motion to assist the vulnerable aged, to develop services for them, and to seek protective environments in which they can navigate more readily. In assisting older persons, however, we have also accepted and reinforced an image of the later years as being dependent, helpless, wanting, and fearful of new ideas, environments, or life situations (B. Kahana, Kiyak, & E. Kahana, 1979).

Typically, environments are considered by gerontologists either as posing constraints, impediments, and assorted problems for older persons or as providing them with comfort and continuity (Lawton, 1980). Environmental change, in the form of institutionalization, urban renewal, or condominium conversions, is usually considered a threat to the older

AGING AND MILIEU:
ENVIRONMENTAL PERSPECTIVES
ON GROWING OLD

person's stability. The future of the older person is often seen as only a spectre of decline or, hopefully, as long as possible, a maintenance of the status quo.

Our basic tenet in this discussion is that environmental change may also be viewed as a potential avenue for personal control and hope for improving one's future in later life. Voluntary relocation allows older persons to plan for a more satisfying future, improve their living situation, and increase person–environment (P–E) fit. Furthermore, such positive, self-initiated change may be accomplished without reliance on city planners, social workers, or gerontologists. This chapter focuses on the adventurous aged—those who may seek environmental discontinuity in later life often with a surprisingly well-founded hope that, even in old age, things may get better in the future.

During recent years, we have conducted a series of research projects exploring environmental influences and coping among the elderly. In projects ranging from studies of the effects of age segregation on the elderly (E. Kahana & B. Kahana, 1971) to surveys of service needs and utilization of the elderly (E. Kahana, 1974), and to studies of adaptation to institutional life (E. Kahana & B. Kahana, 1978; Kahana, Fairchild, & B. Kahana, 1982), a repeated pattern emerged underscoring the importance of diversity and individual differences in coping patterns and environmental preferences of the aged. Our findings suggested that many older persons, even among those in stressful life situations and with limited personal resources, fail to conform to generalizations which gerontologists have patterned for later life and do not fit the mold of later-life attributes.

The conceptual framework of person–environment congruence which has been used in considering the interactive nature of P–E transactions (E. Kahana, 1975a) has implicitly recognized the importance of individual differences in responding to environmental stimuli. It is interesting to note, however, that data regarding the psychosocial strengths of the elderly impressed us from several studies including those which did not implicitly stress a congruence perspective. In our latest study, we have specifically looked at a group of older people whom we term the "adventurous aged" and who exemplify atypical behavioral patterns during the later years (E. Kahana, B. Kahana, & McLenigan, 1980).

In this chapter we would like to share with you the data, the questions raised, and the avenues of further inquiry suggested by our work with these atypical aged. We will also focus on environmental implications of studying the adventurous aged and the ramifications of considering such a group for the congruence model of P–E fit. We also wish to stress that, even though we are considering atypical older people and those with special life-styles, their orientations are viewed as the types of responses and behaviors of which most older persons are capable.

It should also be noted that there is a very urgent political and historical need for considering perspectives of the well elderly. With the need for economy in research funding stressed by the Reagan administration, the pattern that has been set is one of reducing or eliminating support for the social sciences (Holden, 1981). It is now argued that limited sources for aging research must be directed at reducing the ravages of organically caused diseases. The trend in the diverse funding agencies is toward pathology and disease being combated by future research in "hard science," whereas social science research is seen as having fewer payoffs and lower priorities. However, a return to a medical or pathology model of aging holds serious dangers for the field of gerontology by further reinforcing inaccurate negative stereotypes about aging. Older persons are also likely to accept negative stereotypes and self-evaluations and exhibit patterns of learned helplessness and increased dependency (Seligman, 1975).

An exclusive or primary focus on pathology and on problems experienced by the elderly is likely to result in additional unintended and dangerous outcomes. First, recognizing that research funding has an important role in shaping the types of research done we may see more studies focusing only on the ill, institutionalized, and vulnerable aged, providing experts and the public with a distorted, pessimistic view of the later years. Furthermore, focus on a pathology model of aging is likely to yield greater demand for costly services. In contrast, recognizing and studying the factors that lead to wellness, independence, and contributory roles may help prevent the need for extensive supports.

CONTINUITY, CHANGE, AND FUTURITY IN THE LATER YEARS

Effects of Relocation

The generally accepted view in gerontology has been that older persons, whose adaptive capacities are diminished, tend to exhibit a lack of future orientation (Kastenbaum, 1966), seek to maintain continuity with the past (Rosow, 1967), and are resistent to change. Relocation among the elderly has been typically seen as resulting in negative physical and psychological consequences (Lieberman, 1969, 1974). The body of knowledge stressing the negative consequences of relocation may be viewed as a specific case of the more general notion that significant life changes are stressful and lead to negative psychosocial and psychological outcomes for the aged (Dohrenwend & Dohrenwend, 1974).

More recently, it has been recognized that under some circumstances, relocation need not result in negative outcomes (Carp, 1968; Lawton & Yaffe, 1970). In attempting to reconcile contradictory findings about the impact of relocation on older persons, Schulz and Brenner (1977) argue that control and predictability serve as the major mediators of the older person's response to stress. They borrow from the stress paradigm utilized in psychology and suggest that behavioral control may reduce uncertainty about the nature and timing of the threatening event.

Schulz and Brenner (1977) have made an important contribution toward providing a conceptual framework for understanding the impact of relocation and environmental changes on older persons. Nevertheless it is interesting to note that they still consider environmental change only as a noxious stimulus and a potentially negative event which may be rendered less problematic when control and predictablity are introduced.

This generally negative view of environmental or personal changes during the later years is also reflected in work concerned with personal and/or environmental continuity during later life which is approached from diverse conceptual and empirical perspectives within the field of gerontology.

Personal Change

Changes occurring within older persons are generally viewed as negative or detrimental, and stability is considered to be the most positive response to the aging process (Riley & Foner, 1968). Furthermore, when changes do occur, they are generally seen as outside of the older person's control and volition. These theories generally reflect the view held by sociologists since Durkheim (1897) stated that change is problematic. The necessity of role redefinition in later life is also stressed in the work of Peck (1968). In elaborating on Erikson's (1950) concept of ego integrity in late life, Peck stressed that successful aging may be achieved when older people resolve three crises. These include an abandonment of work preoccupation, body transcendence, and ego transcendence (i.e., an emphasis on one's contribution to others). The importance of contributory roles for successful aging has also been stressed by Midlarsky and Kahana (1981), based on studies of altruistic behavior among older persons.

The lively controversy regarding stability versus change in human personality is still raging, and it provides social scientists and the public with frequent evidence of both change and stability. Recent longitudinal studies specifically focusing on later life (Costa, McCrae, & Arenberg, 1980) have emphasized stability of personality into old age. Thus evidence of stability has been reported for diverse traits ranging from extroversion–introversion, to neuroticism, and, to a lesser extent, even an openness to new experiences and excitement-seeking. It has been argued that data which may be interpreted as evidence of stabililty by some may also be viewed as evidence of change by others. Thus, Brim (1976) has suggested that, when one looks at stability, in fact one looks at the people who in effect have gotten stuck. He argues that our focus must be on change rather than on stability. Levinson, Darrow, Klein, Levinson, and McKee (1978) question the validity of paper-and-pencil tests as reflecting stability. Potential growth, according to Levinson, must be considered in a holistic manner. He challenges developmental psychologists by suggesting that a true developmentalist cannot lack a concern for human potential for growth and change.

Sociologists have generally not recognized utility of change. Marris (1975) developed a theoretical framework concerning change and loss as a universal experience. He argues that adaptations are required, socially and psychologically, because of the loss of past reality and the necessary construction of new realities. A crucial theme of the framework is that the anxieties of change center upon the struggle to defend or recover a meaningful pattern of relationships after a life transition. He argues that all of us have a need for continuity in our relationships with our environment. Marris maintains that transition involves a break in our thread of continuity or else a serious threat to its existence.

The issue of the threat to personal identity and continuity posed by retirement during the later years has been discussed by Atchley (1977). Atchley argues with the position advocated by S. Miller (1965) that retirement involves a breakdown of identity for older persons in our society. Atchley points out that older people can typically cope well and even look forward to the discontinuity posed by retirement and the opportunity to adapt to a new leisure-oriented life-style. Nevertheless, these adaptations are seen by Atchley as involving maintenance of interpersonal continuity and the carry over of work-related skills and attitudes into leisure activities. He thus proposes a theory of "identity continuity" after retirement through leisure roles shared with one's retired co-workers. Thus, leisure is seen as a bridge providing continuity between pre- and postretirement periods.

Futurity

Closely related to considerations of the impact of change during the later years is the question of personal desirability of change and the concept of futurity. Older persons have been found to project themselves into a much more limited time span than younger persons when asked to describe important future events in their lives (Kastenbaum, 1966). The general consensus among gerontologists has been that older persons lack futurity (Kalish, 1977). This position is based in part on the limited probabililty that older persons would live a substantial number of additional years in good health. A perception of this limited futurity of the aged has been cited as a reason for society's not investing major resources in older persons. Kalish (1977) attributes the relatively low achievement motivation of older persons to this lack of a sense of futurity. According to him, the older person is rendered helpless to achieve, since whatever is attempted will be transient and unfinished.

Research evidence for a limited sense of futurity among the elderly has come primarily from a set of studies (Back, 1966; Kalish & Reynolds, 1976) using hypothetical problems to determine how older persons would spend their time if provided with information that they had only a very short time (30–60 days) to live. Older people in these studies were less likely than younger ones to indicate that they would change their activities.

In a study of 226 community residents, Spence (1968) examined the role of futurity in the adaptation of older persons. In examining the relationship of different approaches to planning for the future, he found that those who were future-oriented were more likely to be satisfied than those who were complacent. Specifically, the composed planners were much more likely to be satisfied than the complacent, and the unsettled were more likely to be satisfied than the disgruntled. Interestingly, Spence also reports that, as people age, it is those who desire change who continue to plan. In this sense, futurity is seen as related to a desire to effect environmental change.

In contrast to the prevailing view on the generally negative impact of change on older people, a few researchers have recognized the potential value of personal and an environmental change during later life. One of the earliest references to the value of flexibility in later life comes from the work of Havighurst and Albrecht (1953). They suggest that deliberate cultivation of flexibility after age 50 in preparation for retirement may enhance adaptation to new roles in later life. Spence (1968) outlines a dynamic model of engagement in the later years. He suggests that there is a constant reinterpretation of self and situation with consequent modification of actions which comprise the dynamic nature of major life roles.

He suggests that, with termination of major work and family careers, a new flexibility develops during the later years. Geographic moves and life-style changes are facilitated by this new flexibililty.

Positive Functions of Change

After a careful search, a number of relatively isolated references to the positive functions of change in later life have been located. Schonfield (1973) utililzed a similar set of assumptions in his research proposing that future commitments should enhance adaptation in later life. In this context, planning ahead and a desire for change may be seen as related to successful aging. It is important to note that the value of futurity, activity, and stimulation may be seen as sharing a kinship with tenets of the activity theory of aging.

Streib (1977) emphasized that, in spite of well-documented role losses during the later years, old age can also provide a period of new role opportunities. Given good health, some social support and person innovation, it is possible to alter role sets in later maturity. Lowenthal, Thurnher, and Chiriboga (1975), in their longitudinal study of life-change transitions, have found that people in the preretirement stage showed more systematic changes in values than any other age group, portraying major shifts in five of seven value categories. Major changes reflected a decline in instrumental–material values and an increase in social service and ease–contentment values.

Although the authors originally anticipated that young persons who had their whole lives ahead of them would anticipate more change than older persons with a more limited futurity, findings did not bear out such expectations. Furthermore, insight, competence, and hope tended to characterize those anticipating further changes in the future during later life. Among women, those with greatest confidence in their ability to control the environment were most likely to anticipate changes for the future.

In a study of life transitions, Lowenthal (1971) investigated different lifestyles that constitute adaptive strategies after relocation. New leisure roles assumed by older persons were found to have greater importance. Lowenthal (1971) suggests that, following role losses which may have been experienced prior to relocation, new environments may afford many opportunites for re-engagement, primarily in social and leisure activities.

Although focusing on the reduction in social roles and interpersonal involvements often characterizing older persons, psychologists have seldom focused on the reverse pattern of seeking engagement, involvement, and stimulation during the later years. Yet Wohlwill (1966) argues that a large portion of everyday human activity is related to heightening the level of incoming stimulation.

Lawton (1980) has pointed to the applications of Helson's (1964) adaptation level theory to the aged. According to that model, deviations from adaptative level (or, in our scheme, from complete congruence) are evaluated positively within a certain range. Deviations that exceed an optimal level, in contrast, are experienced as unpleasant.

Carp and Carp (1980) have validly criticized activity–disengagement and futurity theories for failing to account for individual differences in patterns of successful aging. It appears however that concerns of futurity may be usefully incorporated and may enrich a congruence model of aging which is predicted in a recognition of individual differences.

Role Continuity in Later Life

Rosow (1974) proposes a theory of role transition–continuity in his work on socialization to old age. He argues that, contrary to all other age-related role transitions and status sequences in American society, socialization to old age does not have complementary rites of passage, social gains, and normative preparation. In this sense, he views old age as characterized by major role discontinuity. Discontinuities in later life are primarily composed of social losses. According to Rosow there is little cultural preparation and facilitation or attribution of meaning to these discontinuities. Role losses are not seen by Rosow as encompassing potentially desirable freedoms from responsibility. Furthermore, the role of individual differences in the extent to which culturally prescribed passages into old age are needed or desired are not discussed.

Hagestad (1980) criticizes Rosow for overemphasizing "immutable structural" roles and directs attention to primary roles and relationships and also to the ongoing process of role negotiation. Our view of adjustment as an outcome independent of coping processes is inconsistent with Rosow's (1967) original operational definition of adjustment as represented by maximum continuity in life patterns. Nevertheless we find that Rosow's 1974 formulation about late life as shaped by individual choice and personal initiative to be consistent with a potentially positive view of change which is within the older individual's reach and control. It is important to note that both Rosow and his critics have considered continuity from the relatively universal vantage point of role theory. We suggest here that the nature of continuity may be more profitably approached from the vantage point of individual differences and environmental opportunities to meet varying personal needs for continuity.

Environments may be profitably considered, in a broad sense, to encompass diverse social and psychological opportunities. In discussing the first concept of congruence presented at the Environmental Design Research Association meeting a number of years ago (Kahana, 1975a), Rapaport commented that symbolic and dynamic dimensions may be lacking in the model. Our data on the adventurous aged also points to the great importance of considering congruence in symbolic aspects of person–environment. Furthermore, consideration of adaptation in a longitudinal framework leads to a consideration of P–E fit in a dynamic framework.

It is proposed here that self-initiated environmental change may provide a possible and meaningful avenue for the elderly to extend themselves into the future, to find meaningful new stimulation and roles, and to enhance their satisfaction during later life.

In the following section, we will focus on self-initiated environmental change in the form of long-distance migration among the aged. We will apply the conceptual considerations noted thus far regarding the roles which futurity, change, and stimulus-seeking have in contributing to later life adjustment. Finally, we will attempt to expand the congruence model of P–E fit to incorporate environmental preferences of the adventurous aged.

THE ADVENTUROUS AGED

Desire for Environmental Change among the Elderly

There has been an increased interest in recent years in interurban residential mobility and in the identification of those characteristics underlying the relocation desires of Americans (Golant, 1971; Wolpert, 1965). Currently, 20% of the population of the United States changes residence annually. Although many moves are made by a small number of highly mobile persons, one-half of our entire population moves within a 5-year period (Simmons, 1968).

Younger persons are the most mobile, and the frequency of relocation among adults declines steadily with age (Goldscheider, Van Arsdol, & Sabagh, 1965). Of all persons aged 65 and over in 1974, only 16.9% moved as compared with 56.9% of the general population and 61.1% of the 20–24 age group (U. S. Bureau of the Census, 1974).

Data about the elderly's desire to change residence have important implications for both the applied and theoretical aspects of gerontology. Nelson and Winter (1975) have indicated that, if planners are expecting to adequately meet the housing needs of the aged, they must obtain precise information about why older people move from their homes. Without current data concerning those factors which make residential settings unattractive to senior citizens, adequate planning of new housing is difficult. The study of residential relocation among the elderly, however, is relatively underdeveloped in contrast to other areas of sociological and demographic inquiry (Ashley & McFarland, 1968; Lawton, Kleban, & Carlson, 1973). To date, the majority of mobility studies concerning the aged have focused on relocation to congregate care facilities, reporting on adaptation to institutional settings (Aldrich & Mendkoff, 1963; Goldfarb, Shahinian, & Turner, 1966; Lieberman, 1961; Miller & Lieberman, 1965). Understanding of the factors which give rise to voluntary relocation desires among community elderly is still very limited.

Voluntary Relocation and Migration of the Aged

It is well known that significant numbers of Americans choose to spend their retirement years living on Social Security benefits abroad. In fact, international migration by the aged has been identified as a major trend of the future, as larger proportions of Americans are reaching retirement age and as the mobility of the aged increases (Belbin, 1972). Nevertheless, there have not been systematic studies thus far which provide data for understanding the characteristics and adaptation of older persons relocating abroad. Similarly, migration to warmer regions within the United States has become a significant trend among older persons (Golant, 1975). A large proportion of these older persons settle in retirement communities. However, there is insufficient information about the successes and failures of this group who undertake major environmental experiences (Lowenthal & Chiriboga, 1972; Sheley, 1974).

In addition to the importance of understanding the dynamics of international and regional migration among the aged, studying the adaptation of this group provides a unique opportunity for gaining insights into theoretical issues about the effects of voluntary relocation and processes of environmental adaptation following self-initiated changes in habitat and life-style.

Research on Americans retiring abroad and in Florida provides an opportunity to gain information about aged persons exhibiting characteristics and strengths which are usually not associated with the aged. Instead of a traditional focus on older people who fit the stereotypes of being disengaged and unable to form any new attachments, older persons choosing to relocate to distant regions assume a great deal of control over their environments. Information regarding the effects of voluntary relocation to new residental environments by older persons should be useful to planners of new communities and housing facilities for the aged (Lawton, 1980).

The study of migration among the aged also incorporates a sociological orientation to adaptation. As Brody (1970) points out:

> A shift in residence involves not only new places but new faces and new norms. Movement over distance implies the crossing of social system boundaries whether the systems are defined in terms of national entities, regional subcultures or immediate friendship and kinship networks. The migrant leaves behind the supports and stresses of the donor system from which he departs . . . at the same time he is excited by the new stimuli and opportunities and fearful of new threats and the unknown in his new milieu [p. 15].

The Case of the Israel-Bound Elderly Migrant

An elderly person emigrating from the United States to Israel represents an interesting case study illustrating the search of some older persons for discontinuity, challenge, and environmental change. The typical Israel-bound emigrant undertakes a move for ideological, if not idealistic, reasons. He or she willingly joins the struggles of a small war-torn country. The person gives up many of the comforts of an established home to integrate socially into a melting pot of diverse cultures. This emigrant expects to face hardships and anticipates having to make some major readaptations; there is a sense of adventure in the desire to move.

Those relocating to Israel view themselves, for the most part, as "going home" to live their remaining days in the land of their people and to actualize their prayers and religious wishes. Isaacs (1967) outlines the essence of relocation to Israel as the desire to express one's Jewish identity, or "shared sameness" in Erikson's (1950) terms. The emigration is seen as enhancing ego identity and self-esteem by the individual's integration into the Jewish culture of Israel.

Relocation to Israel requires major readaptation, especially in adjusting to different social conventions. It may be argued that identification with the people and the land allows the individual to anticipate hardships and to cope with a more difficult life-style. The major adaptive tasks are in coping with a foreign sociocultural environment and in recognizing that "Jewishness" alone does not prepare the emigrant for living in Israel.

The Case of Florida-Bound Migrants

In contrast to retirees emigrating to Israel, the Florida-bound migrant is motivated less by ideological reasons and more by a desire to spend retirement years in a warm, tranquil environment. He or she wants to leave behind the heterogeneous milieu of the city life and opt for an adult age-segregated environment.

The Florida-bound older person often welcomes the end of the need to work and of involvement with children and grandchildren, although many of the movers welcome visits from family during the holidays. Going to Florida may have been a life's dream or a relatively recent desire, but, in any event, many view it as a gift they give themselves after the hardships of younger years. There is an interest in self-actualization via new or renewed leisure activities, diet, and exercise, and appreciation of nature. There is an anticipation of a move into a more comfortable, new and modern (although often smaller) residence.

There is also a desire to establish a new life-style *apart and separate* from younger people and a positive identification with one's age cohort, "the young-old." Many older persons pride themselves in no longer listening to the news and wish to construct a leisure world where neither nature's hardships nor society's problems can affect them.

There are some noteworthy similarities among those who relocate to Israel and Florida. Risk-taking is a common feature of both these groups. They do not mind having to learn new features of behavior, adaptation, and life-styles. Both groups feel capable of emotionally investing themselves in their new environments and are willing to part with many of their lifelong neighbors and friends as well as family.

Futurity, Desire for Change, and Satisfaction among Long Distance Movers

When older persons seek to relocate voluntarily, it is interesting to note that the major motivating factors are not posed by the constraints of the old environment but by the attractions of the new one (E. Kahana, B. Kahana, & McLenigan, 1980).

The following table presents a diametric representation of the relationships suggested between futurity, desire for change, and satisfaction among long-distance movers.

		Environmental change	Environmental continuity
Future orientation	→ Seeking new lifestyles Δ in preferences	High satisfaction	Low satisfaction
Past–Present orientation	→ Seeking continuity No Δ in preferences	Low satisfaction	High satisfaction

Those movers who persistently seek to diminish discomfort or incongruence by undertaking relocation have been found in our research to be more often disappointed with the results of the move than those who sought to enrich their lives and looked for new environmental opportunity in a salient area.

For the adventurous aged and for those exhibiting future orientation in planning their moves, areas of environmental opportunity to meet their need for self-expression are most likely to result in environmental satisfaction. In considering determinants of satisfaction and adjustment subsequent to voluntary relocation, it appeared that future-oriented older persons sought and needed environmental opportunities providing them with new experiences and challenges. In contrast, older persons exhibiting a greater past or present orientation sought continuity in terms of salient life-styles. When individuals seeking new opportunities of self-expression could not find them or when those requiring continuity experienced too much change, dissatisfaction resulted. Specifically, persons relocating due to specific environmental dissatisfactions (e.g., high crime rates or inconvenient apartments) often reported disappointment with their move. For them the new environment was seen as presenting too many unanticipated changes or inconveniences. In contrast, those seeking new activities and opportunities tended to be pleased with their moves even when their new life-styles presented greater inconvenience or discomfort than their prior living situations. Thus, relocation is usually based on the pull of the new environment rather than the dissatisfactions with previous living arrangements.

Patterns of Relocation Adaptation

Data from our still ongoing longitudinal study of adaptation to voluntary long-distance moves (E. Kahana, B. Kahana, & McLenigan, 1980) reveal that long-distance relocation typically represents the culmination of long years of planning and preparation for older persons and often involves some trial periods such as being a "snowbird" in Florida or a temporary resident in Israel. Those who relocate portray a wide range of adaptive styles. New activities and life-styles often represent changes in macro adaptations. In contrast, strategies for coping with concrete stresses and problem situations appear to be rooted in traitlike constellations of coping abilities. Interestingly, many who make long-distance relocations seek discontinuity and measure their success by new challenges and the interesting level of their new lives, rather than by the lack of adaptive tasks. Readaptations are most difficult for persons who are not enthusiastic about the move at the outset.

Our findings have generally confirmed hypotheses about different life-styles subsequent to the relocation for both Florida-bound and Israel-bound persons. These different life-styles represent alternative pathways to self-actualization and to Erikson's (1950) stage of "Integrity." It was typical for the Florida-bound respondents to say, "All my life I have done for my children and family, now it is time to do for me!" This orientation was then followed by various efforts toward self-improvement, education, diet, exercise, and learning new skills.

In contrast, the Israel-bound respondents typically reasoned, "All my life I have done for my children and my family, now it is time that I do for others!" Although many emigrants to Israel opted for a leisure-oriented life-style, this group appeared more altruistic and often gravitated to social and volunteer activities. Israel-bound respondents often moved for ideological reasons seeking fulfillment of a dream to live in a Jewish state. Florida-bound respondents appeared more pragmatic about their moves citing concrete environmental and even financial advantages with a minority moving for health reasons.

Longitudinal data is available for subjects reflecting the first 6 months after the move. In addition, we have cross-sectional data on people who have lived in Israel for 1–5 years.

Although 21% of the premove group listed their health as excellent, 42% of the group that moved within the past 6 months said their health was excellent. There are two explanations for the phenomenon. First, among those planning to move, those in better health are actually more likely to move. Second, the period immediately following the move represents a period of a "high" for long-distance relocators. The stresses and hassles associated with the move actually appear overshadowed by the sense of gratification from "dreams" realized and a euphoria related to a sense of internal control—"I have done it." There tends to be a sense of satisfaction that enables the individual to transcend or deny many of the day-to-day problems confronted in the new environment.

In terms of reported changes in health, 19.4% reported an actual improvement in health during the period following the move. It is interesting to note that only 5.6% indicated improvement in health for a comparable period during the premove period. With regard to a reported decline in health, the proportion for premove and postmove groups are identical (16.1% for each).

When activity patterns in the new environment are compared for recent movers and for those residing there for 1–5 years, some interesting patterns emerge. Only a small proportion actually continue to work for pay after relocation. About 9% work for pay 3–6 months after arrival at their new environments compared to 17% of those in residence 1–5 years after the move.

Religious participation represents an important outlet for about one-third of the sample. Such participation appears to be stable in that the same proportion reports being involved 3–6 months after the move as are involved 1–5 years later. There appears to be a dramatic increase, however, in volunteer activities for long-term relocators, thus 3–6 months after arrival, only about 16% report at least some involvement, whereas 1–5 years after the move, 67% of respondents engage in some volunteer activity. Thus, volunteering and contributing represent a meaningful and important new outlet for the older relocator. Our respondents generally appeared highly motivated to assume contributory life-styles and to improve living conditions in their new environments.

Activity patterns of the Florida-bound elderly revealed a similar pattern to the Israel-bound aged. Working for pay was even less prevalent among the Florida-bound than among the Israel-bound; thus only 8–10% engaged in work for pay both during the immediate postmove and the long-term move group. Participation in religious activities showed a modest increase when compared with immediate postmove to the long-term postmove period.

Our study also explored predictors of positive postrelocation outcomes for 259 older Americans who relocated to Florida retirement communities. Outcome variables included high morale, improved health, and satisfaction with life in Florida. Stepwise multiple regression analysis revealed different significant predictors for these diverse outcome variables. Those in better health, females, and married persons exhibited high postmove morale as did those who felt enthusiastic about relocation before their move. Improvement in health was significantly related to the age, the sex of the respondent (female), the perception of the move as *not* permanent (snowbirds), and the positive views of life in Florida. Interestingly the length of residence in Florida served as an important predictor of satisfaction with life there as did enthusiasm with the move and a feeling that it required few readjustments.

These data suggest that voluntary relocation results in high levels of satisfaction for most aged undertaking such moves in spite of the major readaptation required from them. Positive attitudes and expectations serve as important determinants of coping with long-distance relocation.

Typologies of Successful Relocators

Although quantitative results will have to await the conclusion of longitudinal data collection, our extensive fieldwork and preliminary data have provided some exciting glimpses into the typologies of long-distance movers to Israel and Florida and into some of the life-styles open to older persons who undertake long-distance moves. These patterns appear relevant to older persons who voluntarily undertake residential moves to diverse settings. Interestingly, they also cut across residential moves to Florida and to Israel. Among the *well adjusted* we found four typologies:

1. *The Explorers*: These older persons seek and often find a new lifestyle, a different routine, and a different environment from that to which they have been accustomed. They look for new stimuli, new activities, and enjoy travel. They do not prepare carefully for the move, may even relocate on an impulse, but relish the surprises that await them. They do not put a high premium on material possessions or physical comforts and score high on risk-taking. They may view retirement as a liberating opportunity for a new beginning and for adding a new dimension to their lives.

2. *The Helpers*: These older persons seek fulfillment in their later years through altruistic endeavors. They find joy in "doing for others" on an organized or individual basis. They frequently engage in volunteer activities and seek to relocate to a situation where they can remain useful. They are highly instrumental, find it difficult to adjust to retirement, and seek a meaningful substitute for the world of work. Relocation may actually result in more different circumstances for this group, but they measure their success in terms of challenges found and contributions made.

3. *The Fun Seekers:* This group of older persons succeeded in finding gratification in a leisure-oriented life-style by seeking out environments that provide balmy weather and maximize leisure options and recreational facilities. They often looked forward to retirement years as a period for a well-earned vacation and welcome relinquishing work and family obligations to actualize themselves with self-improvements and a fun-seeking life-style. They enjoy sharing leisure activities with others of similar interests, tend to be highly sociable, and seek association with other older persons of like background and interests.

4. *The Comfort Seekers:* This group, during their retirement years, often rented apartments in crowded, unsafe neighborhoods and lived under trying economic circumstances. They planned, saved, and dreamed for years of a first new home in a new, clean community and safer neighborhood as the reward of a lifetime of hard work. They seek comfort and rest and spend much time in decorating and enjoying their new apartments and revel in the improved physical environment that their new life-style provides. Warm climates are seen as increasing their comfort. These people may be in frail health; they are older and enjoy a relatively disengaged, quiet life-style.

IMPLICATIONS OF VOLUNTARY RELOCATION
FOR THE CONCEPT OF PERSON–ENVIRONMENT FIT

Our initial study of the congruence concept (E. Kahana, Liang, & Felton, 1980) dealt with the P–E fit model in one narrow range of environments and with a relatively homogenous population of institutionalized older persons. The measures utilized in our initial analyses were restricted to personal preferences for (P) and staff judgements of the environment (E).

It is important to emphasize that the model of P–E fit outlined earlier may be applied to a broad range of definitions of both person and environment. The value of the model is seen in its applicability to diverse populations, dimensions, and measurement strategies. Data from our recent study of the adventurous aged who voluntarily initiate life changes serve to point the way toward expanded use of the P–E fit model.

Application of the P–E fit model to diverse populations of elderly has important implications both for assessment of personal characteristics and for consideration of environmental features. In terms of environmental features, it should be noted that institutionalized aged have relatively little freedom of choice in creating their own environment or in leaving the incongruent environment. Based on the environmental docility hypothesis (Lawton & Nahemow, 1973), one could expect that these aged will be especially vulnerable to environmental influences. Typically, these elderly are relocated involuntarily to a situation that may be expected to present greater P–E incongruence than did their original home environment.

In our previous research considering dimensions of P–E fit in institutional settings (Kahana, Liang, & Felton, 1980), we have primarily focused on aspects of the environment which are likely to pose areas of incongruence for residents of congregate facilities—an environment typically characterized in terms of the constraints that it posed. Community settings are less likely to pose direct constraints on behavior. Recent studies have employed similar P–E fit concepts to older populations living in residential housing sites (Kiyak, 1978) and to community-living older persons (Carp & Carp, 1980). The latter populations dictate separate assessment strategies for each individual's environment.

Our study of older persons undertaking long-distance moves has considered much older persons who voluntarily relocated from one community to another. Although our earlier work on congruence focused on the vulnerable aged, we are now interested in extending the notion to the competent and well aged. Continuity has, in the past, been defined as a major form of congruence (Rosow, 1967). However, adventurous older persons often seek discontinuity. Discontinuity between previous life-styles and current life situation may be differentiated from previously suggested models of P–E fit. Furthermore, consideration of an active search for discontinuity raises questions about linear models of P–E fit. In extending P–E fit research to diverse populations of aged we may obtain new information regarding the range and variety of the models. In the initial empirical study (E. Kahana, Liang, & Felton, 1980), P–E fit was essentially considered in a static fashion. It is important to note, however, that the model readily lends itself to dynamic interpretations.

Given certain levels of P–E fit at any moment in time, the question arises as to the effects of change in environments or of change in personal needs and preferences on fit and on subsequent outcomes. In this framework, any environmental change or manipulation may be viewed as impacting on P–E fit. Relocation of older persons may be considered as a prime example of such an alteration of P–E fit. Although the environmental impact of relocation is readily observable, it is useful to note that relocation may be a function of changed personal needs and preferences as well.

Forced relocation, such as that experienced by most institutionalized older persons is likely to lead to low levels of congruence. In contrast, voluntary relocation generally implies expectations of enhanced congruence between the new environment and the older person's needs. In populations of older persons seeking to relocate, lack of congruence between person and environment may lead to relocation decisions. When the new P–E fit does not meet expectations, negative outcomes are likely to result. Thus, it is important to look not only at *postrelocation* P–E fit, but also at the relative increase or decrease in fit and the discrepancy between expected and actual fit. Preferences and needs for environmental continuity versus change may in themselves become important aspects of P–E fit in relocation studies. In this context independent assessments of continuity preference are suggested rather than simple assumptions about the volition of the move.

In considering a congruence model to predict environmental satisfaction subsequent to voluntary moves, a dynamic approach must be used that takes into account both changes in personal preference and changes in environment. Thus, an environment meeting the initial preferences of a respondent may, in fact, prove to be incongruent subsequent to a self-initiated move.

Environmental characteristics, presses, and opportunities which fulfilled the older person's long-term needs and preferences have been traditionally considered as important for environmental satisfaction among older persons. In considering P–E fit congruence, subsequent to long-distance moves, we cannot assume that long-term patterns of preference were to be matched with environments. Instead, expectations for new patterns of fit may need to be met. Thus, a person who lives in an age-integrated environment and is satisfied may have developed new preferences for an age-homogenous environment and may seek to fulfill those preferences by moving to a Florida retirement community.

Different dimensions of P–E fit are likely to be salient to different groups of aged. The dimensions posed in the original formulation of the P–E fit concept considered those dimensions of fit that were hypothesized to be especially salient to institutionalized aged and to vulnerable older persons (E. Kahana, 1975b). Selection of these dimensions by no means implies the assumption that they include all major determinants of morale.

In institutional settings, environmental dimensions reflecting constraints and personal dimensions reflecting varying degrees of impairment or deficiency become salient. Consideration of P–E fit in community samples representing competent older persons requires a choice of different dimensions of fit. For example, environmental opportunities (Lawton, 1980), as well as environmental constraints, may be profitably incorporated into consideration of fit for such populations of competent aged.

Based on our research on older persons who were voluntarily relocating to Florida and Israel, eight areas of environmental opportunities appear to be particularly salient for the adventurous aged. Respondents were asked to check those areas where a P–E fit was most important to them and where mismatch presented the greatest problems. Based on open-ended responses for 40 older persons, a checklist of areas of potential match and mismatch was obtained. Added to this list were also applicable dimensions of the original model. The resulting list of dimensions was then given to a second subsample of 60 older persons; they are (a) age segregation–homogeneity; (b) activity–participation; and (c) social interaction–integration.

Additional dimensions of preference relevant to the adventurous aged include those in areas of environmental stimulation. These dimensions fit well with stimulus-seeking behaviors discussed by Wohlwill (1966); they include (a) challenge–adventure; (b) novelty–variety; (c) control–choice; (d) helping–giving; and (e) functioning–planning. Environmental opportunities which fulfill the older person's needs in these areas appear to be particularly likely to result in self-fulfillment and satisfaction.

Both individual and environmental factors may mitigate the importance of congruence for outcomes. Among individual variables, competence may be one of the most important. We have argued that for the most vulnerable persons (e.g., those bedridden in a nursing home) personal (P) variables, such as health, may become so overwhelmingly important that effects of

P–E fit wash out. On the other end of the spectrum for the most competent persons with rich personal resources, P–E fit is likely to be high because of their ability to manipulate their environmental context. The adventurous aged may even seek to decrease congruence and continuity in a search for autotelic experiences in new environmental contexts.

This orientation is exemplified in the response of one older man who relocated in Israel after retiring as a pharmacist: "Retirees should have a sense of adventure. At our age, it is a privilege to start a new life. When I lived in New York, I was not active. I was not used to getting up and speaking before people, and I didn't belong to any organization. In Israel I am involved and it feels wonderful."

CONCLUSIONS

Our aim in this chapter was primarily to call attention to an atypical and, thus far, overlooked pattern of aging—one that does not support commonly held notions of later life motivations and life-styles. We attempted in this effort to point out some of those factors that may explain alternative pathways to successful aging. In particular, concepts of futurity, change, and stimulus-seeking may be useful in considering the adaptation of this group. These concepts are not seen as representing an alternative universal prescription for older persons. Rather, they are viewed as important areas of potential diversity which are best conceptualized in the framework of a congruence model. We hope that focusing on this alternative pattern will generate systematic future research and enable us to examine evidence which may broaden our view of the range of aging experiences and patterns of successful aging. A recognition of a more hopeful pattern of responses to later life may also provide an incentive to many older persons who have been led to believe that their options were severely limited. They may look toward expanded life-styles by recognizing that a sense of futurity may be as much a liberating frame of mind as a limiting sense of reality.

For the adventurous aged, the later years pose a new opportunity for freedom from obligations and role prescriptions, affording them with a second career in living. This may be a chance to become physically fit, to fight for a favorite cause, or even to try to improve the world. The adventurous aged, in fact, may seem to embody and give meaning to the old adage that life begins at 60. Although the search for new life-styles, exemplified by this group, may be relatively infrequent among the elderly, the adventurous aged pose a challenge to gerontologists to reexamine our stereotypes and to consider alternative pathways to integrity in the later years.

The subjective nature of time and futurity is aptly illustrated in a little poem written by the 13-year-old daughter of a friend:

Past
is nothing but the future gone away.
One minute from now—
Now its one minute from then.

Future
is nothing but the past before it happens
Time before it becomes the present just to become the past.

Present
is nothing.
By the time you finish saying, "No time like the present"—
it's already become the past.

Time
is
nothing.

—SUSAN MIDLARSKY
Grade 8

REFERENCES

Aldrich, C., & Mendkoff, E. Relocation of the aged and disabled: A mortality study. *Journal of American Geriatric Society,* 1963, *11,* 185–194.

Ashley, E., & McFarland, M. The need for research toward meeting the housing needs of the elderly. In C. Tibbits & W. Donahue (Eds.), *Social and psychological aspects of aging.* New York: Columbia University Press, 1968.

Atchley, R. Retirement: Continuity or crisis? In R. Kalish (Ed.), *The later years: Social implications of gerontology.* Monterey, Calif.: Brooks/Cole, 1977.

Back, R. Meaning of time in later life. *Journal of Genetic Psychology,* 1966, *109,* 9–25.

Belbin, R. M. Retirement strategies in an evolving society. *Retirement,* 1972, 175–196.

Brim, O. Male mid life crisis—a comparative analysis. In B. Heff (Ed.), *Growing Old in America* (Vol. 2). New Brunswick, N. J.: Transaction Books, 1976.

Brody, E. *Behavior in new environments: Adaptation of migrant population.* Fresno, Calif.: Sage Publications, 1970.

Carp, F. M. Person–environment congruence in engagement. *The Gerontologist,* 1968, *8,* 184–188.

Carp, F. M., & Carp, A. *Person–environment congruence and sociability.* Unpublished manuscript, Wright Institute, Berkeley, Calif., 1980.

Costa, P., McCrae, R., & Arenberg, D. Enduring dispositions in adult males. *Journal of Personality and Social Psychology*, 1980, *38*(5), 793–800.

Dohrenwend, B. S., & Dohrenwend, B. P. *Stressful life events: Their nature and effects.* New York: Wiley, 1974.

Durkheim, E. *Le suicide.* Paris: Etude Sociologigue, 1897.

Erikson, E. *Childhood and society.* New York: Norton, 1950.

Golant, S. M. Adjustment process in a system: A behavioral model of human movement. *Geographical Analysis*, 1971, *3*, 203–220.

Golant, S. M. Residential concentrations of the future elderly. *The Gerontologist*, 1975, *15*, 16–23.

Goldfarb, A., Shahinian, S., & Turner, H. *Death rates in relocated aged residents of nursing homes.* Paper presented at Gerontological Society Meetings, New York, 1966.

Goldscheider, C., Van Arsdol, M., & Sabagh, G. Residential mobility of older people. In F. Carp (Ed.), *Patterns of living and housing of middle aged and older people.* Washington, D. C.: U. S. Government Printing Office, 1965.

Hagestad, G. *Discontinuity versus flexibility: The need for a social psychological approach to men's and women's adult roles.* Paper presented at the Gerontological Society Meetings, San Diego, 1980.

Havighurst, R., & Albrecht, R. *Older people.* New York: Longmans Green, 1953.

Helson, H. *Adaptation level theory.* New York: Harper & Row, 1964.

Holden, C. Dark days for social research. *Science*, 1981, *211*, 1397–1398.

Isaacs, H. *American Jews in Israel.* New York: John Day, 1967.

Kahana, B., Kiyak, A., & Kahana, E. Changing attitudes toward the aged. *National Journal*, November 1979, pp. 1913–1919.

Kahana, E. *Service needs and service utilization of urban aged.* Final progress report submitted to National Institute of Mental Health, December 1974.

Kahana, E. Environmental adaptation of the aged. In T. Byerts (Ed.), *Housing and Environment for the elderly.* Washington, D. C.: Gerontological Society, 1975. (a)

Kahana, E. Matching environments to needs of the aged: A conceptual scheme. In J. Gubrium (Ed.), *Late life: Recent developments in the sociology of aging.* Springfield, Ill.: Charles C Thomas, 1975. (b)

Kahana, E., Fairchild, T., & Kahana, B. Measurement of adaptation to changes in health and environmental changes among the aged. In R. Mangen & W. Peterson (Eds.), *Handbook to research instruments in social gerontology.* Minneapolis: University of Minnesota Press, 1982.

Kahana, E., & Kahana, B. Theoretical and research perspectives on grandparent: A theoretical statement. *Aging and Human Development*, 1971, *2*, 261–268.

Kahana, E., & Kahana, B. *Strategies of aging in institutional environments.* Progress report submitted to National Institute of Mental Health, 1978.

Kahana, E., Kahana, B., & McLenigan, P. *The adventurous aged: Voluntary Relocation in later years.* Paper presented at Gerontological Society Meetings, San Diego, November 1980.

Kahana, E., Liang, J., & Felton, B. Alternative models of person–environment fit: Prediction of morale in three homes for the aged. *Journal of Gerontology*, 1980, *35*, 584–595.

Kalish, R. *The later years: Social applications of gerontology.* Monterey, Calif.: Brooks/Cole, 1977.

Kalish, R., & Reynolds, D. *Death and ethnicity: A psychocultural study.* Los Angeles: University of Southern California Press, 1976.

Kastenbaum, R. As the clock runs out. *Mental Hygiene*, 1966, *59*, 332–336.

Kiyak, A. *Person–environment congruence as a predictor of satisfaction and well-being among institutionalized elderly.* Unpublished doctoral dissertation, Wayne State University, Detroit, 1978.

Lawton, M. P. *Environment and aging.* Monterey, Calif.: Brooks/Cole, 1980.

Lawton, M. P., Kleban, M., & Carlson, D. The inner city resident: To move or not to move. *The Gerontologist,* 1973, *13,* 443–448.

Lawton, M. P., & Nahemow, L. Ecology and the aging process. In M. P. Lawton & C. Eisdorfer (Eds.), *Psychology of adult development and aging.* Washington, D. C.: American Psychological Association, 1973.

Lawton, M. P., & Yaffe, S. Mortality, morbidity and voluntary change of residence by older people. *Journal of American Geriatric Society,* 1970, *18,* 823–831.

Levinson, D., Darrow, C., Klein, E., Levinson, M., & McKee, B. *The seasons of a man's life.* New York: Knopf, 1978.

Lieberman, M. The relationship of mortality rates to entrance to a home for the aged. *Geriatrics,* 1961, *16,* 515–519.

Lieberman, M. Institutionalization of the aged: Effects on behavior. *Journal of Gerontology,* 1969, *24,* 330–334.

Lieberman, M. Relocation research and social policy. In J. Gubrium (Ed.), *Late life: Communities and environmental policy.* Springfield, Ill.: Charles C Thomas, 1974.

Lowenthal, M. F. Intentionality: Toward a framework for the study of adaptation in adulthood. *Aging and Human Development,* 1971, *2,* 79–95.

Lowenthal, M. F., & Chiriboga, D. Transition to the empty nest: Crisis, challenge or relief? *Archives of General Psychiatry,* 1972, *26,* 8–14.

Lowenthal, M. F., Thurnher, M., & Chiriboga, D. *Four stages of life.* San Francisco: Jossey–Bass, 1975.

Marris, P. *Loss and change.* Ann Arbor: Anchor Press, 1975.

Midlarski, E., & Kahana, E. *Altruism and the aged.* Paper prepared for American Psychological Association Meetings, Los Angeles, September 1981.

Miller, D., & Lieberman, M. The relationships of affect state and adaptive capacity to reactions to stress. *Journal of Gerontology,* 1965, *20,* 492–497.

Miller, S. The social dilemma of the aging leisure participant. In A. Rose & W. Peterson (Eds.), *Old people and their social world: The subculture of the aging.* Philadelphia: F. A. Davis, 1965.

Nelson, L., & Winter, M. Life disruption, independence, satisfaction and the consideration of moving. *The Gerontologist,* 1975, *15,* 160–164.

Peck, R. Psychological developments in the second half of life. In B. Neugarten (Ed.), *Middle age and aging.* Chicago: University of Chicago Press, 1968.

Riley, M., & Foner, A. *Aging and society* (Vol. 2). New York: Russell Sage Foundation, 1968.

Rosow, I. *Social integration of the aged.* New York: Free Press, 1967.

Rosow, I. *Socialization of old age.* Berkeley, Calif.: University of California Press, 1974.

Schonfield, D. Future commitments and successful aging. *Journal of Gerontology,* 1973, *28,* 189–196.

Schulz, R., & Brenner, G. Relocation of the aged: A review and theoretical analysis. *Journal of Gerontology,* 1977, *32,* 323–3333.

Seligman, M. E. P. *Helplessness: On depression, development and death.* San Francisco: W. H. Freeman, 1975.

Sheley, J. Mutuality and retirement community success: An interactionist perspective in gerontological research. *Aging and Human Development,* 1974, *5,* 71–80.

Simmons, J. Changing residence in the city: A review of inter-urban mobility. *Demography,* 1968, 622–651.

Spence, D. The role of futurity in aging adaptation. *The Gerontologist*, 1968, 9, 180–183.

Streib, G. *The later years: Social applications of gerontology.* Monterey, Calif.: Brooks/Cole 1977.

U. S. Bureau of the Census. *Current population reports*, Series P-20, 273. Washington, D. C.: U. S. Government Printing Office, 1974.

Wohlwill, J. The physical environment: A problem for a psychology of stimulation. *Journal of Social Issues*, 1966, 22, 29–38.

Wolpert, J. Behavioral aspects of the decision to migrate. *Papers of the Regional Science Association*, 1965, 15, 159–169.

V

PERSPECTIVE

14

Emergent Themes and New Directions:
Reflection on Aging and Milieu Research

GRAHAM D. ROWLES   RUSSELL J. OHTA

In little more than a decade there has been a rapid proliferation of research on the theme of environment and aging (e.g., Altman, Wohlwill, & Lawton, in press; Atchley & Byerts, 1975; Byerts, Howell, & Pastalan, 1979; Golant, 1979; Lawton, 1980; Windley, Byerts, & Ernst, 1975). As a result, this domain has gradually emerged as a subfield within gerontology with its own cadre of prominent scholars, including Lawton, Pastalan, Kahana, Howell, Byerts, Newcomer, Carp, Cantor, and Gubrium. As the subfield has grown in significance it has, in common with all new research areas, evolved its own array of dominant themes and controversial issues. In this concluding chapter, we briefly review the recent history of the field, argue that the current state of aging–environment research presents us with a critical dilemma, and suggest ways in which the contributions in this volume constitute both an acknowledgment of the dilemma and a quest for new beginnings.

WHERE WE STAND

There are at least three justifications for engaging in research on the relationship between old people and their environmental contexts. First, from a theoretical perspective, the acute sensitivity of old people to small environmental changes makes them an ideal study population for exploring subtleties of the individual–environment transaction. Second, old age may represent a phase of life characterized by distinctive normative

AGING AND MILIEU:
ENVIRONMENTAL PERSPECTIVES
ON GROWING OLD

developmental transitions in the nature of the individual–environment transaction worthy of study in their own right. Finally, aging–environment research may be justified in terms of practical concerns of society with the living conditions of its elderly members that have made work in this domain a matter of great contemporary relevance.

The third rationale provided the main impetus for the burgeoning of the field during the 1970s. Societal concern for the problems of housing the elderly and improving the quality of institutional environments resulted in large-scale research funding during this era for specific design and evaluation projects. The Gerontological Society of America, through its Housing and Environment for the Aging Project (1971–1975) and a subsequent Curriculum Development in Environment and Aging Program (1975–1978), played a major role not only in encouraging basic research but also in providing impetus to the translation of findings into design alternatives and policy strategies.

One consequence of this funding emphasis was a somewhat circumscribed definition of the primary themes and controversies that were to provide the intellectual focuses of the emergent field. The issue of residential segregation versus community integration of the elderly became a critical concern because it was of direct relevance to the agencies commissioning the research (e.g., Lawton & Yaffe, 1979; Rosow, 1967; Sherman, 1971; Teaff, Lawton, Nahemow, & Carlson, 1978). The question of relocation and its impact on the old person became a central theme in aging–environment research for similar reasons (e.g., Aldrich & Mendkoff, 1963; Borup, Gallego, & Heffernan, 1979; Bourestom & Pastalan, 1981; Carp, 1966; Tobin & Lieberman, 1976; Wittels & Botwinick, 1974). In short, expediency came to determine substance. It resulted in a plethora of studies of high-rise housing projects, institutional environments, and other segregated settings. There was a regrettable paucity of aging–environment research on the majority of older people living out their days in community environments—in urban neighborhoods or rural communities where they had resided most of their lives.[1]

As the field expanded beyond its initial focus on specific policy questions and sought to develop understanding of the old person–environment relationship in broader context, a series of definitional issues became important. On the most basic level, how was environment to be defined? In everyday contexts we talk of people and environment as distinct entities, as somehow mutually exclusive. Yet this was clearly a false dichotomy. If we were to avoid this metaphysically complex and ultimately

---

[1]This selective myopia was, of course, reinforced by the fact that institutionalized and segregated populations were far easier to study in terms of obtaining satisfactory samples and undertaking survey research.

irresolvable issue by acknowledging the ultimate oneness of person and environment, while retaining the distinction for purposes of operational definition, we were confronted by other issues. What was the form of the person–environment (P–E) relationship? Should we adopt a determinist stance, viewing the old person as merely a passive respondent to environmental conditions beyond his or her control ($E \rightarrow P$)? Should we focus on the way individuals molded the settings in which they resided as, through use and the attribution of meaning, they transformed spaces into places ($P \rightarrow E$)? Or should we seek insight within an intuitively more attractive but operationally more complex transactional framework, acknowledging the dynamic reciprocity between the two elements ($P \rightleftharpoons E$)? Increasingly, as the field matured, emphasis shifted to the latter perspective (Ittelson, 1975).

Rapid expansion of the aging–environment field inevitably led to the quest for theory (Windley, Byerts, & Ernst, 1975). The 1970s resulted in several theoretical models. Pastalan (1971, 1975) postulated an "age–loss continuum" in which aging was viewed in terms of progressive lifespace contraction in association with a series of losses, including children (leaving home), spouse, age peers, health, physical mobility, income, and social roles. Reviewing the implications for environmental participation in lifespan perspective, Pastalan (1971) noted that "at infancy lifespace scarcely extends beyond the body; it expands as the senses develop and reaches a maximum in adulthood where it remains relatively stable and then with old age gradually diminishes until ultimately it stops at the body once again [p. 2]."

Lawton and Simon (1968) proposed an "environmental docility hypothesis" which posited that, as the individual ages, personal competence declines and external or environmental influences become progressively more pervasive in limiting activity and determining the old person's lifestyle and level of environmental participation. This perspective was subsequently elaborated in Lawton and Nahemow's "ecological model of adaptation and aging" (Lawton, 1975, 1980; Lawton & Nahemow, 1973). An additional level of complexity is provided in Kahana's "environmental congruence model" (Kahana, 1975). Old people are acknowledged to have highly individualistic sets of needs and preferences that, under ideal conditions, are consonant with facilitating characteristics of the environmental context. When such a balance is achieved (for example, when an individual's privacy needs are satisfied by the potential for privacy provided by the architectural design and social ambience of an environment) a state of congruence exists. Kahana's model is of particular interest as it explicitly incorporates a variety of social and psychological dimensions such as privacy, autonomy versus control, potential for individual expression, and so on, that provide for a more comprehensive definition of the old person–environment transaction. Emphasis shifts from primary concern with the built environment. A more explicit extension of this shift of emphasis is provided in Gubrium's (1973) "socioenvironmental theory of aging," a perspective focusing on sociological dimensions of the old person–environment transaction. Finally, Rowles (1978) has proposed a "hypothesis of changing emphasis" in which an array of consistent changes with advancing age are postulated to occur in four distinctive domains of the old person–environment transaction—action, orientation, feeling, and fantasy.

While the flurry of activity during the 1970s has had demonstrable impact in terms of policy, it has also focused the field in a manner that has entailed long-term costs. Indeed, the research agenda has reached an impasse, and as we enter the 1980s, aging–environment research faces a fundamental dilemma.

On the one hand, particularly as policy imperatives become less insistent and research funding decreases, researchers are becoming more aware of the shortcomings of studies that explore single aspects of the old person–environment transaction, such as the design of the dwelling, or architectural barriers to mobility, or patterns of shopping behavior. These studies lack a sense of the total context. The fragmentation of research, so necessary for methodological reasons, obscures aspects of relationships and the ultimate wholeness of the phenomenon that may be critical for understanding it. It is becoming increasingly apparent that to fully understand the old person–environment transaction, it is necessary to adopt a holistic stance, utilizing a broader definition of milieu such as is incorporated within this volume. It is desirable to incorporate consideration of societally determined norms of "appropriate activity" (Ostrow, Chapter 10), changing sex-role expectation (Livson, Chapter 9), and other social, cultural, and political components of the individual's total milieu, into consideration of the old person's environmental context.

On the other hand, the quest for more holistic interpretation raises the specter of sterile "grand theory" (Mills, 1959) of developing fuzzy conceptual frameworks that are so complex and all-embracing that they cannot be empirically researched even with the most advanced computer technology. The complexity of some of the more recent aging–environment theories reflects this tendency. The dilemma, then, is one of reconciling the two levels of inquiry.

The chapters in this volume express an acknowledgement of the dilemma. They represent a "stepping back" in an effort to explore expanded definitions of aging and environment relationships and yet, at the same time, to preserve the integrity of empirical research by framing it within operationally manageable bounds. Within this rubric, the contributors not only elucidate important subdilemmas in the field but also provide a set of fresh perspectives to facilitate reaching out in new directions.

EMERGENT THEMES AND NEW DIRECTIONS

First, as is apparent from our listing of theoretical perspectives on aging and environment, the gerontological literature is permeated by an ethos of "losses" or "decrements" with advancing age. The contributions in this volume by Ohta and Kirasic (Chapter 6), Rowles (Chapter 8), and Kahana and Kahana (Chapter 13), suggest a rather different perspective. Ohta and Kirasic demonstrate that, contrary to the indications of laboratory research, elderly individuals are surprisingly competent in everyday spatial situations. Rowles illustrates the ability of rural old people to harness a wide array of indigenous social support networks and the implicit support of a familiar physical setting in developing life-styles characterized by high levels of subjective well-being. Kahana and Kahana find that relocation often provides considerable potential for personality growth which should not be disregarded by gerontologists examining the effects of environmental discontinuities on the elderly. Moreover, in contributions ranging from Datan's discussion of Leland (Chapter 3) to Nahemow's case study of a patient's self-awareness of her symptomatology (Chapter 11), there emerges a strong sense of self-determination in the environmental participation of old people that questions prevalent stereotypes of environmental passivity. Future aging–environment research can profitably focus on the issue of the way in which old people actively mold not only their physical contexts but also the psychological and social milieu in which they reside. How is it that so many old people, through personal adaptation, rationalization, sometimes even creative self-delusion, are able to create lifeworlds conducive to a sense of well-being?

Several contributors highlight the confining effects of societally determined norms of appropriate behavior on the old person's life-style and potential for growth. In so doing, they reinforce the need for studies incorporating alternative definitions of the aging–environment transaction that embrace the impact of societal social norms. Ostrow (Chapter 10) demonstrates that clear beliefs about age-appropriate physical activity serve to regulate involvement in physical activity across the life span. Livson (Chapter 9) focuses upon the impact of changing sex roles as components of the social environment of later life and explores their implications for older women. The chapter by Nahemow (Chapter 11) reveals the potentially harmful effect of normative expectations implicit within the social ambience of the traditional patient–physician exchange and the relationship that this may bear to the issue of patient compliance. The implication is that old people would benefit from changes in current societal expectations based on age, sex, and medical roles. But how is such a liberation of milieu to be implemented? The task is a monumental one with far-reaching implications not only for the milieu in which old people reside but also for the entire structure of society.

These essays provide reinforcement for the perennial plea for investigation of aging–environment transactions in a wider range of settings. Beyond mere admonition that we move outside the housing project and long-term-care facility and consider old people in the neighborhoods and community environments where the majority reside, this volume indicates the need for more descriptive exploratory studies of aging–environment relationships in hitherto little researched microenvironmental settings including community health clinics and physicians' offices. There is a special need for greater discrimination among different geographical scales of analysis in interpreting the qualitative characteristics of the old-person–environment transaction (Rowles, Chapter 8). An old person may, for reasons of physical incapacity, be unable to cross a room; yet this same individual, if provided the appropriate assistance in boarding an airplane, may experience little difficulty in traversing a continent. Clearly, there may not only be great variation in the nature of the old-person–environment transaction in different environmental contexts, but also there may be considerable variations in the nature of the transaction at different scales within the same setting.

A fourth recurrent theme is epistemological—the issue of reconciling objective, directly observable dimensions and subjective aspects of the old person–environment transaction. Several essays illustrate the need to incorporate subjective dimensions of experience in understanding old people's relationships to their environments. For example, Lawton (Chapter 4) discusses the necessity of considering the cognitive meaning with which individuals imbue the everyday activities in which they engage. He suggests that such variable meanings are integrally related to well-being. Regnier (Chapter 5) illustrates the ways in which old people's neighborhood images often differ markedly from those of urban planners, differences that may have critical implications for policy. Implicit in these chapters is both a concern for individual variability and an acknowledgment of the need to explore worlds within the head, to seek insight into the meanings, values, and intentions that permeate the old-person–environment transaction. In previous work, Lawton (1970) took a first step in seeking to operationally disentangle objective and subjective dimensions of environmental experience by distinguishing among personal, suprapersonal, social, and physical environments. Rowles (1978) has also sought an integration of the subjective and objective domains. However, the dilemma of reconciling subjective and objective dimensions of person–environment transactions has still to be satisfactorily resolved.

More comprehensive concern with the person, incorporating a phenomenological perspective, facilitates a far more subtle understanding of the old-person–environment transaction and is closely linked to a fifth theme to have emerged from the preceding chapters—the ultimate interdependency of person and place. This is a theme that has received attention from geographers and merits incorporation within aging–environment research in gerontology (Buttimer & Seamon, 1980; Ley, 1977; Tuan, 1977). The concern in this literature is not merely with the reciprocity that exists between the two elements. Rather it is with the way in which for many people, especially those who may have resided in a setting for a considerable period of time, the two are fused to provide a holistic sense of "being in place." This sense of integration is the essence of the attachment to place so often noted but so infrequently researched in studies of old people's relationships to their environments. The importance of "being in place" is most easily revealed when it is threatened. Datan (Chapter 3), in poignantly describing the critical impact of a relatively short distance of separation on her family's close personal friendship with Leland, conveys something of this sense. In seeking to describe the aura of humanity, caring, and tranquility that would characterize a therapeutic hospital environment for a psychiatric geriatric patient, Kastenbaum (Chapter 1) also appears to be advocating the quest for understanding the kind of ambience that will promote a sense of "being in place" and hence foster recovery. The question is ultimately one of the meaning of place—how it is created, its experiential components, and its relationship to well-being. This theme is pursued in some depth by Howell (Chapter 7). Her discussion is an attempt to probe the essence of what may be one of the most critical issues in aging–environment research, an issue with far-reaching implications for policy, ranging from the design of housing to the efficacy of relocation.

Throughout this volume there have been repeated allusions to the role of time in influencing the quality of the old-person–environment transaction. The passing of time is an important aspect of the changing milieu inhabited by Leland and Gidon and the relationship it fosters (Datan, Chapter 3). Lawton (Chapter 4) focuses on the role of time as a constraint on activity patterns. Howell (Chapter 7) illustrates how personal history dimensions of involvement in place are critical components of understanding its changing meaning to the old person. Finally, the Lohmann's

(Chapter 2) remind us that the policy milieu in which old people reside is in a constant state of flux. Clearly, future research can profitably focus on the theme of temporal change in aging–environment relationships. This emphasis will be particularly important as research shifts away from funded studies of housing policy-related questions toward consideration of both the "developmental" and the "ideal study population" rationales outlined at the beginning of this chapter.

In sum, we believe that an appropriate response to the central dilemma posed by the current status of aging–environment research may be to review our progress and set out on a more modest course. This course will involve neither the abstraction and generality implicit in the search for grand theory nor the short-term responsiveness of accommodation to the demands of funding agencies (in this regard the drying up of funding sources may represent an opportunity rather than a problem). Instead, it will involve refocusing the aging–environment research paradigm, incorporating perspectives and approaches that have been held in abeyance or ignored in previous research. To set out in the new directions indicated in the essays of this volume is not merely a challenge. In a larger sense it is a responsibility, for ultimately we are charged with nothing less than the potential for determining the milieu in which we all may grow old.

REFERENCES

Aldrich, C. K., & Mendkoff, E. Relocation of the aged and disabled: A mortality study. *Journal of American Geriatric Society*, 1963, *11*, 185–194.

Altman, I., Wohlwill, J., & Lawton, M. P. (Eds.). *Human behavior and environment: The elderly and the physical environment.* New York: Plenum, in press.

Atchley, R. C., & Byerts, T. O. (Eds.). *Rural environments and aging.* Washington, D. C.: Gerontological Society, 1975.

Borup, J. H., Gallego, D. T., & Heffernan, P. G. Relocation and its effect on mortality. *The Gerontologist*, 1979, *19*, 135–140.

Bourestom, N., & Pastalan, L. A. The effects of relocation on the elderly: A reply to J. H. Borup, D. T. Gallego, & P. G. Heffernan. *The Gerontologist*, 1981, *21*, 4–7.

Buttimer, A., & Seamon, D. (Eds.). *The human experience of space and place.* London: Croom Helm, 1980.

Byerts, T. O., Howell, S. C., & Pastalan, L. A. (Eds.). *Environmental context of aging: Lifestyles, environmental quality and living arrangements.* New York: Garland STPM Press, 1979.

Carp, F. M. *A future for the aged.* Austin: University of Texas Press, 1966.

Golant, S. M. (Ed.). *Location and environment of elderly population.* Washington, D. C.: V. H. Winston & Sons, 1979.

Gubrium, J. F. *The myth of the golden years: A socio-environmental theory of aging.* Springfield, Ill.: Charles C Thomas, 1973.

Ittelson, W. H. Some issues facing a theory of environment and behavior. In P. G. Windley, T. O. Byerts, & F. G. Ernst (Eds.), *Theory development in environment and aging.* Washington, D. C.: Gerontological Society, 1975.

Kahana, E. A congruence model of person–environment interaction. In P. G. Windley, T. O. Byerts, & F. G. Ernest (Eds.), *Theory development in environment and aging*. Washington, D. C.: Gerontological Society, 1975.

Lawton, M. P. Ecology and aging. In L. A. Pastalan & D. H. Carson (Eds.), *Spatial behavior of older people*. Ann Arbor, University of Michigan–Wayne State University Institute of Gerontology, 1970.

Lawton, M. P. Competence, environmental press and the adaptation of older people. In P. G. Windley, T. O. Byerts, & F. G. Ernst (Eds.), *Theory development in environment and aging*. Washington, D. C.: Gerontological Society, 1975.

Lawton, M. P. *Environment and aging*. Monterey, Calif.: Brooks/Cole, 1980.

Lawton, M. P., & Nahemow, L. Ecology and the aging process. In C. Eisdorfer & M. P. Lawton (Eds.), *The psychology of adult development and aging*. Washington, D.C.: American Psychological Association, 1973.

Lawton, M. P., & Simon, B. The ecology of social relationships in housing for the elderly. *The Gerontologist*, 1968, 8, 108–115.

Lawton, M. P., & Yaffe, S. *Victimization of the elderly and fear of crime*. Philadelphia: Philadelphia Geriatric Center, 1979.

Ley, D. Social geography and the taken-for-granted world. *Transactions of the Institute of British Geographers*, 1977, 2, 498–512.

Mills, C. W. *The sociological imagination*. New York: Oxford University Press, 1959.

Pastalan, L. A. *How the elderly negotiate their environment*. Paper prepared for Environment for the Aged: A Working Conference on Behavioral Research, Utilization and Economic Policy, San Juan, Puerto Rico, 1971.

Pastalan, L. A. Research in environment and aging: An alternative to theory. In P. G. Windley, T. O. Byerts, & F. G. Ernst (Eds.), *Theory development in environment and aging*. Washington, D.C.: Gerontological Society, 1975.

Rosow, I. *Social integration of the aged*. New York: Free Press, 1967.

Rowles, G. D. *Prisoners of space? Exploring the geographical experience of older people*. Boulder, Colo.: Westview Press, 1978.

Sherman, S. R. The choice of retirement housing among the well elderly. *International Journal of Aging and Human Development*, 1971, 2, 118–138.

Teaff, J. D., Lawton, M. P., Nahemow, L., & Carlson, D. Impact of age integration on the well-being of elderly tenants in public housing. *Journal of Gerontology*, 1978, 33, 126–133.

Tobin, S. S., & Lieberman, M. A. *Last home for the aged*. San Francisco: Jossey–Bass, 1976.

Tuan, Y. F. *Space and place: the perspective of experience*. Minneapolis: University of Minnesota Press, 1977.

Windley, P. G., Byerts, T. O., & Ernst, F. G. (Eds.). *Theory development in environment and aging*. Washington, D.C.: Gerontological Society, 1975.

Wittels, I., & Botwinick, J. Survival in relocation. *Journal of Gerontology*, 1974, 29, 440–443.

Author Index

Subject Index